The Ultimate Grain-Free Cookbook

SUGAR-FREE, STARCH-FREE, WHOLE FOOD RECIPES
FROM MY CALIFORNIA COUNTRY KITCHEN

ANNABELLE LEE

Skyhorse Publishing

Skyhorse Publishing books may be purchased in bulk at special discounts for sales promotion, corporate gifts, fund-raising, or educational purposes. Special editions can also be created to specifications. For details, contact the Special Sales Department, Skyhorse Publishing, 307 West 36th Street, 11th Floor, New York, NY 10018 or info@skyhorsepublishing.com.

Skyhorse® and Skyhorse Publishing® are registered trademarks of Skyhorse Publishing, Inc.®, a Delaware corporation.

Visit our website at www.skyhorsepublishing.com.

10 9 8 7 6 5 4 3 2 1

Library of Congress Cataloging-in-Publication Data

Names: Lee, Annabelle, (fashion model), author.
Title: The ultimate grain-free cookbook : sugar-free, starch-free, whole food from my California country kitchen / Annabelle Lee.
Description: New York, NY : Skyhorse Publishing, [2018] | Includes bibliographical references and index.
Identifiers: LCCN 2018005611| ISBN 9781510729490 (hardcover : alk. paper) |
ISBN 9781510729483 (ebook)
Subjects: LCSH: Gluten-free diet--Recipes. | Sugar-free diet--Recipes. |
LCGFT: Cookbooks.
Classification: LCC RM237.86 .L43 2018 | DDC 641.5/639311--dc23 LC record available at https://lccn.loc.gov/2018005611

Cover design by Mary Ann Smith
Cover photograph by Jacob Lee

Print ISBN: 978-1-5107-2949-0
Ebook ISBN: 978-1-5107-2948-3

Printed in China

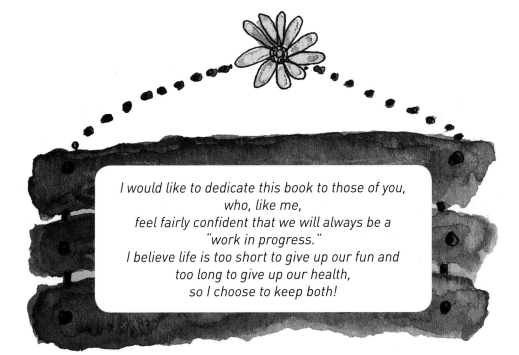

I would like to dedicate this book to those of you,
who, like me,
feel fairly confident that we will always be a
"work in progress."
I believe life is too short to give up our fun and
too long to give up our health,
so I choose to keep both!

Contents

· · · · · · · · · · · · · · · ·

Preface

. . . .

The journey to bringing this book to print has been a bit of a long and winding road for me. I'll save you the details; however, I want you to know that over the years that have passed during this hike, my purpose for bringing you this book has not so much changed, but has grown. It's grown into something much more meaningful to me than simply sharing some thoughts and recipes. Lord knows, there are enough great recipes floating around to fulfill almost anyone's desires. So, simply bringing you more recipes or telling you to eat more fruits, vegetables, protein, and healthy fats is kind of preaching to the choir for many of you. What can be a bit difficult is figuring out a sustainable way to do this in our fast-paced world full of temptation, misinformation, and confusing diet suggestions, right?

My hope is that this book will actually help to change the process and make navigating what should be an enjoyable part of your life easier. I hope this book helps you feel better, have more energy, and even lose some weight, without stressing over perfect meal plans and hard to follow diet-cult strategies. I hope you'll learn that, while breaking emotional ties to food is important, enjoying your childhood favorites with my recipes can be fun and even healthy. I hope to encourage you to have more confidence and courage in your kitchen, by simply learning easy and unique ways to prepare real *human* food, the delicious gifts from nature that are meant to provide humankind a happy, healthy life.

Over the years I've learned that the Universe is certainly not on my timeframe, and while it can be excruciatingly frustrating at times, I've also learned to *trust* the Universe, just as I've learned to trust the divinity of nature for my food source. Some great things happened during the time I was not-so-patiently waiting for publishers and contract changes. For one, the natural foods market has exploded, giving us more buying options than ever. Among other foods, we now have an array of whole food flours and sweeteners to choose from, with more competitive pricing, making this type of baking even more fun. When I wrote my cupcake book *The California Country Gal's Sweet Secrets: Real Food Cupcakes*, I used blanched almonds and shredded coconut and the food processor. Now, most of these recipes can be made with ground flours and your blender. I also decided to include My Favorite Basics section to show you what has helped make living a "whole foods" lifestyle easier for me.

Well, it may be true that all good things come to those who wait. While I was waiting on publishing changes, I know more of you have been waiting on a book like this. So, I welcome you to *My California Country Kitchen*, and I hope you'll find it's been worth the wait.

Wishing you lots of love, sunshine, and good health,

Annabelle
xo

Introduction

. . . .

I'd like to begin by answering a few questions you may have: Am I a doctor, a scientist, a nutritionist—or even a veterinarian? No. Am I a celebrity or VIP? Well . . . no. Am I a triathlete, bungee jumper, or marathon runner? Umm . . . no. Well then, who am I? Outside of my family, who loves me for being me—and maybe my dogs who might miss a meal if I'm not around—I'm really just a curious, health-conscious person by nature, who took some time out of my life to read a lot of books and papers to educate myself about health, food, and nutrition, while experimenting in the kitchen. This was important to me because I wanted to raise healthy children and for many years I'd also been managing what doctors refer to as "auto-immune" conditions.

For decades, I had mysterious knee pain with swelling, along with widespread body and joint pain. Eventually, I had wacky hormone levels, sleepless nights, tummy troubles, and other delightful symptoms. Tests confirmed past viral/bacterial infections and nutritional deficiencies, and, finally, a doctor of rheumatology suggested I had lupus. Lupus, like other "mystery" illnesses, is usually diagnosed on symptoms and a positive blood marker that indicates an autoimmune attack in the body somewhere. While I'm not sure I agree with this specific label, it was clear my body needed help. Prior years of my own research had already led me to conclude that a healthy body is far too smart to suddenly begin attacking itself; therefore I've come to believe the vast majority of these types of diseases manifest from previous or current infections brought on by common (and some not-so-common) pathogens and toxins. Depending upon the type of pathogen, where it migrates to, a person's individual weaknesses (genetic and deficiencies), and the germ's ability to hide, transform, and adapt for its survival (hence, "super bugs") determines the illness. With these thoughts, I chose to decline a form of oral chemotherapy and painkillers, which was mainstream medicine's treatment offered to me. Instead I embarked upon more research and a determination to vastly step up what I already thought was a fairly healthy lifestyle, all in an attempt to change and control my symptoms without the help of Western medicine's drugs. While I don't know that I will ever completely clear my body of resistant pathogens, my vigilance to correct my body's weaknesses and heighten my immune system has remarkably reduced my symptoms and kept me from even so much as contracting a cold or flu in over a decade.

I have always had rather lofty goals for myself, and to this day I aspire to: be healthy, feel vivacious, look good, give and receive lots of love, and reach a state of happiness and contentment that allows me to believe that in the end I won't have a sea of regrets. So, who am I? I'm just me, a simple gal who was raised (mostly barefoot) on California soil and sunshine.

Part 1:
Living a California Country Life

Chapter 1:
The Joys of Country Life

About sixteen years ago, my husband and I embarked upon a rather intrepid journey when we decided to move our family of four young men to the southern California countryside where, with the help of a few sub-contractors, we built our own home. We also built several out buildings, installed a five-acre fence, a septic system, and drip lines. We planted over 120 trees and a vegetable garden, learned to keep goats, a pet pig, raise chickens (keeping chicks in the house is *not* recommended), and most recently hired a crew to dig a new well because our original one was running dry. These last dozen years have been the most exhausting, frustrating, exhilarating, and rewarding years of our lives. Our boys are now grown but the memories of their adolescent adventures in the country are often dinnertime conversations . . . like the time someone nearly stepped on a rattlesnake, or when dad tumbled off the roof (into some soft dirt, thank God!), or when the dirt bike jump twenty feet in the air took our son left and the motorcycle right, and when our dog, Honey, once chased three coyotes down the road. We recall standing our first walls of the house and installing drywall (that one nearly ended our marriage) and when we carried a thirty-foot beam and used the pick-up truck to help get it into place. Installing a seven-foot wide window on the third floor during a storm wasn't such a good idea, but we did it. We learned to operate a tractor and other heavy equipment. Our sons encountered a huge millipede in the bathroom, a scorpion in the laundry room, and, imagine me being surprised by the tarantula in the kitchen! Somewhere along the way my husband even earned the nickname "Animal." You simply won't find memories like these in most suburban settings. Notice I didn't necessarily refer to all of these as "fond" memories, but they are *my* memories, *our* memories, nonetheless, and I wouldn't trade them for anything. Ahh, the joys of country life.

I haven't always been a country bumpkin, though. I grew up a bit of a San Diego beach bum and went on to become a Los Angeles city slicker. Then, by the time I was twenty-one, life had taken my new, small family from our California home to New York City where we lived, worked, and ate for almost a decade. There I learned the ways of the city and experienced wonderful restaurants with chefs that opened my eyes to what *real* cooking meant . . . to prepare food myself—from scratch. As a teenage wife and mother, for the most part I had cooked and baked like my mom had, rarely using a cookbook except for referencing, finding true joy in creating a dish myself. Often I used the typical ingredients Mom used, convenient packages and cans, with some fresh items thrown in for good measure. Though Mom would hop on health kicks now and again, mostly she believed what our government and big business would hype, and like so many Americans back then began a love affair with processed foods. As a young mom, I began reading the ingredients on labels and all the words I'd never heard before just didn't sound like food for my family. I realized that the convenience of opening packages and cans was not the best option to keep a healthy body. Then, I read a book that described how margarine contained nickel and that the chemical used to flavor pineapple ice cream was basically anti-freeze, so I *rarely* brought processed foods into our home after that.

After our stint on the East Coast, we moved back out West and continued living a typical family life with four active boys, a mortgage, stressful jobs, yada-yada (I learned that in New York). As time went by and my boys turned into young men, I noticed I had put on a pound or two (okay, more like ten or twelve), and my body just wasn't running as smoothly any more. What on Earth was going on?

In both New York and Los Angeles, I worked as a fashion model, so I have always been conscious of my weight, and my now-growing waistline was not appealing to me. Was this menopause? Egad, NO! And if it was, why? Before the chemical food era most women seemed to cross that threshold without a hitch. Well, I may just be your "country gal next door," but I must tell you that when declining health and a growing belly opened my eyes enough, I finally realized my "healthy diet" wasn't making me healthy at all. I began looking more and more at mainstream food and the government's food pyramid as a *taker* of health and real whole foods as a *giver* of health. I decided to step up my research of nutrition with my creative spirit in the kitchen and teach myself how to bake and cook with common, inexpensive, "real food" ingredients, so that my family could continue to enjoy the same beloved comfort foods they were used to. When I changed my cupboards and my buying habits, it changed my life.

When I began cooking, baking, and eating beyond gluten-free and even beyond grain-free, now filling my cupboards and tummy with *real* whole foods, my lifestyle naturally transitioned to one that went *beyond* dieting. I no longer needed to make sure I maintained my weight (as a model, this was, of course, important to my job), as the foods I ate maintained it for me. Did I give up comfort foods? Nope! I discovered I could use *real* foods to replace the refined flours, starches, and often even the oils typically used in recipes. The results have been so wonderful I've never looked back.

Moving to the country is a choice we've always been happy with. Living where we can have our own chickens to provide eggs, the ability to grow our own vegetables and fruit, and where we can buy fresh raw milk, cream, and cheese from our neighbor has its obvious rewards, but there have certainly been years when I had to rely on our farmer's markets and the organic produce aisle. Though sometimes confusing, we are lucky for the vast choices available to us today so that we don't all have to live on a farm to be healthy. However, we do have to make the commitment mentally and financially to purchase high-quality, organic, fresh, free-range, and locally whenever possible. If we encourage our friends and community to participate, it will help to move society back towards health instead of the slippery slope it's now on.

Country Living Evolved

It's kind of funny to me that I never felt truly "countrified" until the day we brought home our first chickens. I love raising happy chickens (and you thought California just had happy cows). It's amazing to see the different personalities of all the animals and to learn how smart and even loving they can be. For this reason, while I may eat a little meat on occasion (usually just fish and occasional bacon, but please don't tell my pet pig Chuckles because I realize it's very disrespectful to him), unless great misfortune requires it, I certainly prefer to never actually raise any animal for their meat. I'm okay with feeding and caring for them in exchange for their eggs or cream and entertaining antics, however I'm afraid I would quickly become a vegetarian should I need to "process" my own meat. Besides, as nature intended, meat would run from me while an apple would patiently wait for me to pick it. Much easier and more inviting, don't you think? Nature's divine intelligence has already selected the perfect diet and food pyramid for us, and truly, for many reasons, we do not want to stray.

Eventually, research and exciting kitchen experiments had me wanting to shout my discoveries from rooftops, so with my dear Animal's encouragement, www.californiacountrygal.com was born. Now, before you start thinking I have an endless supply of energy, let me just tell you that I can also be just as lazy as the next gal.

I must admit, between regular chores, the website, all of my kitchen experimenting, meddling in my children's lives, and gossiping with friends means I can sometimes get overwhelmed. There are times I just want to be able to reach into my cupboard and find a mix that will give me delicious and good-for-me breads, pizza dough, and lots of other goodies in a jiffy. So, I decided to take the time to create that perfect baking mix, which we now ship nationwide and to Canada. We also now sell our line of both vegan and Paleo baked breads, buns, and baguettes in southern California and hope to someday reach your town. Then we can *all* enjoy delicious and healthy *real bread* at our lazy fingertips, any time of the day or night.

Who Do *You* Want to Be?

Now that you know a little bit about my background and why I'm writing this book, an equally important question may be: Who are *you*? Are you the person you want to be? Or are you a person who has been led down the modern food path of *least* resistance and *most* disease? Are you the person who is ready to change that path? Will you take the road labeled "pain and disease" or the one labeled "health and vibrancy"? Surprisingly, it has always been your choice—like Dorothy and her ruby slippers giving her the power to go home—you just haven't known it because "big business" with "big advertising" campaigns, skewed and confusing studies, and media hype (even disagreements between professionals) have all kept you misinformed. All you have to do is trust in Mother Nature and believe in yourself. Because *believing you have been given the power* is your biggest step to changing the road you're on. Now, all you need is a little old-school teaching, and you'll be on your way. It may be the road less traveled, but I promise you, it's the road that will take you home.

Let's Get Real

Probably much like yours, mine has been a journey towards trying to look and feel my best while also striving to raise a healthy family. In a confusing, expensive, and polluted world, we all know this is not an easy process. Along the way I've let go of diet crazes and plenty of inaccurate and misleading information, such as "eat low fat, lots of whole grains, and half the egg." I no longer need to remember all the reasons *why* I should trade out that box of cake mix, or even some of the ingredients Gramma used in her baking; it's now so ingrained in me that I just do it. These days *I trust no one but Mother Nature*.

Once I learned to change my pantry from items that were really non-food ingredients to *real*-food ingredients, my life transformed as well. My ultimate reward was to actually see the pounds drop off, feel my health improve, and my energy increase, which gave me gratification knowing I was giving my family what they needed to thrive.

There's nothing wrong with eating simply—enjoying a steamed vegetable, maybe an egg or two, a slice of cheese, and salad greens. However, we've become a species who has spent centuries devising creative ways to fill our bellies and satisfy our taste buds. As cities developed, savvy business people discovered there was a lot of money to be made feeding people who didn't live in conditions where they could grow or supply their own food. They also found that certain "foods" and ingredients would keep their customers coming back for more, again and again. Modern humans have become accustomed to eating dishes like pancakes, pizza, lasagna, hamburgers, wraps, biscuits, casseroles, cakes, and cookies—all foods made with addictive, simple and complex, starchy, sugary, processed carbohydrates. A truly simple meal is rare these days. Even the raw food community may spend hours dehydrating vegetables so they can recreate something similar to childhood memories. Let's face it: We like the flavors and textures we grew up with and change is not easy, even when we learn that the "food" we've been consuming is greatly contributing to—if not causing—our aches, ills, and even our nation's epidemic diseases.

Although the real food ingredients I use are all gluten-free and Paleo-diet friendly, they are a bit different from the typical grain/gluten-free and Paleo ingredients, as I firmly choose not to use high-glycemic sweeteners, refined starches or, even the newest trending Cassava (yucca) flour (because of its toxic level of arsenic before it's refined). I will explain why the trend of omitting wheat and other grains while adding refined starch is a big mistake—for your health and your waistline.

When striving for a healthier diet, breads, crackers, crusts, wraps, cookies, and cakes are usually the most difficult to give up or replace. Lifelong habits, food addictions, misinforma-tion, and confusion make this no easy task. My goal is to help you understand *why and how* to make the necessary changes by simply using real food ingredients, *without* following a one-way, diet-cult strategy. The "whole food" ingredients used in my recipes are full of vitamins, minerals, protein, and resistant fiber that can actually help people lose weight naturally, and the great tastes and textures will astound you.

Along with other fruits and veggies, the main ingredients in my recipes include blanched almonds (or blanched almond flour) and other nuts, coconut, zucchini, new potatoes, and the yellow sweet potato. I also use plantain and sweet potato flour (the whole, ground food). It should be easier to buy many different whole food flours in the future but for now mashing a banana is simply easier (and cheaper) than finding banana flour, so most recipes use the whole food. The foods I use each have an impressive nutritional resume, as well as plenty of much-needed fiber, without any harsh, heavy whole-grain taste. When blended together in the right proportions, the tastes of these whole-food ingredients meld together to create delectable baked goods.

You and your family will never feel deprived of classic "comfort food" dishes or even guess you're actually eating to promote a long, healthy life. You'll discover how simple changes to your pantry and baking techniques allows you to enjoy delicious bread and decadent desserts and be healthy, too.

So, throw out what you think you know about baking, get out your blender and food pro-cessor, and roll up your sleeves, because I'm going to show you how to enjoy your guilty indulgences—without the guilt!

Chapter 2:
Eating REAL Without Dieting

··

The more I researched food, the more fascinated I became as I realized that we are now *sicker than we've ever been.* We have constant struggling weight issues and new diseases cropping up regularly. There's a pill for everything (with a list of side effects), but there rarely seems to be a cure. After decades of research and hundreds of millions of dollars spent, cancer is still running rampant in our society. We have epidemic proportions of obesity, diabetes, autism, ADHD, bi-polar disorder, allergies, Alzheimer's, fatty liver, heart disease, bowel disease, fibroids, an out-of-control growing list of "auto-immune" disorders, osteoporosis, infertility, and pharmaceutical addictions. There's confusion and disagreement amongst scientists and medical professionals as to how and why we fall prey to these conditions. Skewed "studies," fake news, and media hype fuel the confusion. *Dietary beliefs are at the forefront yet seem to be more hotly debated than ever before.* Personally, after my experience, I wholeheartedly believe that what we put into our bodies has a direct impact on our health and longevity. Once I made the decision *not* to put my life and health purely in others' hands (no matter what fancy titles they have) and to instead take as much responsibility as possible by making my own educated choices, many things happened. I had more energy, those extra pounds disappeared, my skin became less dry, my hair less brittle, and my aches and pains subsided greatly, as well as my knee swelling. I knew I had chosen the path I would stay on for the rest of my life.

The Not-So-Sweet Secrets of the Food Industry

With the end of World War II, the rationing of sugar ended. Because sugar, starch, and wheat flour were the cheapest ingredients that could be put into *everything* and be made to taste like just about *anything*, they became the darlings of the processed food world. Unfortunately, they can also be health-destroying and addictive. Sugar, wheat flour, and extracted starches are still used abundantly today in virtually all our packaged and pre-made foods. Just because a label reads "organic cane sugar" or tapioca/arrowroot "flour" doesn't mean these refined, partial "foods" are okay for your body, *especially* on an everyday basis.

When faulty studies and publicity fueled the big "fat lie" of the 70's, which erroneously demonized saturated fat, the food industry began removing the natural fat from their products. To replace the flavor and texture appeal they lost, they chose to add the cheapest, most addictive ingredients available: sugar, starch, wheat, and refined salt. Wheat flour and extracted starches, such as those used abundantly in gluten-free baking (often called "flours" or "powders") break down in our bodies and turn to sugar as quickly as eating table sugar. *Now, think about what you're doing when you combine refined flours with sugar and/or starch for baking. You're doubling and tripling your trouble!* Think whole grain is better? Whole grain flours may contain more fiber but the hulls also contain most of the anti-nutrients such as phytates and specifically difficult protein lectins designed by nature to protect the seeds of these grasses in order for it to propagate.

So What's the Problem with Grains?

Grains have *never* been ideal human food.
- Some animals are meant to eat grains and grasses. Birds have beaks and gizzards. Cows, goats, and sheep have multiple stomachs and continuously growing teeth. But the human digestive system is not designed to properly digest grains or "cereal" grasses.
- Grains are seeds of grasses that contain "anti-nutrients." These anti-nutrients were designed by mother nature to withstand digestion so they can remain intact and be planted in the ground (right along with their built-in fertilizer).
- Grains are less nutrient dense than fruits, vegetables, nuts, seeds, and leafy greens, which all contain adequate fiber for our system.
- Anthropological records indicate that early peoples had virtually no dental problems until the adoption of agriculture.
- Grains may have historically staved off hunger, but they are not a true human food group.

Grains aren't what they used to be.
- Grain, specifically wheat, is now 50% of the modern American diet, a gross increase over the small amounts eaten by a few hungry groups of early humans.
- The vast amount of modern grain is cross-bred and genetically modified without human testing, and if not organic, sprayed with herbicides and pesticides.
- Long, hot storage of grains can breed cancer-causing fungal aflatoxins.
- Unscrupulous food companies exploit the addictive properties of wheat and sugar by sneaking them into virtually all of their processed foods.
- The "low fat" craze fueled big business to add wheat, starch, and sugar to their products to make up for the loss of flavor and satiety once the fat was removed.

Grains don't help your body thrive.
- Removing the hulls/husks, soaking, sprouting, grinding, and cooking grains reduces some of the anti-nutrients, such as phytic acid; however it does not reduce specifically damaging lectins or the high starch content that quickly increases blood sugar.
- Eating grains blocks mineral and other nutrient absorption in humans, leading to deficiencies.
- Many grains contain proteins that damage human intestines, which can cause permeability and wide spread inflammation.
- Grains, such as wheat varieties, have peptides that bind to the opiate receptors in the human brain, which can trigger addictive impulses.
- Wheat, rye, barley, and rice contain agglutinin, a toxin that is completely resistant to human digestion.
- Studies show that many health conditions including weight control, allergies, digestive disorders, and even autism symptoms can noticeably improve when grains are removed from the diet.

Problems with Other "Foods"

Extracted, Refined Starches and Sugar

It was once thought that these "complex carbohydrates" digested slower and thus didn't affect our blood sugar adversely. However, we now know that isn't the case. Some starches actually raise our blood sugar quicker than sugar. Carbohydrates are chains of simple sugars and depending upon the molecular makeup of the chain and what has been done to it (cooking, refining, or further processing) determines how it is assimilated by the body. Maybe grandma used to treat you to tapioca pudding, or thicken her pies with it. Arrowroot—you might think it's good for you, simply because so many healthy and gluten-free baking books use it instead of tapioca. Often these two are referred to as "flours" or "powders," but what they truly are is a pure starch, extracted from the root of the toxic cassava plant for tapioca or any number of different plants from around the world that is then labeled as "arrowroot." The starch is extracted in the same manner in which both corn and potato starch are extracted from those vegetables. Extracted starch is used for many things, including making glue, plastic, and stiffening shirt collars at the cleaners.

You may have heard about foods that contain small amounts of "resistant" starch, which can act like a beneficial fiber in the colon. Depending on the food it comes from, the method of extraction and how it's prepared depends on how resistant to digestion it is. We're simply not meant to extract starch from its source and eat it, especially in large quantities. Plant foods with starch were meant to be eaten in their entirety so our bodies would obtain all of the compounds needed to properly digest and assimilate it. If we rely on starches to replace our beloved gluten in wheat, we are only jumping from the fire into the frying pan.

Because our bodies break down refined carbohydrates (sugar, white flour, starch) as quickly as it breaks down table sugar, the combination of sugar, flour, and starch in your baking only triples your sugar load. Virtually all the epidemic diseases we deal with today are linked in some way to excess sugar in our bodies. Sugar is the preferred food for cancer and pathogenic yeasts. Recent studies report that high blood sugar, vitamin D deficiency (why are we still told to stay out of the sun?! Soak up the sun in doses that don't burn you), and lack of physical exercise are the *three most prevalent* determining factors of cancer patients.

Our digestive systems use carbohydrates for quick energy by converting them into glucose and glycogen. The body will send this glucose directly to the muscles during exercise; otherwise it remains in the bloodstream, wreaking havoc until being escorted into our cells with the release of insulin. Because we can't store many carbohydrates, our liver works to convert the extra glucose to fat (which we know we have almost an unlimited ability to store), contributing to fatty liver disease, another growing epidemic.

There are now many delicious and safe sweeteners to replace sugar and I recommend many, but you're free to do your own research and choose what sweeteners work best for you. Read your labels and when making gluten/grain-free recipes, consider passing on the ones that use starch as a main ingredient. You won't get what I call a "Starch Belly" and your body (and waistline) will thank you for it. I, personally, would not replace sugar with sucralose (Splenda), as the nation's number-one-selling artificial sweetener has had few human studies of safety published.

Fats and Oils

Fat is high in calories but eating fat does NOT make you fat! Human breast milk contains more cholesterol than almost any other food. More than 50% of its calories are from fat, mostly saturated, and are essential for brain health development and growth. Now, I realize you're probably not a nursing child; however, we NEED fats to survive. Fats carry our fat-soluble vitamins and minerals into our tissues, organs, and bones. Saturated fatty acids make up 50% of our cell membranes. Fats allow the body to make hormones, protect our digestive tract and liver from toxins, and surround our heart muscle. Saturated fats also allow better utilization and retention of the essential fatty acids. So, why would we want to consume "low-fat" anything? Saturated fats are the most stable fats and are resistant to oxidation as it ages, is heated, or is inside our body. The cheap non-food oils such as canola (what's a canola, anyway?), cottonseed (still in many processed foods—who eats cotton?), and soybean (GMO, no thanks) oxidize on the shelf and in our bodies, so they're not in my cupboards. Who wants oxidized oils in their body? Not me! I seldom heat my oils and prefer to bake, poach, or simmer my food and finish a dish with a drizzle of virgin olive, avocado oil, or butter.

Dairy Products

Many people lack the gut flora and enzymes needed to break down the sugar in milk and are considered "lactose intolerant." Other than the lovely gassiness it causes, lactose is fairly harmless. Ancient cultures often cultured their milk products before consuming them so that the good bacteria in the milk could gobble up the sugar and transform the milk into things like yogurt or kefir or clabbered milk, making it easier to digest. The whey protein in cow milk contains lactoferrin, which has many documented health benefits, ranging from weight loss to bone strength to anti-viral effects and even better sleep.

However, these products will still contain the casein protein. While the whey protein appears to be harmless to human health, casein protein shares structural similarities to the gluten/gliaden protein in wheat. Research also shows the casein protein to be most harmful when it's separated from the natural fat in the milk, so I *never* buy "low fat" anything. Happily, butter and heavy cream contain very little lactose sugar or casein protein and are usually very easily digested, even by those who are sensitive. Cream and butter also contain butyrate, a fatty acid that nourishes and balances the pH in the colon. So, I realize I'm not a baby cow, but I do enjoy some full-fat, organic, and grass-fed dairy products.

I also love a blend of coconut/almond/macadamia nut, which is easily substituted for both cow milk and cream in basically any recipe.

Why I Eat Organic

Fact: Until about 1945 *all* produce was organic. As if the onslaught of chemical foods weren't enough, research confirms pesticides to be harmful to human health (duh!). Between synthetic pesticides, GMOs, antibiotics, and hormones, there are a vast amount of toxins that can enter the body through foods. Moreover, our air, water, food, homes, cars, personal care items, cosmetics, and yards are full of chemical toxins. Well over 200 common toxic chemicals have been found in the cord blood of newborn babies. The constant exposure to these substances means our bodies carry their burden. Escaping these toxins may be next to impossible at this point in time, but helping our bodies to cleanse them out is within our ability. However, this takes your knowledge and commitment to do so on an ongoing basis, not just the occasional, popular "cleanse," which can result in flu-like symptoms because the body becomes over-burdened trying to flush the toxins out.

Keeping Our Gut Healthy

Have you ever wondered why certain foods seem to bother some people and not others? Why some gain weight easily and others don't? Why are certain people more prone to allergies? The answers to these questions are directly related to the amount and types of bacteria we house in and on our bodies, mainly in our intestines, the lifeline of our body. The health of its microbiome is intimately connected with the health of the rest of our body. We are colonized on every inch of our body by bacteria, inside and out. In fact, astonishingly, our human cells are outnumbered by these bacteria 10 to 1. They actually communicate with each other as well as with our cells. The vast majority is friendly bacteria that *want* a healthy host, and their ability to communicate, like our own cells, enables them to perform the job that has been intended for them. Without them, we would die.

When our intestines are full of a healthy balance of microflora, these beneficial bacteria will happily help us digest our food, continually creating essential nutrients and antioxidants to keep us strong and healthy. The anti-inflammatory compounds they produce act like antibiotics, working to dissolve fungi and bacterial and viral cell membranes. These friendly microbes are our first line of defense against disease. When this balance is disturbed, it allows opportunistic pathogenic varieties to proliferate, causing digestion and overall health to suffer greatly. What can kill or damage our friendly microflora enough to allow pathogenic varieties to take over? First, and foremost, our "standard American diet" provides an abundance of certain organism's favorite foods: sugar and starch. Also, antibiotics, birth control, steroids, pharmaceuticals, gluten, a bout of "food poisoning" and other infections, hormones, fluoride, chlorinated water, a food supply laced with GMOs, chemical toxins, and food additives, nutrient and mineral deficiencies, and even stress can disrupt the friendlier bacteria we want to keep.

Our gut is home for many yeasts and bacteria that would usually live symbiotically in the human digestive tract. Many are non-aggressive fungi that basically have the role of janitors in that they clean up excess sugars and other debris. However, constant processed carbs and sugar in our modern diet provide enormous amounts of excess food for them to proliferate and become pathogenic. Now, after decades of creating the conditions listed above and passed on through generations, we have weakened our constitution and promoted a massive overgrowth of dangerous yeasts and bacteria, promoting a permeable gut lining that can allow food and waste particles and more dangerous microbes to pass through.

If we aren't eating the food to nurture and replace good microflora, we are weakening our immunity and losing our first line of defense. There are trillions of bacteria in our digestive system, and we desperately need the good varieties to line and protect this incredible system. The latest research is now connecting the types and amounts of flora in our guts with virtually all the current epidemic diseases, including obesity. The friendly microflora on the vegetables multiply when cultured and these fermented foods, like those our ancestors ate, contain far more strains of healthy microbes than do probiotic capsules. Capsules contain only a few dozen strains of bacteria, while a healthy gut houses many hundreds of different strains, most of which science knows little about.

Because of so many negative changes to our modern food, water, environment, and medicine, we must remember to nurture our friendly bacteria daily. I share a few culturing recipes in this book, but most of these recipes concentrate on omitting grains, sugars, and refined starches, also imperative for a healthy tummy. Using more whole foods as ingredients, with their natural fiber, will help to feed the good bacteria our body needs. There are many books and blogs that have more recipes for cultured and fermented condiments to accompany your meals. If you choose to buy your yogurt, sour cream, or sauerkraut, make sure the company promotes "live cultures."

Healing My Body Through Food

By the time I'd reached my fortieth birthday, I felt poorly on many levels and seemed to begin aging overnight. At the time I was eating what I would call a typical healthy diet, meaning that sometimes it was organic, sometimes not, and I was drinking mostly tea, but there were also days I might've had a soda or a meal from a package, and I also ate treats that were sweetened with coconut or cane sugar because I didn't want an artificial sweetener. I ate pasta and whole-grain bread. But I also ate lots of fruits, veggies, and whole fat foods (because I never bought in to the low-fat craze). I *thought* I was eating healthier, but my body had finally hit a brick wall. My hormones were completely out of whack and I became susceptible to infections. The mysterious episodes of knee swelling would come and go randomly. My knees had been an issue since the birth of my first child, when I had contracted my first and only UTI (urinary tract infection) and had been given antibiotics while pregnant. Over the years my knees have been drained and tested by numerous doctors to no avail.

Later in life I came down with a bad case of food poisoning from a restaurant and not long after began experiencing widespread pain throughout my body. It felt like experiencing the most intense workout at the gym for the first time—or getting hit by a bus. Only I didn't work out, and it hurt to even raise my arm. I sought help, but my past experiences gave me little faith that the medical community would come to my rescue. Unfortunately, I was right. Their solution was to prescribe me hormones, painkillers, anti-depressants, sleeping pills and, finally, chemotherapy to try to combat the "auto-immune" symptoms, all of which were of no interest to me. I even wound up in the ER a couple of times, once with fluid around my heart that couldn't be explained and once when my symptoms got so bad I couldn't walk alone and my husband had to carry me down the stairs. The doctor on call suggested I was "faking" my symptoms when he couldn't find anything "wrong" with me. I haven't seen a doctor since.

Now, with more than a decade of research and plenty of trial and error behind me, I've decided my best shot is to accept human health as a universal law that mimics our planet. When not mistreated or overwhelmed, it will cleanse and renew itself, allowing for the natural balance of life on earth. We've been given all that we need to maintain it. If we screw it up, be it from ignorance, laziness, or lack of resources, it doesn't matter, there is little forgiveness. I knew my best form of control was what did or didn't go into my mouth. At this point I began to become more vigilant and less tolerant of my weakness for an occasional Oreo (which, at that time, just kept the fire smoldering). It wasn't long before my body began to respond and I truly felt the beneficial effects of eating an abundance of fruits and vegetables and other real *human* food. Eating only real food balanced my weight, increased my energy, and dramatically improved my health.

I believe that choosing to be happy doesn't mean life is perfect, it just means we've chosen to look past life's imperfections. With this thought in mind, I've also chosen to look past conflicting "diet-cult-strategies" to find my happiness. I've never been a fan of following a specific diet, especially the ones that have us counting carbs from vegetables as the same as carbs from Frosted Flakes. Who wants to cook or meal prep all day or all weekend? Not me! Whoever convinced us we needed three square meals or six small meals a day must've owned a restaurant. Eating so much, so often, keeps us thinking about food all day, exposes us to loads of toxins, produces enormous amounts of waste products and has digestion working

24/7, using vast amounts of energy. All of these, in my opinion, keep us so focused on food and food planning that it creates an emotionally stressful condition, leading to even more issues regarding the act of eating, which should be peaceful and enjoyable. We want life and eating to be happy, satisfying, and healthy. We want to create a culinary lifestyle we will be able to happily keep for a lifetime. We want peace of mind and happy food thoughts.

Viewing food as real or not real has actually *simplified* my approach to eating, by allowing me to let go of other conflicting (diet) strategies. Viewing most pre-made, processed, and denatured food as nothing but empty calories with damaging ingredients also helps control compulsive habits. Real food, on the other hand, is a basic need, just behind air and water. Yes, we could probably survive for some time on Marshmallow Fluff, but eventually we wouldn't be doing so well.

Eating Real Foods Is Easier Than You Think

How many diet books do you suppose have been written in the past, say, forty years? I'm going to venture to guess that there have been hundreds of diets developed and thousands of books, many variations on one original idea and most contradicting each other. Often they have strict dietary guidelines and difficult to follow rules and menus. Should we be Vegetarian, Flexitarian, Vegan, Raw, Paleo, or just Low-Carb and Gluten-Free?

Even the educated, health-conscious consumer has trouble keeping track of which new super food or supplement to buy next. Never mind the dent in the pocketbook these items can make. As we stare at the aisles in our natural foods store, how do we remember which supplement to buy, and why, from study to study, year to year, illness to illness? We wonder, *does my body absorb this laboratory-made product and use it efficiently?* Yes, the road to improvement can be daunting—until you realize it has been offered by Mother Nature since the beginning of time and is literally at your fingertips right now. If you're suffering from a chronic illness, diet alone is often not enough, but without correcting your diet and nutrient deficiencies, your body will not have what it needs to fight the infection or disease and allow other treatments to improve or help heal your condition.

When I realized that there were great ideas and good research behind many ways of eating, I began to borrow and combine several of them into a lifestyle that's easy and enjoyable for me to keep. And the knowledge I've acquired along the way has helped to give me the power to break bad habits. Through the years I've found what works beautifully for me is *not* a strict, *one-way diet-cult strategy*, but a commonsense approach to eating in today's world. It's simply back to nature plus a couple of modern conveniences: the food processor and the blender. Yes, it's possible to enjoy your favorite comfort foods while actually *improving* and not jeopardizing your health.

What *Are* "Real" Foods?

The heading may sound like a silly question, but when people ask me how I eat and I answer, "Well, basically I just eat real food," I'm often met with a blank stare. I describe *real food* as food that is meant to be eaten by humans. Typically, this means foods that are grown or raised naturally and organically in nutrient-dense soils, preferably picked at the peak of their growth (and sometimes even foraged from the wild) tops my list. These are foods that are safe to eat raw and don't need to be specially treated in order for us to eat them. Also, these foods are mostly prepared and eaten in ways that don't completely denature or devoid them of all of their life-giving nutrients, enzymes, and naturally good micro-organisms. This means we need to incorporate a higher percentage of raw foods into our daily meals. I do this by simply using my blender for quick juices, smoothies, raw (warmed) soups, salad dressings, and a serving or two of cultured veggies. Knowing that I get plenty of raw foods in an easily digestible form during the day gives me more flexibility and peace of mind when dinnertime rolls around. Whether I feel like an elaborate meal or a simple one and whether I'm eating out or at home, I feel confident my body already received ample nutrition that day.

Prior to the Age of Agriculture, dairy and wheat, two of the most prevalent food allergens today, were not even part of the human diet. However, since fresh fruits, vegetables, and meats weren't always plentiful, other food sources were sought out *simply to fill our ancestors' bellies*. While small amounts of wheat and other grains and cow milk may have been an easy solution to hunger, they were also undoubtedly different years ago. Many of our great-grandparents grew up on fresh milk and bread. A century ago, these foods were clean and organic and unaltered. Wheat hadn't been bred and crossbred to become the modified wheat we have today. Our ancestors also knew to soak their grains, nuts, and seeds so they could digest them better and benefit from what nutrients they did offer. Most nuts and seeds were designed by nature to *not* be digested so their life cycle could continue. Eating large amounts of seeds, even sprouted, of inedible grasses is not good human food, in my opinion. Our ancestors never consumed the denatured pasteurized and homogenized dairy we have today. They raised animals that naturally grazed and usually cultured their milk products into things like sour cream, yogurt, and clabbered milk.

These days, enormous advertising campaigns, food addictions, bountiful grocery stores, busy schedules, and even the way we learn to cook have made it all too easy for us to make the poor decision to grab the package of processed food instead of the fresh produce and free-range meat. Real, whole, natural foods contain a multitude of vitamins, minerals, amino acids, enzymes, phytonutrients, and all the other co-factors that act in synergy and as catalysts in any number of bodily functions—from something that may *seem* basic, such as digestion, to the more difficult to understand processes, such as hormone production or brain chemistry. Processed foods and isolated supplements simply don't possess the life-giving mysteries contained in a piece of beautiful, ripened fruit.

When we make time to prepare our own food whenever possible, it means we *know what we're eating.* We can't simply rely on the organic food aisle because misleading labels often make it impossible to really know what we're buying. The FDA may deem small quantities of certain additives and chemicals safe for humans, but have they ever taken into consideration (or do they care?) the impact of *all* the various additives *combined* effects, the buildup in our tissues day after day, as well as the stealth, addictive properties many have? Recently, there have been many great new food companies popping up truly bringing better convenience products to us but I would still encourage all of us to rely first on organic Mother Nature, *not* the organic food aisle.

When I dine out, I choose a restaurant in my town that uses fresh, local ingredients. Eating some meals out is fun, of course, but unless you're lucky enough to have an organic "farm to table" restaurant in your town, you should take precautions. It's not that eating non-organically once a week is going to kill you (at least not right away), but once you know better, you just won't want to put the toxic seed oil many restaurants use as a salad dressing on their GMO salad into your body. I usually just bring my own salad dressing and my bread.

Organic versus GMO

Organic fruits and vegetables have been shown to produce specific enzymes that target fungal growth as well as inhibit the ability for angiogenesis (blood vessel production) in tumors. These abilities are un-comparable in non-organic produce. Organic produce and animal products are free from pesticides, genetically modified organisms (GMO), antibiotics, and growth hormones. *High quality, nutrient-dense food allows us to eat less while satisfying our needs.* Testing has shown that the nutrient quality of produce grown in pesticide-herbicide-ridden soils is highly inferior to those grown organically. Those chemicals also saturate the plant and are passed into our livestock feed and into our bodies, where their ill-effects have been linked to many medical issues, as well as the possibility of those we aren't even aware of yet. GMOs have been banned in Europe for more than a decade. Animals fed a non-organic, unnatural, grain-based diet full of toxic oils, hormones, and chemicals and contaminated with fungi *are what they eat, and so are we.* Personally, I prefer not to put any of this in my body, if I can help it, so I choose not to buy foods that are not organic, *whenever possible.*

Products labeled "Certified Organic" or "100 Percent Organic" don't contain GMOs. Some have trickier labels that may say "Made with Organic Ingredients," and they are allowed to contain up to 30 percent of non-organic ingredients and additives. These labels are *supposed* to use 100 percent non-GMO ingredients. Some companies are now labeling their products as "non-GMO," which is at least helpful.

Nearly every non-organic product in America today containing wheat, corn, soy, cotton-seed, or canola oil, and even rice, is contaminated with some form of genetically modified engineering. Besides the fact that we don't know exactly how our bodies process GMOs, or what their long-term effects are, they also contain antibiotics. Where else does this lead? Well, these genetically modified plants produce pollen that is not only transferred by birds and insects but also becomes airborne, cross-contaminating other crops and *forever* changing our landscape.

With our busy schedules and tight budgets, it's easy to fill up on convenience foods. This doesn't leave much room to eat the quantity and quality of fresh fruits and veggies our bodies need to look and feel great. That's why I add juices and smoothies to my day as well as keep a stash of homemade goodies in the freezer. If you get a few like-minded friends together, and each of you takes an hour out of your weekend to make a healthy, freezable dish from scratch, you can all share in the benefits.

The "Good Food" Movement: Eat Mostly Seasonally, Locally, and Organically

Growing our own food and supporting our local farmers in supplying us with healthy foods is the first step towards a real food lifestyle. Start with small changes: You *can* forgo the drive-thru and stop at your market. Speak to the manager and select as much food supplied by your local community as possible. You *can* adjust your budget to buy organic at least 80 percent of the time. There are significant differences between the nutrients obtained from a chemically raised tomato and an organic one. Why eat produce with half the nutrient value, when you can cut out your morning latte and put that money towards your local Farmer's Market or CSA (Community Supported Agriculture)? It's better to spend a little extra on real, good food instead of spending it on doctor visits later. A small, local farmer is more likely to use nutrient-dense soil and sustainable practices like crop rotation as opposed to large industrial farms. Also, the less travel time, the better for all.

Your backyard is a great place to learn about planting your own small garden and reaping the benefits. If you don't have much space, planter boxes or vertical set-ups can give you a good amount of produce. My nephew and his family live in Orange County (or, the OC if you watch un-Reality TV). He and his master gardening wife put me to shame with their creative use of every inch of space in their suburban back yard. They grow more vegetables than I ever have, keep chickens, and even a bee hive! (Don't know how legal that is in the OC, but their neighbors aren't complaining and I'm not handing out addresses.) Our garden varies from year to year, and I won't tell you we haven't battled pesky varmints on occasion, but we usually manage to grow something and buy organic for whatever else we need. If you're short on time or don't think you have a green thumb, I say just "fake it till you make it" (I guess that's the Californian in me) and start a neighborhood garden exchange. You grow the tomatoes and each of your neighbors grows and contributes different crops. It doesn't take much space or time to do this, but again there is a desire and commitment needed. Learning with your children is fun and more rewarding than it is work. Children especially love it when they realize the zucchini they grew in their garden is in their cupcake. Do you have room in your backyard for a couple of laying hens? They're easy to keep and fun to raise, if your area allows it. If not, try your best to seek out your local farmer, visit their farm, and teach your children where their food comes from and why it's important to know.

Real Foods *Are* Super Foods

I believe *all* edible plant foods cultivated in optimal conditions and consumed at their peak of freshness should be considered super foods. Just because we've recently discovered another potent anti-oxidant in an obscure plant from somewhere on the other side of the world (often brought to us in a processed form at an unaffordable cost) doesn't necessarily mean the latest age-defying discovery won't be found tomorrow in a sun-kissed, fuzzy peach (or another unassuming fruit or vegetable) right in your own backyard. Truly, the ultimate "fast food!"

Most of us would agree that it can be a bit overwhelming to understand and remember the intricate workings of the human body and mind, and how it relates to what the last diet book said, or what the newest in the ever-changing field of science has found. Attempting to incorporate this all into daily life is not only impossible but also often defies practicality and a family budget. However, no one looks forward to a revolving door to the doctor's office and living on prescription pills, so we must do what we can *now*. We *can* break the habit of grabbing a package, even if it says organic or gluten-free. We *can* choose to eat from the garden because broccoli, for instance, contains a substance (isothiocyanate) that sparks hundreds of genetic changes by activating genes that fight cancer while deactivating genes that promote tumors. *But we don't need to know and remember all of this or the long names and details*. We just need to know this type of *real food*, mostly plant, is what we should be eating. It's okay to choose an *occasional* package, just carefully read the label before buying. By cultivating a desire to help ourselves and our family feel better, look better, and live longer, we will gain the willpower needed to change our thinking, our habits, and the future of our health.

It's *Your* Ultimate Choice

Ultimately, we have choices, and my choices have brought me to the lifestyle I keep today. I haven't owned a bathroom scale in over two decades, and my favorite pair of old (and I mean *old*) blue jeans that I use to remind me when I've over-indulged too many times still fit. I have a healthy weight constitution and a feeling of abundance, not of denial. It has truly put the joy back into mealtime for my family and me. This is my hope for you, too.

We all have busy lives in this hectic world, but if making a hair appointment, work obligations, or a soccer match is more important to you than what's on your dinner table, then you can probably plan for your health and energy to suffer. Now is the time to change that. With technology, science, and medical advancements, we have the ability to live a much longer and better quality of life today than our ancestors ever did, *if* we take charge of what we put into our bodies *now*, so our bodies can heal and begin to thrive. *No matter what our age, it's never too late to start a new beginning.*

Chapter 3:
Cleanse Your Body and
Reset Your Life

. . . .

For many years I convinced myself that as long as I ate mostly good, fresh food, "a little of this" and "a little of that" wasn't a problem. I was wrong. Somewhere along the way, my knees got worse. I contracted a C-difficile infection, which causes serious inflammation in the colon when dangerous bacteria release toxins that attack the lining of the intestines. The pain and swelling spread to other joints and soft tissues. Of course, the medical community offered drugs, as I said earlier, one being a form of oral chemotherapy, to help control my conditions. I had already tried numerous cleanses, probiotics and antibiotics, and intense herbal and other types of therapies, but I found that while I would feel better for a short time, my symptoms always returned, and generally they were even worse. *I'm too young to act like an old lady,* I thought. I was too vain to allow others to see that even getting up from a chair was often excruciating. At times I felt pretty hopeless, especially when I came to understand that these virulent germs become resistant to various treatments and evolve into even more hardy strains. If you have similar or other "auto-immune" symptoms and choose a pharmaceutical treatment to assist you, implementing a cleanse and clean-eating lifestyle will help to curb side effects and bolster your healing.

After each cleanse and/or therapy I employed, I would ultimately resume my typical way of eating, which didn't include *enough* healing raw fruits and veggies and still included small amounts of coconut sugar and refined starch. Eventually, I realized that even in small amounts these non-foods were literally stoking chronic infections in my body, causing constant damage and weakened immunity. It was a pattern that needed to be changed.

Most good healing plans to help people regain their health and vitality suggest about 90 days as a minimum commitment to reset your body. That may be true for many, but depending upon your particular issues, how widespread and deeply they've been imbedded in your system, it could be much longer. It's also impossible to maintain the health you've regained by returning to your old lifestyle. After a body and mind reset, maintaining a "Real Food Lifestyle" forever isn't difficult, because by simply eating real food and using recipes like these, you should always feel completely satisfied and content.

Many of the cookbooks and websites devoted to gluten/grain-free eating began because someone became sick. If that's not the case with you, why wait until poor health is an obvious concern? *Everyone,* young or old, sick or healthy, will benefit by omitting all non-organic produce and livestock as well as wheat and most other grains, processed sugars, and low-fat, denatured dairy from their diets. Once you see and feel the difference, you'll never want to go back to your old way of cooking and eating.

These days, I like to perform a mini reset four times a year, with the change of the seasons. I take an hour or two to give my kitchen a little "rebirth" and look forward to the new crops of seasonal fruits and veggies we'll be adding to our meals. Because I'm happy with how I eat, these little resets seem to be more emotional, psychological, or spiritual for me rather than physical. Nonetheless, they give me that time to slow down and refocus, so I really look forward to them now. What grows in each season depends upon where you live. For instance, I've actually been able to grow certain tomatoes year-round here, while I probably wouldn't be able to do that if I lived in Wisconsin (unless I had a greenhouse, I suppose). The best way to discover what's in season in your area is to visit your farmer's market. While I'm all for world trade and getting along with our neighbors, I still prefer not to buy zucchini that's been shipped from Mexico and grass-fed meat from Australia, when I can support more local efforts. Being aware of what is grown locally to us will automatically help us buy what is fresh and in season in our area, possibly encouraging us to try a fruit or vegetable that we might not otherwise choose. This also gives our body a wider variety of nutrients when we're encouraged to change up our selections. Never had figs? What do you do with persimmons? Lucky for us, we now have search engines at our fingertips! This is not to say that I don't ever buy frozen berries or mangos and bananas shipped from South America, but I like to support local agriculture as much as possible.

What I Learned from My Own Clean Up

I have witnessed firsthand that natural treatments not widely shared in our society work miracles. One time my son's dog's tumor was killed and removed by using Blood Root salve after the veterinarian had no treatment to offer. Another son and my husband used Manuka honey to kill their deadly "super bug" (MRSA) skin infections when their antibiotic treatment didn't work. Supporting my body to heal and maintain health without damaging it with pharmaceuticals is always my first preference. In a nutshell, this is what I've learned over the years:

- We can't fix our health, or weight problems, with a seven-day or even a thirty-day cleanse/detox. It's a good start, but it takes a full commitment to reset and heal the body, and the timing will be individually specific to each of us, *so patience and perseverance are key.*
- The chances of a chronic, stealth infection being at the root of many problems, including "auto-immune" issues, is high. The many different strains of Epstein-Barr virus, *Staphylococcus aureus* (commonly know as MRSA, and is *not* just a skin infection), cytomegalovirus, herpes, mycoplasmas, various strep and staph infections, and fungi, only name a few organisms we know of that can cause ongoing issues.
- Generations living on earth today have inherited nutrient deficient bodies, unhealthy gut flora, and infections causing widespread inflammation and literally changing our genome.
- Toxins from "modern conveniences," overuse of antibiotics, chlorine, "fake" foods, widespread germ exposure/food poisoning, damaged guts, "dirty" vaccinations, heavy metals, medications, and lack of accurate detection, understanding, and treatments, leave us weakened and susceptible for co-infections and for these microbes to flourish.
- Aside from chronic infections, chemicals, and damaged digestion, nutritional deficiencies further deplete us and promote glandular and hormone imbalances, having profound effects on body systems, immunity, and weight-loss factors.
- It is imperative that we have a healthy, functioning lymph (our blood's drainage system) and digestive system lined with beneficial bacteria. Besides immunity, these bacteria greatly affect metabolism and weight.

- We need raw food enzymes to help our body with the process of digestion. Culturing and fermenting foods enhance enzymes and provide life-giving probiotics for our gut, more than probiotic pills provide.
- We eat too much. And most of what we use to void our hunger is devoid of nutrients that feed our cells. Our bodies signal that they are hungry, because we are starving our cells of nutrients while providing them with too much sugar/refined carbs in the form of grains and starches. This fattens, ages, and continues to sicken us.
- We need nutrient-dense, easy-to-digest foods, so the vitamins, minerals, enzymes, amino acids, fats, proteins, healthy carbohydrates, and all their cofactors can be broken down by our stomach acid and gut bacteria and fed to our cells and organs, allowing them to regulate each system and create constant energy.
- Organic fruit (remember, anything with seeds is considered a fruit) contains numerous disease-fighting benefits. Don't let the diet police scare you into believing that the studies done on laboratory-made fructose is the same as the natural fructose in fruit.
- We need plenty of natural, saturated fats. We *don't need* grains and extracted starches. Saturated fats are building blocks for brain cells and hormone production. Decades of low-fat eating has helped produce a generation of young women with fertility problems now.
- We must maintain blood sugar and insulin levels in a normal range (with the right eating habits) in order to maintain health. Both raise acidity and deplete minerals, hindering our natural ability to detoxify and making us prone to aging and disease.
- Feeling tired, fatigued, plump, bloated, hot, cold, depressed, or achy, is *not* normal, no matter what your age, as they are not signs of aging. They're signs of a struggling body.
- A decision to help your body heal and return to optimal health needs to be followed by a simple strategy in order to stay the course and make it your new lifestyle.
- Our thoughts are affected by the health of the body and mind. Deficiencies and imbalances can create unhealthy thoughts and actions. Our thoughts and how we perceive our environment can literally change our genes.
- If your body has a chronic infection/illness many natural modalities along with diet may greatly improve your condition—however, the amount of improvement/recovery will be unique to you and your illness.
- True cravings are the result of addictions or deficiencies.

Pamper Your Belly

To improve my overall health, my first order of business was to pamper my belly—because a damaged gut cannot absorb nutrients efficiently. Even if you think you don't have gut issues, my guess would be that you're so accustomed to your routine that you may not even realize you're not running as efficiently as you should be. Improving gut function allowed me to create energy for my body to then begin to clean and heal from the inside. The best defense against pathogens and toxins is to keep immunity strong, so invaders are beaten before they're able to make our body their home. If you have a damaged gut, it cannot protect the rest of your body. I found that a diet that included processed carbs and GMOs (designed to blow up the stomachs of insects), the unnatural fructose in processed foods, gluten/gliadin proteins in wheat and other difficult to digest proteins in other grains, past infections, antibiotics and other medications, fluoridated water and toothpastes, and a lack of raw food enzymes had lowered my stomach acid and changed my intestinal microbiome. Studies show certain bacteria strains can even be responsible for adding on and keeping those extra pounds.

Low stomach acid (often misdiagnosed as just the opposite) means poor digestion of proteins, less bile and enzymes released, and allows pathogens that enter through the mouth to continue their journey. This creates mineral and other deficiencies and can have a domino effect in the body. When the large intestine has an overgrowth of bacteria or lacks the correct essential bacteria and cannot produce the enzymes necessary to break down carbohydrates, it can cause extreme amounts of painful symptoms. It's very frustrating and confusing when even healthy fruits and vegetables seem to cause issues. If this is the case with you, you can have your doctor test for fructose malabsorption, but a temporary food elimination plan is a reliable way to detect which foods are most problematic for you. Even probiotics and healthy cultured foods can cause problems if you're suffering from a bacterial imbalance. There are herbs and enzymes that can help, but a juice fast works wonders here, particularly celery and cucumber juice. Juice gives you nutrients without the fiber to feed the bacteria, giving your body time to heal and correct the issue. For very difficult issues there are more extreme treatments a good functional medicine doctor can suggest.

No matter what the cause, the simple fact is that whatever your situation may be, you still need to receive adequate nutrients to improve and promote healing. The good news is that given the opportunity our mucosal linings heal fairly rapidly, and once you've changed your diet and your symptoms wane, it's likely you'll be able to enjoy these foods again.

To begin with, I used an "elimination diet" approach by eliminating anything I thought could aggravate my gut for about four weeks. This included a lot of healthy foods too, so basically all I ate during this time was gently simmered non-starchy vegetables and broth, fruit, and eggs. Some of you may need to eliminate eggs in the beginning. After four weeks I added different foods back into my diet and noted any reaction. If you research an "elimination diet" or an "auto-immune protocol" there are many books and online sources to walk you through this stage. Once you determine offending foods, continue to eliminate them until you are healed enough that they no longer bother you. For me, onions, garlic, and mushrooms were the worst offenders.

You Hold the Key to Boosting Immunity

Aside from exposure to bacteria and viruses, fungal mycotoxin infections often go undiagnosed and untreated by modern medicine. Mycotoxin-producing fungi have been found in many areas of our food supply, from the soil foods are grown in, to grains, beans, nuts, coffee, dairy, corn, and even some fruits. It's impossible to know when you may be exposed. Mycotoxins are released by mycoplasmas, which are parasitic in nature and cause widespread inflammation as a body attempts to combat the invasion. Mycoplasmas are particularly difficult to detect because they lack a cell wall and are easily able to change forms and evade the immune system. While some other countries screen for up to eight different species, the United States currently only screens for aflatoxins (the most carcinogenic substance known on earth!) and allows a small percentage to contaminate our food and livestock feed supply. The mycotoxins as well as their spore form are both heat stable and, astonishingly, cannot be killed through regular cooking methods. This information is not meant to scare you but, instead, to encourage you to be aware of the need to know your food supply chain whenever possible and *to nurture and protect your immune system so it can protect YOU.*

Tips to Enhance Your Immunity
- Drink freshly juiced celery/cucumber and bone broth (or veggie equivalent on page 190) with sea salt to help correct, heal, and optimize your digestion.
- Keep your inner "garden" strong by omitting sugar, grains, refined starches, and most processed "food."
- Include cultured and fermented foods and drinks in your diet as soon as your tummy can tolerate it.
- Correct deficiencies by drinking fresh juices and smoothies.
- Use high quality, multi-vitamin/mineral supplements.
- Feed the "firmicute" bacteria, a species that promotes a balanced weight, with polyphenols found in berries, coffee, and chocolate.
- Exercise, outside in the sunshine whenever possible, to get your lymph fluids moving and for more vitamin D.
- Drink real mineral water by adding liquid plant minerals to filtered water.
- Use mineral-rich, high quality sea salt liberally.
- See a dentist regularly to catch any gum disease early (the same bacteria found in gum disease has been isolated from plaque in arteries).
- Manage stress with exercise, creative visualization, mini-meditations or prayer, finding something to laugh about, deep breathing, and tapping (I like to gently tap my fingertips on my face to relax—don't laugh, try it right now!).
- Get adequate and peaceful sleep by learning to manage stress and not staring at blue light (TV, computer, cell phone) until all hours. Most of us no longer make enough melatonin and supplementing can be very helpful for sleep in particular.
- Take immune-boosting herbs and teas with a dose of spirulina.
- Add an anti-viral/bacterial supplement containing oregano oil, black walnut, garlic, clove, olive leaf, turmeric, etc. to your routine for prevention, especially when eating out. Charcoal or psyllium can help sweep the intestines of possible unwanted guests as well.
- Relax, forgive, use meditation/prayer to open your heart to give and receive as much love as possible (human, nature, and animal).
- Accept that you can't go back and change the past but you can start now to make the future you want.

Whether you're dealing with an "auto-immune" infection or just discouraging the next cold virus, this is the best way to ward off any of these dangerous invaders. Eat to protect and nourish your gut lining, keep your blood clean and full of alkalizing minerals and nutrients, and live a life that supports your immune system. Keep it as strong as it can be to discourage the ability for germs to take hold.

Why I Believe in Fasting

Fasting is an essential tool I used for my own body/mind reset and continue to use today. I decided to begin my reset with a fast after realizing Western medicine's solution for me was a chemo drug and not what I had in mind to help me. Fasting has been used throughout history to improve mental, physical, and spiritual health, and recent studies cite various health benefits. How it works: Our cells generally burn glucose, which the body makes from carbohydrates for fuel. During a water-only fast, your body will generally use up its glucose stores in one to two days. After this, your liver will then begin to turn fatty acids into something called "ketones" to use as fuel. Brain cells burn ketones very efficiently, which may contribute to the clarity and sometimes euphoric feelings a fast often brings on (once you're past the first couple of difficult days).

Supporting this is the brief omission of food, which conserves energy because it rests the digestive organs and keeps toxins from constantly rolling in. This extra energy allows the body to use its natural resources, such as enzymes and white blood cells, to help eliminate things like metabolic waste, damaged cells, pathogens, and other toxins. The more alkaline your blood and lymph system, the better (think minerals, green juices for alkalinity), as this toxic load being dumped is very acid forming, and acid blood will inhibit the body from dumping more toxins into it. Fasting also reduces the amount of opportunistic fungi and bacteria in the colon as they lose their food source. By the third day, the body should begin to burn fat for its fuel, so the toxins that have been stored in fat cells should now be able to be dumped at a high rate of efficiency. Some people experience flu-like symptoms from "carb withdrawal" and toxin release, which should clear after a day or so, depending on your body. During this time, I make sure to help my body to keep its detox pathways open as much as possible by drinking plenty of alkalizing fluids like mineral-enriched water. I like to use a brush on my skin both before and during my showers to stimulate my lymph system.

Though you're not eating at this time, the bowels should still be eliminating; if not, stir a little psyllium, vitamin C, sea salt, or magnesium into water to assist in this. An infrared sauna, or a good dose of sunshine, stretching, yoga, prayer/meditation, bathing, and reading, are perfect accompaniments to fasting. If you choose to follow a similar path and you're used to exercising, a little moderate exercise during this time is fine.

If you're relatively healthy, fasting is a safe, natural way to complement a life change. As I mentioned, this process takes a couple of days, so you won't be eliminating a lot of toxins until then. If the thought of a water fast is too scary, a fresh juice fast provides your body with nutrients without the burden of digestion and is a bit easier, especially if you're new to the idea of fasting.

What is Intermittent Fasting?

For me, intermittent fasting is just a fancy term for skipping breakfast. It just means to incorporate longer periods between meals on a consistent basis. Whether it's skipping a meal, or fasting one day a week, or both, it has been shown to have numerous health benefits. I usually only have smoothies/food during the hours of 12–6 or, maybe as late as 2–8 (depending on my schedule) instead of eating all day long.

I believe eating this way has mental and emotional benefits as well, as I've witnessed personally. My body has the time to rest between digestion, my mind isn't constantly thinking about what to eat. With full-day fasting I quickly learned that regular feelings of hunger are just because my stomach was used to getting food in a certain pattern and it would tell my brain it's hungry. I also discovered that I am not going to die without food for a day. As a matter of fact, hunter-gatherers often went long stretches without food; it's not an unnatural way of living—it's just counter to what we've been taught in this land of abundance.

Don't tell the diet police I've skipped breakfast for the better part of my life. I now often include one day a week, usually Monday, as what I call a *rest* day rather than a *fast* day. That's because as I see it I don't have to go to the trouble involved with eating. No shopping, cooking, or dirty dishes! I drink plenty of mineral water, herbal tea, or green juice, and plan something

I look forward to around dinner time. Maybe a massage or a movie or a bath and a good book. Sound crazy? Think about it—you will learn to embrace the slight hunger pangs your previous habit was to squelch, by turning your thoughts instead to how good it feels to clean out and give your gut a rest. You won't feel bloated because you overate, and you don't have to spend any time in the kitchen or waiting at a restaurant. Soon, I believe you will even begin to look forward to this day. Have a family that doesn't want to fast? That's okay; they can eat a delicious sandwich made with my healthy bread recipes, so you don't have to spend time in the kitchen or smell something cooking.

What Is Ketosis and "Keto Adapted" and How Is It Beneficial?

The "elimination" and "ketogenic" plan are the "diets" I followed to clean up my body and begin to bring my health back. While going Keto seems to be a popular weight-loss strategy these days, I did it to help me feel assured I had cleared (or at least sent into remission) as many sugar-consuming pathogens as possible that may have taken up residency in my body. Remaining on a Ketogenic Diet for a period of time has been shown to be extremely beneficial in managing many diseases, from epilepsy to even cancer, as well as for speedy weight loss. A Ketogenic Diet is essentially a very low-carb (approximately 5–10 percent), high-fat (approximately 60–70 percent), and moderate protein (25–35 percent) diet that forces the body to break down fats into ketones to burn for its fuel rather than a constant flow of readily available glucose. For instance, for a woman who weighs 150 pounds and eats approximately 1600 calories a day, this would equate to 136 grams of fat, 74 grams of protein, and 20 grams of net carbs (carbs minus the fiber).

The goal is to actually keep your body pumping out ketones, so you know your cells aren't using glucose for their energy. It also means if there's a glucose-eating pathogen lurking in a cell, you won't be feeding it. Frequent eating of carb-rich foods reduces the body's ability to burn fat and to lose its ability to produce ketones. Once we correct this, we become "fat adapted" and our bodies will easily use fat as a primary fuel source, reversing many health issues caused by the abundance of glucose.

So, the reason I suggest a Ketogenic Diet for an additional cleansing period after fasting (or, if you choose not to fast) is this: When carbohydrates are consumed, insulin escorts as much of the sugar as it can into the cells to use for energy. Some of it will be converted to glycogen and stored in the liver and muscles for later use, released between meals when blood sugar is low and during exercise. Meanwhile, the yeasts are consuming as much as they can gobble up, while the body begins to store the rest as fat. All carbohydrates, simple or complex, are broken down by the body into glucose. So, by omitting all sugar and all processed carbs, there is no quick, easy food for the fungi or cancer to eat and no extra fat to be stored. *Cancer and fungi cannot burn ketones for food, so they begin to die. Plain and simple.* Unfortunately, when cancer has been fed long and abundantly, it will spread and grow its own blood vessels, making it much more difficult to kill.

Once your body is "fat adapted," it can easily switch from burning ketones to glucose and back again. *This is the natural state your body should've been in your entire life* and how humans were meant to eat *before* the "eat three meals a day" mantra and refined grains, sugar, starch, and processed foods came into play—all of which keep our blood sugar soaring. Once adapted, to remain on a ketogenic diet, most people report keeping their net carb count to about 50 grams per day, ideally from just organic fruits and vegetables and not grains or processed foods.

During this time, I choose to omit dairy, however the difficult part for me was limiting fruits and vegetables because of their carb content. It is logical to me that (organic) fruits and vegetables are not an enemy just because they have fruit fructose and carbohydrates. While it's my humble opinion that omitting grains and processed carbs is what makes this diet so successful, I heeded this scientific approach and did not try to change it up. I admit that physically counting my macro nutrients (fat, proteins, carbs) was irritating and aggravating. I used "keto test strips" (you can purchase them at your local pharmacy) to make it easy to make sure I produced adequate ketones for about a month after my fasts. There are several books and websites devoted to the Ketogenic Diet which can explain it in much more detail.

Once the body is rid of fungal overgrowth, adding plenty of (organic) fruits and vegetables to the diet is, I believe, the most beneficial and enjoyable way to eat. Fruits and veggies have been proven to have many disease-fighting and cancer-fighting abilities. Organic fruits that provide natural fructose also make substances that defend them from fungi. These substances are passed on to our bodies when we eat the fruit. Laboratory-made fructose is *not* the same.

The other carbs? Grains and starches have few, if any, benefits and unless you are a bird, they are *not necessary in any way*. Even the so-called "good whole grains" benefits are *not comparable* to fresh organic fruits and veggies, and can do more harm than good. There are only two reasons you crave these carbs:

1. Processed, starchy carbs are addicting.
2. The yeast and fungi are messaging via your vagus nerve (that runs from your gut to your brain) that they want food.

Because of the detoxification the body undergoes during the time it's adapting to ketosis, you may not feel too great. This is one reason I recommend a fast, because it brings you into ketosis quickly, however the flu-like symptoms may be intensified with a fast, so a quiet Friday through Sunday is a good time to start.

Like I mentioned, you can take longer by just eliminating most carbs instead. While it generally takes anywhere from 3 or 4 weeks (or longer) to become fully keto adapted, everyone's different, and the way you go about it could either prolong your pain or ease the symptoms. Also, taking enzymes at this time of change is really important, because your body will need to start producing plenty of fat-burning enzymes (lipase) instead of the ones that burn carbs (amylase). You may have headaches and be generally pretty cranky for a few days, not just because your body is adapting, but also because you'll likely be experiencing some withdrawal symptoms from your body's dependence upon sugar and carbs. Eating more good fat (fatty meats and fish, butter, eggs, nuts, sour cream, raw cheese, avocado, coconut) will stabilize your blood sugar and help cut your cravings. Fat is also very satiating, not to mention yummy.

Real Food for Life

Once I finished my reset plan, I began what I call my "Real Food Life." This means I'll have lower carb and higher carb days now, which come mainly from my veggies and fruit. A dietary lifestyle has to be practical to live by 24/7, becoming our lifestyle so that we never feel like we're on a *diet*. This lifestyle works for me and brings a sense of peace instead of tension to my mealtime. I feel healthy, happy, and incredibly indulged with my eating pattern *and* the food I eat. With these recipes in this book, it's easy to bake my own breads, pastas, and desserts. I often freeze some, so I can have an even quicker pizza crust or treat available.

Just a precaution: If you're prone to hypoglycemia (low blood sugar), which can happen when someone who's been eating a high-carb diet drastically reduces their carbohydrate intake or goes on a fast for the first time, the drastic reduction of food and/or carbs has not given the body enough time to create the right enzymes (remember to take enzymes) or metabolic state to burn fat for fuel. If you feel dizziness, nausea, or shakiness, eat or drink a little something and lay down.

The Benefits of Healing Broth and Spirulina

Broth, slowly cooked vegetable or bone broth, is very healing and comforting to the digestive system and has loads of benefits for the entire body. Bone broth is full of vitamins, minerals, amino acids, gelatin, collagen, and more good things. It's very healing to the gut tissue, heart, skin, muscles, and bones. While bone broth contains collagen, the vegetarian version contains foods that promote our body to produce collagen. There's obviously plenty of debate as to which is the better choice and that is clearly up to you and your individuality. The point is, choose one and drink it during this time, then implement it into your everyday lifestyle.

I always keep spirulina around during a reset or fasting period. I add it to my healing broth recipe (page 190) to make it easy to drink daily. Spirulina is a blue-green algae that is best harvested from deep Hawaiian waters or grown organically. This algae is thousands of years old and, like mycoplasmas, lacks a cell wall, as true algae do. High in minerals and amino acids, spirulina is 65–71 percent protein.

Spirulina has been consumed for thousands of years by people all around the world. It has been shown to significantly improve the immune system, increase endurance, thin the blood, and help break down clots and eliminate heavy metals and toxins. Sadly, our freshwater lakes, which also grow spirulina, are contaminated now, but spirulina grown organically or from deep, pristine waters is a powerful blood cleansing, chelating (heavy metal remover), and alkalizing agent. Does it taste good? Not so much, but then you don't need much, and if you don't make the broth, there are other ways to disguise the taste (fresh lemon juice works for me)—unless, of course, you like the taste of algae.

If fasting in any form is just not appealing, no worries—you can still detox and reset your body. It may take a bit more time with changes occurring more slowly, but it may be the best way for you. In this case, I would suggest following a ketogenic plan for 6–12 weeks.

Why I Consume Cultured and Fermented Foods

With the popularity of over-the-counter probiotic use now, it's obvious that people are finally beginning to understand the importance of maintaining a healthy balance of bacteria in the gut. Research is showing that the types of microbes we house will even regulate our metabolism and fat absorption. Ever wonder why some people are just thin and others aren't no matter what they seem to eat? The foods we eat will allow certain types of bacteria to flourish, and these bacteria even affect our cravings.

Eating fresh from your organic garden is best and safest way to eat, though not very practical for most people these days. Garden foods contain wonderful micro-organisms right on their skins that flourish in our bodies. It's clear we don't get enough of them anymore, so using the ancient method of food preservation is a wonderful way to up the beneficial bacteria in our system.

Fermented foods have been part of humankind for thousands of years. Dozens of cultures have used this process for preserving foods before refrigeration was available. High in enzymes, these foods are teeming with essential bacteria that help with digestion, make essential nutrients, eliminate toxins, strengthen our immunity, and cleanse our cells. From sauerkraut to salsa or pickles (the real kind that are naturally fermented with bacteria and not made by using heat), to kimchi, kefir, and kvass, you're bound to find something you like. These condiments round out a meal and pair perfectly with fats, cheeses, eggs, meat, salads, beans, and potatoes. Take them in small amounts at first, until your body is accustomed to their powerful cleaning abilities.

Capsules with only a small number of microbes known to be beneficial (even beneficial bacteria can overgrow and become pathogenic) cannot compare to the power of raw, cultured vegetables, which contain far more strains of beneficial bacteria than found in a bottle. We need a diverse microbiome for optimum health and immune protection. Fermented veggies also provide us with a great source of vitamin K_2, which escorts calcium out of our blood and into our cells where it belongs, reducing the risk of artery disease, blockages, or clots. If your gut microflora has been disrupted, it may be the root of any number of issues, including weight control and disease.

Fermented and cultured foods are easy to make. While I've included a few of my favorite cultured recipes here, you can also find books on the subject and many recipes on the Internet. These days they're even easy to buy. Be sure you purchase a good brand that provides hardy strains of friendly microflora. Cruciferous veggies in particular, like cabbage, ferment wonderfully and are high in the super anti-oxidant glutathione, which has shown to detoxify by-products of toxic fungal wastes.

Gluten-Free and Paleo Versus Simply Real Food

While gluten has been found to be damaging to humans, the habit of replacing gluten with refined starches or starchy flours in gluten-free baking is not promoting health or weight balance in general. Many gluten-free and Paleo cookbooks rely heavily on extracted starches, starchy flours, and high-glycemic sweeteners, such as coconut sugar, to make their baked goods. Remember, when you combine these things, it's quite a sugar slam that your bloodstream is getting. A person who follows a lifestyle filled with refined starches or starchy flours will likely be nurturing a simmering fungal overgrowth. If these baked goods are a once a month treat, it might not be a huge concern. But if your family is anything like mine, we like to enjoy treats much more often than one time a month!

Taking a little time out of life to follow a short-term plan that assists your body in regaining its natural state of health and balance *before* it becomes overwhelmed is something I believe you'll never regret. Once I did that, rather than joining a specific dietary group, I just choose to *keep it simple*:

1. Eat the *real, whole, organic, foods* Mother Nature provides.
2. Enjoy the sunshine and outdoor activities.
3. Love big and find something to laugh about.

It really is just a simple lifestyle that I live and using these recipes makes keeping this lifestyle easy because I don't feel like I'm giving up or sacrificing anything. We have bread, sweets, cheese (dairy or vegan is your choice), creamy sauces, and all the comfort foods we like, with a ton of full flavors.

Let the Sun Shine On

The media (and our California Tourist Board) likes to portray a California that is mostly a glitzy "Tinsel Town," with money, celebrities, Valley girls, and health nuts. Yes, California has its share of us "kooks" and being touted as the sixth largest economy in the world yields some power, I suppose. But *my* California is full of a kind, diverse, active, and intelligent demographic of people who may appear a bit out-of-the-box, but are also often at the forefront of good change.

There's nothing better than sharing good food and drink with good company, and while it's understandable many of us have dietary guidelines we like to follow, we don't want to cast a dark cloud over a joyful dinner table. We all need to remember that a common desire in humans is to bring people together, which, I believe, is usually why we argue. We want the other person to see and understand our way of thinking, our "side." When the other person doesn't come over to our side, no matter what the reason, we need to be gracious, especially when it involves something as fundamental as choosing which foods to put into our bodies, or not. The dinner table is a wonderful place to learn to embrace each other's differences rather than (find more ways to) put wedges between us. The last thing we ever want to do is cause angry feelings in ourselves or *anyone else* because of our conflicting eating choices. This comes to mind when I see T-shirts with provoking slogans or negative comments on social media. Let's live and teach by good example.

It's not cool to make someone defend their choice or to try to force someone to eat or not eat something. However, if eating something is not life-threatening, I've found that relaxing my rules on occasion is the best choice for me. I don't have celiac disease, I just prefer to fill my belly with more nutrient-dense foods than grains. A slice of regular pizza at my niece's birthday party is not going to kill me, but for some it could make them very sick, so understanding and acceptance is key.

We can all help to bridge these gaps. It's not difficult to prepare a meal without meat, but it may take some extra effort if you're not used to it. If you're vegan and eggs or dairy are served at the table, just smile and be happy that nothing had to give its life for the meal; and if there's meat served, remember we're all different and any evolution is on our own timeline. Let's be thankful and allow meals to connect us again because teaching and learning can move mountains. With patience, they can also change habits, opinions, and the food on the dinner table. Bon appétit!

Chapter 4:
My California Country Kitchen

When I made the decision to improve my health I eliminated many items from my diet that I believe are harmful—oils such as canola, soy, and most seed oils, grains, sugar, and starches. Fortunately, we now have several options that taste great and won't destroy our health to replace these common baking ingredients. However, most gluten/grain-free baking ingredients include various starches to replace the gluten. Unfortunately, I found that using these starches and starchy flours and "flour-blends" caused me to gain a little tire around my mid-section. The starch I now use in my baking comes from the whole fruit or vegetable, not the extracted starch sold on the grocery store shelves.

Preparing classic American and other comfort foods were always at the top of my list, because raising four boys meant a lot of BBQs, birthdays, and other occasions where feeding and satisfying a crowd was pretty common in my household.

The high-powered food processors and blenders available today make it easier than ever to use whole foods in so many ways. They're terrific to help us get an abundance of nutrients in our bodies that we may not otherwise eat, and it keeps us from cooking everything to death. The best news is that you don't *ever* have to feel like you're depriving yourself or your family, because when you're using these recipes, your meals will not only be packing a ton of nutrients but also taste delicious.

If you eat organically and from your local community, your chance of eating seasonally improves. Visiting the farmer's market in your area is helpful for learning your area's growing patterns. Produce in season is usually a bit less expensive, and because it doesn't have to be shipped many miles, it's also at its peak of freshness, taste, and nutrient levels. I keep frozen (organic) produce in my freezer as well.

Your Real Food Pantry

While traditional gluten-free and even most Paleo baking strives to duplicate wheat's taste and texture with a whole lot of refined starches and starchy flours, I've chosen a different path. Over the last decade I've worked with dozens of alternative flours and discovered many different flavors and properties in them. Whether grain, nut, seed, vegetable, or fruit, each of these have distinct flavors, textures, and properties they bring to a dish—all of them lacking the stretchy gluten that wheat flour (all-purpose and whole) provides. It was easy at first to reach for the gluey, sticky, blood-sugar-spiking extracted starches used in traditional gluten-free baking, because they so closely mimic gluten. But after less than a month of experiments, guess what I noticed? Yep, I was developing a belly! At first I thought it was just my age (let's just pretend I was 40ish), stress, lack of exercise . . . *anything* but what I thought was my "healthier" way of cooking and eating! But Noooo, it was none of those. It was "Starch Belly" . . . definitely Starch Belly.

I thought I might wither away without breads and pastas and baked goodies. I *knew* my family would. Yikes! Then, I had a miraculous light bulb moment in my little brain, and so I began experimenting with easy-to-come-by, *real*, whole fruits and veggies, with all of their naturally delicious and balanced amounts of fibers, juices, oils, and whatever other wonderful things Mother Nature used to make them. Add in some coconut and nuts, and I was amazed! I found that I could use these whole foods to replace typical white and wheat flours. The fresh fruits and vegetables usually provided enough liquid and fiber that could replace added oil and milk. As years passed, almond flour and coconut flour became less expensive, fresher, and easier to buy, so I began adjusting many of my recipes for their use instead of the shredded coconut and whole nuts I usually used. I was also thrilled when I discovered I could actually buy plantain and sweet potato flour, but because those are not readily available yet, I'll need to save most of those recipes for another book! The taste, texture, and benefits to my family that these ingredients provide assures me I will never bake another way again.

Most of the ingredients I use should be quite easy for you to find. Many of them are common items that are easy to grab and will become your new staples, *instead of* starchy flours, sugar, milk, and unstable oils. Simply keep these ingredients on hand in your pantry, refrigerator, or freezer. Remember, try your best to always buy organic and preferably from your local area farms.

Almond flour, coconut flour, erythritol/monk fruit, stevia, and psyllium husks are found in natural foods stores, in the organic or gluten-free aisle of your supermarket, and online. The brand you buy is often very important because they can vary greatly. So, for these items in particular, I would stick to my suggestion in my Resources (page 296). While I enjoy legumes, you'll notice I don't bake with bean or other typical "ancient grain" or gluten-free flours, such as rice or sorghum or flour "blends," as I don't care for their various properties or don't believe them to be beneficial for us.

The ingredients I most commonly feature in these recipes include:

- Blanched almond flour
- Unsweetened shredded coconut and coconut flour
- Walnuts, pecans, brazil, and other nuts
- Sweet potatoes and yams
- Veggies and fruits (zucchini, yellow squash, beets, carrots, eggplant, winter squash, apples, cherries, berries, dates, and citrus fruits)
- Dehydrated sweet potato powder
- Psyllium husk powder
- Chia
- Eggs
- Egg white powder
- Butter
- Heavy cream, cream cheese, sour cream (you can also use your favorite non-dairy substitutes)
- Dark chocolate/cocoa
- Pure monk fruit and stevia sweeteners (liquid and powder)
- Date "sugar" (ground whole dates) and occasional erythritol sweeteners
- Sustainably sourced coconut oil and palm shortening
- Sea salt

Note: Cassava or yuca flour (the whole root that tapioca starch is derived from) is becoming popular for gluten/grain-free baking. I've opted to leave it out of my cupboards because the natural root contains a high enough concentration of a toxin that turns to cyanide when eaten raw so that it must be processed in order to be edible and not toxic. The Japanese have banned its use in human food production for years. I don't use or promote any foods that are highly processed in order to be consumed.

Tips for Stopping Starchy, Sugary Carb Cravings in Their Tracks

When your body is cleaned up, your cravings will change or cease. Until then, you may still have yeasts messaging for food, emotional attachments, addiction triggers in the brain, just plain old bad habits, or other reasons that a processed carb craving may hit you. If that happens, and you can't grab a pre-made treat from these recipes, try one of the following:

- First of all, if you always keep on hand ingredients for the sweet or snack recipes in this book (they freeze wonderfully), you can just go ahead and indulge your craving when it hits you.
- Look at that selfie you took that reminds you of how badly you want to change your ways.
- Don't keep anything bad at home that will tempt you.
- Drive to and/or from work a different way so as not to pass the Starbucks, the doughnut shop, or your favorite pizza joint.
- Practice restraint long enough to implement a distraction, such as calling someone on the phone, exercising, meditating, turning on music and dancing, going for a walk, or, if the timing's right, maybe having sex (husbands love this one!).
- Keep beans, hummus, or cooked potatoes on hand, reheat and eat for a filling "resistant carb" snack.
- Eat some fat! Try cheese, avocado, hard-boiled eggs, nuts, a banana with nut butter, a buttery sweet potato, or a homemade shake or smoothie with cream and monk fruit.
- Eat a piece of fruit or drink some sparkling mineral water with lemon.
- Play a game with your kids.
- Use a stress-management technique like tapping (fingers to your face), meditation, or creatively visualizing the person you plan to be, vibrantly running along the beach in your bikini. Smell the ocean!
- Give yourself a manicure or take a bath with essential oils.
- Take a walk or groom your dog and throw the ball with him.

About These Ingredients

. . . .

PLEASE don't skip this section! It's important for you to know *why* you're using these ingredients because it *helps you stay the course* when you're having a "lazy" day and/or prone to weakness. Not only are these real foods super nutritious, but I've also found their flavors and textures blend together beautifully. They're unbelievably healthy and many contain a high-protein profile instead of refined carbs. They actually promote your body to burn fat by encouraging the release of glucagon, which has been called the "weight-loss hormone."

Almonds and Other Nuts

The wisdom of nature is truly astounding. To think that every small almond (or any seed, for that matter) contains the dormant energy and life force it takes to begin to sprout and grow into a great big tree is nothing short of miraculous. All it needs is a little water and moderate temperature, and in a short few hours, it comes to life. Nuts are full of vitamins, minerals, and healthy fats. The good fats in nuts also stimulate the production of a hormone that makes us feel full and even slows the emptying of the stomach.

Consuming soaked and/or sprouted nuts offers your body a softer nut to digest. This means its nutrients are more bio-available (more accessible for your body to use). Because most little nuts desire to become that great big tree, they also contain phytates and enzyme inhibitors, which can bind minerals in the digestive tract and make digestion difficult. In defense of being eaten, even many innocent-looking little sprouts in the plant kingdom can contain potent enzyme inhibitors, which can cause an achy gut.

So what's a nut lover to do? Removing the skins by quickly blanching the almonds or buying blanched almonds or almond *flour* (not what is commonly called the *meal* which contains the skins) is beneficial in a few ways:

1. The highest concentration of these anti-nutrients is contained in the skin. For that reason, I prefer using blanched almonds or almond flour (see Resources) rather than the meal (ground whole almonds, skin intact).
2. They are also easier to bake with and have a delicious, mild flavor.
3. Long, hot storage of nuts, seeds, and grains creates an environment for dangerous fungi to grow, so unfortunately, most almonds are pasteurized and irradiated now because of this issue—another good reason to buy organic, remove the skins, and to know where these items come from.

While I mainly use almonds for their light color, mild taste, and moderate price, many other nuts can be used instead. If you run out of almond flour, it's quick and easy to grind your own blanched almonds. If you buy the flour already ground, make sure you choose a finely ground brand from my Resource page as the results you will get from a coarsely ground flour will not be the same.

Coconut and Coconut Flour

Unless you've been living on the moon for a while, you've probably heard about the many wonderful benefits coconuts offer. Coconut water, meat, oil, and milk/cream (made by blending it all together) has so many uses and healthy properties. Coconut water's mineral and electrolyte composition is similar to human blood plasma. The sterile water from a freshly cracked coconut has even been used in IV form to rehydrate an ill person, acting similar to saline solution.

Pre-WWII, before being introduced to America's processed junk food, the cultures who relied on the coconut as a staple in their diets were lean, healthy people. Coconuts are full of vitamins, minerals, and many trace minerals. Extremely high in fiber with potent antimicrobial and antiviral qualities, coconut even helps strengthen our immune system. It is approximately 60 percent fat, and its main fat, lauric acid, is a medium chain fatty acid that is quickly converted to energy by the liver, speeding up our metabolism and promoting a lean body. The popular MCT oil (which stands for medium-chain-triglyceride) is being used for exactly this purpose and is basically like coconut oil on steroids.

I used to always use whole, shredded coconut in my recipes because coconut flour was defatted and of poor quality. Today's coconut flour is much improved, thank goodness. Now it's made with the whole fruit and smells and tastes like coconut. It's very high in fiber and highly absorbent and the many brands available today can vary greatly depending on the amount of fat removed.

Note: Because of the range in brands at this time, adding a little more or less may sometimes be necessary in some recipes.

> ### Tip
> Our ancestors learned that soaking the nuts in water for several hours leeches most of these compounds out into the water, but this is not always possible. If you want to buy whole almonds, you can blanch them yourself by immersing in boiling water for a minute; drain, cool, and pop out of their skins.
>
> If you prefer to buy raw almonds: For healthier, crunchy nuts, soak them in warm water with a little sea salt for about 8 hours. Germinate them on a paper towel for about 12 hours, and then rub the skins off by rolling them in a clean kitchen towel. Dehydrate them in the oven at the lowest temperature setting with the door ajar.

Eggs

Whatever your ethical belief is regarding raising animals for a food source, one must acknowledge that a chicken raised humanely in a free-to-roam flock can provide unfertilized eggs without a concern of cruelty. For this reason, and the nutrition contained within, as well as its numerous culinary uses, truly makes the egg indispensable in my kitchen. I often put these fresh and clean eggs in smoothies and make meringues and eggnogs, thoroughly enjoying them in their raw form. A raw egg from a healthy chicken raised in proper conditions does not pose a threat of contamination.

High in protein, eggs are little powerhouses of nutrients. Proteins are a combination of amino acids. Nine of these acids are essential, which means we need to obtain them from our diet. If we're low in or missing just one of them, our bodies cannot make the other proteins it needs. Eggs are a rich source of all nine of these amino acids. The yolk is a wonderful source of choline, which is a nutrient vital to heart and brain function, as well as cell membrane health.

Eggs should come from chickens that have been able to roam and enjoy feeding on plants and insects. That's when you can enjoy their eggs, containing the right balance of nutrients and omega 3 oils, rather than their less fortunate grain-fed cousins, whose eggs pass on a highly unbalanced ratio of omega 6 fatty acids.

Psyllium Husks

Used for decades as a dietary soluble fiber supplement, psyllium comes from the *Plantago ovata* shrub and is passed through our digestive system because it is indigestible to humans. Psyllium bulks and softens the stool and has also been shown to attach to mycotoxins in the intestines and escort them out of the body, as well as to regulate cholesterol levels by stimulating the synthesis of bile acids. As a prebiotic it's been shown to increase the beneficial lactobacilli bacteria in the colon as well as short-chain fatty acids. Psyllium, and some other plants, such as figs, okra, chia, and plantain, create a unique fiber known as mucilage with many therapeutic benefits. Depending upon each individual's gut microbial makeup, different fiber sources will have different effects. My experiences with psyllium have only been positive and I much prefer to use it as an aid in grain-free baking rather than extracted starches; however, I've read opinions that it's "not paleo" or it may "increase auto-immune symptoms" (which has not been my experience, nor have my baking mix customers shared a negative experience). As always, listen to your body (especially if you're ill) and buy organic.

I use ground psyllium husk as a binder that somewhat mimics gluten. When mixed with liquid, psyllium becomes sticky and stretchy, adding great structure to breads and pasta as well as chew and leavening in other applications. Buy the organic husk, not the seed, and grind it in your coffee grinder or blender if it's not already ground to a powder. Natural food stores and the internet carry psyllium, and since brands vary greatly, I recommend you choose yours from my Resources page for a purer, light-colored husk. Do not buy psyllium seed, as it can turn food purple!

Sweet Potatoes and Yams

This beautiful, luscious, creamy fleshed, delectable member of the Morning Glory family is not even in the same botanical family as the potato. That means sweet potatoes do not contain alkaloids. (Alkaloids are substances that some people are sensitive to and research suggests they may aggravate arthritis. They are mostly found in the nightshade family: eggplants, tomatoes, peppers, and white potatoes.)

Even though sweet potatoes taste so deliciously sweet, they are high in fiber and slow to digest, which means a slower release of their natural sugars. These yummy tubers are high in a fiber that is classified as a resistant starch, meaning it is not digested into your bloodstream but travels through your digestive system to your colon. There it becomes a prebiotic fiber, feeding good little probiotic bugs in your intestines, thus raising the nutrient absorption of your food, including important minerals like calcium and magnesium. These friendly bacteria make many wonderful substances our bodies need, such as short-chain fatty acids and B vitamins. One of the fatty acids the microflora make with this type of starch is butyrate, the same fatty acid found in butter and heavy cream, which research indicates may block the liver's use of carbohydrates for fuel.

There are different types of resistant starch and whether it's raw, its degree of ripeness, and whether it's cooked, heated, or chemically de-natured, changes the way our body assimilates it and how much it benefits us. Resistant starch has been found to promote weight loss because it's not absorbed into your bloodstream, so it doesn't get turned into fat like other carbohydrates. This has made it another popular "super food supplement" recently—*however,* consuming this without its whole counterpart of dietary components that work synergistically in our bodies may have other negative effects. While research reveals that resistant starch improves blood glucose levels and decreases insulin resistance, in contrast, other starches digest quickly and are sent directly into our bloodstream.

Typically, I use the white or yellow sweet potato and sometimes the orange one, known as the yam here in America (although we often interchange the names). They're both easily accessible. If you encounter any of the various other colors, such as purple (I use these to make beautiful Lavender Cupcakes) or the white variety, by all means be brave and experiment! In addition to all of their other great benefits, sweet potatoes are also high in antioxidant compounds and are a great source of vitamins and minerals such as C, A, B_6, copper, manganese, and iron. Sweet potatoes and yams also increase satiety-producing hormones and stave off hunger because they're bulky and satisfying.

Sweet potatoes and yams add bulk, moisture, fiber, and structure to baked goods. While most of my recipes use raw sweet potatoes, I always keep a stash of baked sweet potatoes (they keep for up to a week in the refrigerator) for a quick snack or side dish.

Summer Squash

Often people think of the winter varieties when they think of squash, such as pumpkin, acorn, or butternut. While I use winter squash in some recipes, I primarily use summer varieties for their great versatility and mild flavors. Zucchini and crookneck, both green and yellow, are two of my favorites. They are low in calories (not that I'm counting, right?) and full of fiber, vitamin C, potassium, vitamin A, beta-carotene, lutein, and zeaxanthin. Research has confirmed excellent retention of antioxidant activity, even after steaming and freezing. Summer squash also provides B vitamins, minerals, and even omega 3 fatty acids (in the seeds) and has an unusually high amount of pectin that has been linked with better insulin regulation.

Summer squash belongs to the same family of plants as winter squashes, cucumbers, and melons and are popular all over the world. Scientists have found squash seeds preserved in caves in Mexico and Central America dating back 10,000 years! I use them in various recipes for moistness, fiber, nutrition, and their mild flavor.

Potatoes

Sadly, potatoes have gotten lumped in with other, less nutrient-dense, starchy carbs and processed foods. Recent studies have revealed about 60 different kinds of phytochemicals and vitamins in the skins and flesh of 100 wild and commercially grown potatoes. Eating a potato is not the same as eating a fast–food biscuit!

Cooked and cooled potatoes have an even higher concentration of resistant starch than Sweet Potatoes (see Sweet Potatoes above). Red potatoes are the least starchy of all the varieties and contain about five times the level of antioxidants compared to russet potatoes. When the cooked potato is cooled, its glycemic score is about 55 compared to a higher score when eating it warm. The starch in the cooled potato becomes even more resistant to digestion. As with the resistant starch in sweet potatoes, resistant starch in potatoes acts like soluble fiber and is a prebiotic in the colon. Many studies have shown it to improve insulin levels and lower blood sugar. It's a rich source of iron, potassium, and vitamins B_6 and C, as well as protein and fiber. It's also very satiating. However, potatoes belong to the nightshade family and contain alkaloids, so if you're sensitive, replace them with a white sweet potato. As with sweet potatoes and yams, potatoes add bulk, structure, and moistness to a recipe, helping to replace refined starch, gluten, oil, and milk.

Whole Fruits and Veggies

Do I really have to tout the health benefits of real whole fruits and veggies in comparison to ingredients such as flour, milk, sugar, bad oils, and starches? I think I've covered that already. Those are the ingredients we replace with our delicious fruits and veggies, which for the most part are not even detectable in the recipe (unless we want them to be).

Aside from coconut, zucchini and yellow squash, sweet potatoes, potatoes, other foods I also often use in baking are pumpkin, apples, bananas, beets and beet greens, baby spinach, dark cherries, berries, citrus fruits, tomatoes, carrots, and avocados.

Heavy Cream

If you don't do dairy at all, I recommend using full-fat coconut milk to replace the cream. The major difference between cream and milk is that milk contains the highest amount of casein protein which can be difficult on human digestion. There is very little casein in heavy cream. The lactose sugar is not as much of an issue because it should be broken down by good bacteria in the gut (if you're missing it, as many are, a good probiotic supplement should do the job). Most people digest heavy cream just fine. Real (raw, if you can find a reliable source) pasture-fed, organic cream is always the best. Pasteurization renders the milk dead and homogenization denatures its molecular structure.

Heavy cream provides the fiber to produce butyrate, a fatty acid that nourishes and balances the pH in the colon, as well as many other functions in the body. Cream from grass-fed (humanely raised, of course!) cows also supplies us the essential fatty acid, conjugated linoleic acid (CLA), which actually helps keep our cells from storing fat. While we can whip up a fluffy topping from coconut cream, in my opinion its taste just can't compare to heavy whipped cream, which also makes sour cream, cream cheese, and butter.

Butter/Ghee

Butter contains only trace amounts of lactose or casein (clarified butter and ghee contain none) and is usually quite easily digested. Butter contains all the fat-soluble vitamins, including high amounts of vitamin A. Butter derived from grass-fed cows is another rich source of conjugated linolenic acid (CLA), a fatty acid found to promote weight loss, as well as lauric acid, which has demonstrated anti-cancer/anti-viral benefits. Butter also promotes our gut bacteria to make butyrate, which nourishes our intestines, and research suggests it may also help block the liver's use of carbohydrates, promoting our cells to burn fat. Ghee and clarified butter have their milk solids removed through heating and are basically identical, other than ghee is often toasty tasting because it is generally cooked longer.

Sea Salt

Once again we've been led to believe salt is bad for us because of testing on highly refined salt, stripped of its natural mineral content, and containing additives (including aluminum hydroxide) to keep it dry in storage, plus bleaching agents shown to raise blood pressure. True high-quality, sun-dried Himalayan or Celtic sea salt contains dozens of minerals and trace minerals our bodies need and is a wonderful addition to food. I use sea salt in just about everything.

Coconut Oil and Palm Shortening

Coconut oil is great for baking. I keep Trader Joe's triple filtered on hand too because sometimes I don't want the coconut flavor. However, using real whole foods that usually bring with them their own natural oils so we don't use as much.

As mentioned earlier, coconut oil is one of nature's rare sources of lauric acid, a medium-chain fatty acid that is quickly digested and sent to the liver where it enters your cells' mitochondria and produces energy. Coconut oil also contains caprylic acid, which is a potent anti-fungal. This is unlike the long-chain fatty acids found in polyunsaturated oils that your body cannot process as well so prefers to store instead.

Palm shortening makes great frostings because of its mild flavor, texture, and its higher melting point than coconut oil. It is simply whipped from palm oil and is *not* a mechanically hydrogenated, fake fat. These days most stores carry both of these, but see my Resources page for my suggestions for companies that employ sustainable and fair trade practices.

Additional Ingredients

I also use the following ingredients in my recipes—many of which are commonly used in baking. Some may be new to you and a couple of them are optional.

- **Baking Soda:** Sodium bicarbonate is a safe leavener (rising agent) when combined with acidic ingredients. Its natural mineral name is nahcolite and is found dissolved in many mineral springs.
- **Baking Powder:** This is a blend of sodium bicarbonate, cream of tartar, and a starch. The starch keeps this combination of an alkaline and an acid from touching until moisture is added. It then gets a second boost of leavening when the heat from the oven hits it. To omit all corn, starch, or concern for aluminum in recipes I make my own baking powder by using 2–1 cream of tartar to baking soda. Sometimes my recipe will make it easier for you by just adding cream of tartar.
- **Coconut Cream and Dried Coconut Milk:** Substitute coconut cream for heavy cream, if desired. Dried coconut milk is an option in a couple of recipes. See Resources page.
- **Cheese:** Real full-fat cream cheeses and cultured raw cheeses are easiest on digestion. Use the cheeses that agree with you or feel free to leave them out or use your favorite non-dairy cheese substitutions.

- **Cream of Tartar:** A by-product of wine making, it's used as an acidic stabilizer to stabilize beaten egg whites or to react with the heat of your oven as a leavening agent for rise.
- **Dark Chocolate/Cocoa Powder:** Dark chocolate has been shown to help restore flexibility to arteries and prevent white blood cells from sticking to the blood vessel walls. It's rich in antioxidants and our gut bacteria create anti-inflammatory compounds after feasting on it.
- **Egg White Powder:** Dried, powdered egg whites promote a good rise in baked goods as well as adding additional structure when gluten is missing. They also absorb additional moisture without thickening an already thick batter. However, in some recipes, it's an optional ingredient—be sure to buy pure egg whites with no additives (see Resources).
- **Gelatin, Agar, and Pectin:** Gelatin is derived from the connective tissues of animals, generally chickens, pigs, or cows. It's what makes bone broth jiggle. Agar is a seaweed that substitutes the properties of gelatin. Pectin is generally derived from apples.
- **Vanilla Extract:** My recipes were most often tested with extracts, however vanilla powder or paste is wonderful. Almond extract is also a favorite of mine.
- **Plantain Flour*:** As much as I love using plantains in my baking, I don't love peeling them, ripe or not. Like sweet potato flour, plantain flour comes from the whole, dried, and ground fruit of the plantain. High in resistant starch/fiber, a plantain is very similar to a banana with a milder taste and less sweetness. I use it in just a couple of recipes in this book, as it's a "new" ingredient for most grain-free cooks and not readily available yet.
- **Sweet Potato Flour*:** Sweet potato flour makes terrific frostings without the need for an isolated starch. Buy from the suppliers listed in my Resources page because they have the best yellow (not from the orange yam) finely ground flour that I've tried.

*Note: Most grain-free bakers are just mastering baking with blanched almond flour and coconut flour. Introducing more whole-food flours, such as plantain and sweet potato, may throw a curve ball to some of you so I use them very sparingly. Watch for more fun with these flours in the near future though.

About Sweeteners

While cane or beet or coconut sugar may seem natural, research has clearly shown that the amounts consumed by the average person to satisfy our exorbitant sweet tooth wreaks havoc in our body. Cooking without added sweetener would be my preference; however it's just not practical for widespread appeal these days. The whole foods add some sweetness to the recipes, but for our modern taste buds we usually want an added boost.

I mostly use pure monk fruit extract (listed on my Resources page) for sweetening. I also use the brands of stevia that use the whole leaf and not isolated extracts. They are safe and the most delicious without an aftertaste. I also love to use dates and date sugar (the whole dried and ground date) and when I need a more "sugar-acting" sweetener, I usually choose erythritol or one of the fiber sweeteners listed below. While palm sugar, honey, and maple syrup are considered more natural sugars to use, they still raise blood sugar, so I don't use them as often. The prices of these sweeteners, like their tastes and cooking properties, vary. All of them, unfortunately, are more expensive than table sugar, but for reduced health problems, *they're worth every penny!*

I've also used and listed some other sweeteners, like Fiber Sweet, which you can read about below (as well as further research, if you desire). I use these mostly in their syrup or liquid form to add chew to recipes.

Monk Fruit/Luo Han Guo

Monk fruit is a vine native to China, and is known as luo han guo. This gourd-type fruit is, like stevia, about 300 times sweeter than sugar, and has a zero glycemic index. This safe sweetener has been used medicinally and as a sweetener in Japan for decades. It's been shown to have antioxidant properties. I use 100% monk fruit (see Resources), which uses very small proportions in recipes, similar to using stevia, and I love it. While today's stevia is really quite good, pure monk fruit is a real game changer.

Please note: My recipes were tested with Lakanto liquid and Pure Monk powder.

Stevia

Also known as rubiana, stevia is an extremely sweet-tasting herb native to South America. It has been used for centuries in other countries and used for decades in Japan. Big business interests kept stevia banned for years from being sold in the United States as a sweetener and could only be sold when labeled as a "nutritional supplement." In more recent years, stevia has become available on our store shelves labeled as a sweetener, just as it should be. But leave it to some of the big companies who are now patenting and promoting products like Truvia, using isolated, highly processed stevia compounds and hiding additives in their "natural ingredients" list.

Stevia has a long and safe history. Research indicating otherwise is unfounded and shown to have used extremely high amounts of isolated stevia compounds, rather than the whole leaf. I always keep the liquid on hand to add just a few drops whenever I want a little extra sweetness.

Please note: My recipes were tested with the Sweet Leaf, Trader Joe's, and Body Ecology's stevia drops. I have noticed that different manufacturers can have different strengths and tastes, depending upon the ingredients they may use as a "carrier." Check your labels.

Dates and Date Sugar

The Hebrews considered the date palm the "tree of life" and their cultivation goes back more than 8,000 years. They're not only grown around the world but they thrive right here in our California desert. Dates are packed with fiber, vitamins, and minerals with a flavor reminiscent of brown sugar. I prefer the milder flavor to that of coconut sugar (which is made from the juice of the blossoms). I often use soft, whole dates in recipes as well as date sugar, which is made with the dried, whole and finely ground dates. I like to use my coffee grinder to grind date sugar into an even finer powder. Because it's the whole fruit, this sugar won't dissolve completely and usually requires more liquid be added to a recipe.

Erythritol

I used to use erythritol more in my baking until I found pure monk fruit extract. Most of my recipes in this book call for pure monk fruit now, not because I don't think erythritol is safe, but because monk fruit has a broader appeal for those looking for healthier sweetener options.

Erythritol is classified as a sugar alcohol (but it's not a sugar or an alcohol, go figure); it is very low on the glycemic index and is safe for diabetics. It's also classified as an "unavailable carbohydrate," because it's mostly absorbed through the small intestine, not metabolized and excreted unchanged in urine. Only a small amount reaches the colon and these zero-calorie carbs are not used as energy by the body, they don't raise your blood sugar, and unlike sugar, yeast and bacteria in the gut do not feed on erythritol.

Erythritol is made by breaking down food starch (usually from corn, so buy organic from my Resources page) into glucose and then fermenting it with moniliella polinis (a microorganism found in honeycomb) until it's broken down into this four-carbon "sugar alcohol." Erythritol is also found naturally in many fruits and vegetables, such as asparagus, grapes, melons, and fermented foods. Because erythritol is fermented, it does not usually cause the gassiness that xylitol or other sugar alcohols can cause. Xylitol and all other sugar alcohols are made through a hydrogenation process. Xylitol has been clinically proven to fight ear infections and improve the teeth and gums; erythritol is showing many of those same promising effects.

Erythritol is about 70 percent as sweet as sugar (when I use it I prefer to exchange it 1 to 1 for sugar, adding a bit of stevia or pure monk fruit sweetener) and is easy to use in baking. An added benefit of erythritol is that it helps baked goods stay fresh longer. You can powder it in your coffee grinder or blender if you'd like to, however in some lower moisture applications it may re-crystallize and have a "crunch" to it anyway (like in frostings). Use it alone, or combine it with another sweetener. It doesn't have an aftertaste, but may have a bit of a cool effect in your mouth.

Syrups and Other Liquid Sweeteners

The granulated sweetener I used to test these recipes was erythritol. IMO and allulose are now available in both granulated and syrup form and are more choices that don't raise your blood sugar. Research leans towards their safety, but there's no long-term documentation yet. However, I know many of you prefer a more natural sweetener like coconut sugar, which I don't use because it does raise blood sugar. So, for this reason I rarely call for a granulated sweetener except for date sugar, instead giving you a wide variety of syrup-type sweeteners to choose from. They all add a sugar-like chewiness that erythritol doesn't. I often use IMO syrup, but there are many liquid sweeteners available these days. Here I share with you the ones I use and why. I prefer the safe, low-glycemic sweeteners. However, I understand that our tastes and preference are varied and that some of you may use sweeteners, such as rice or agave syrup, that I don't use. Feel free to substitute for your favorites, I won't judge you, but the taste of the syrup you use will affect the flavor of the final product.

IMO (VitaFiber or FiberYum Syrup)

These syrups (also available in powdered form) are composed of isomalto-oligosaccharides (IMO), which acts as a prebiotic soluble fiber in our intestines. Currently, IMO is popular in Asian markets, where it's been a normal food component of the human diet for many centuries. IMO occurs naturally in a number of fermented foods, including miso, soy sauce, and sake. It's derived through an enzymatic process converting a starch from non-GMO corn to this low glycemic sweetener. The enzymes convert it to a soluble fiber that is mostly digested by lactobacilli bacteria in the small intestine so it doesn't cause gastric distress that FOS (fructo-oligosacharides) derived from chicory commonly do. It's been shown to improve mineral absorption and cholesterol levels. The research I've seen so far looks good, but it's a fairly new product for me. It's flavorless and less sweet than honey or maple syrup and also comes in a powdered form.

Allulose

Allulose is considered a "rare" sugar with the same chemical formula as fructose. It isn't metabolized by the body so it doesn't raise blood sugar or insulin levels and has few calories. Since our gut enzymes cannot break it down, it can cause bloating, pain, and gas if eaten in large quantities. It's found naturally in fruits such as raisins and figs; however it is derived for the food industry using corn and there is not an organic source available that I know of.

I did not test recipes with this sweetener at the time of writing this book. I have since had good results using this sweetener, but know little about long term use and safety. It's available in both a syrup and a powdered form.

Date Syrup

Date syrup is made by cooking down and straining the dates, which removes any solids and most of the fiber. Recent research has shown this syrup is even more efficient than Manuka honey for killing bacteria! See my Resources page, or, it's easy to make your own by following one of several recipes on the internet. True date syrup is cooked to reduce and condense the sweetness and flavors.

Honey and Maple Syrup

Both honey and maple syrup are sweeter than sugar and contain lots of vitamins, minerals, and amino acids. Maple syrup is made by boiling the sap of the maple tree, and we all know that bees make honey, which is best purchased in its raw, unprocessed form. While considered natural sweetening options, I prefer to use them sparingly, only in small amounts—like in tea and on pancakes.

Molasses and Yacon Syrup

Molasses is a by-product of refined sugar. It contains the vitamin and mineral content that refined sugar loses during processing. Yacon syrup is similar to molasses, with half the calories of sugar. This syrup is derived from the South American yacon root. It's considered a prebiotic, as it is high in FOS, or fructo-oligosaccharides, which feed our gut bacteria. It gives a depth of flavor to gingerbread and graham crackers.

Cassava Syrup

Cassava is not my favorite plant to eat. Sure, cook it, process it, refine and package it on store shelves and its pure starch (tapioca) becomes edible. The newer, fructose-free cassava syrup on the market today is a clear, flavorless option if you don't use IMO syrup. However, as of the printing of this book, I have read nothing about long term testing on this product.

Sweetener Comparisons

	Carbs	Glycemic Index*
Cane Sugar	100%	68
Coconut Palm Crystals/Nectar	92%	35
Erythritol	0%	1
Monk Fruit	0%	0
Maple Syrup	84–93%	54
Raw Honey	82%	35–65
Stevia	0%	0
VitaFiber Syrup	0%	1

*The Glycemic Index is a numerical index that ranks carbohydrates based on their rate of glycemic response or their conversion to glucose within the human body.

Chapter 5:
Equipment, Helpful Tips, and Conversions

. . . .

I've always heard how baking is such a precise science, but I've found that baking with real, whole foods can be a rather *inexact* science, as the sizes, shapes, and moisture content of the whole foods vary. In the beginning, I used measuring cups, but find it easier to use a kitchen scale now (and anything that makes life in my kitchen easier is good with me!). One of the benefits of this type of baking is that most of the ingredients we use don't require additional oils or liquids, because the whole foods already contain them.

Whole foods contain different amounts of moisture, oils, fiber, starches, and sugars. Once you get used to working with them, it's easy to judge whether you need a little more or little less of a particular ingredient. Usually, simply adding an extra egg to loosen a thick batter or adding a tablespoon more of coconut flour to thicken a batter that's too wet, is all that's needed.

You may also notice that most of the recipes call for fairly consistent ingredients, such as almond and coconut flour. For varied tastes and nutrients, many recipes can be substituted with other nuts. Almonds and coconut have become very popular choices for those going grain-free, not just because they're high in protein and fiber, but also because of their mild taste and visual appeal, which gives the most traditional taste and texture of baked goods. Also, when you're first switching over or learning to use different ingredients, I think it's best to keep it as simple as possible.

Real Food Kitchen Equipment

The right equipment can make a huge difference when baking, and below I've listed for you the items I use most frequently. A well-stocked kitchen already has many of these kitchen tools. You'll want to invest in a nice, high-powered, sturdy food processor and blender for smooth batter results in minutes. I use the Cuisinart 14-cup food processor and the Vitamix blender. They've been worth every penny.

- Blender
- Food processor
- Kitchen scale
- Coffee grinder or Magic Bullet
- Spiralizer for veggie noodles
- Oven thermometer and timer
- Cutting board
- Electric handheld mixer
- Muffin pans
- Doughnut pans

- 6- and 8-inch cake pans
- 7-inch springform pan
- Pastry cutter
- Pie pans
- Baking sheets
- Cooling racks
- Microplane zester
- Measuring cups and spoons
- Mixing bowls
- Spatulas, knives, whisks, and wooden spoons
- Colander/sifter
- Silicone baking sheets
- Parchment and waxed paper
- Slow cooker and pressures cooker are great additions
- Lastly, you need an oven (haha) and you need to know how it bakes, as not all are created equal.

Having the items I've listed on hand will make it simple for you to bake the recipes in this book. Most of the equipment is easy to find and fairly inexpensive.

Helpful Tips

Over the years of experimenting in my kitchen with whole foods I've learned a few tricks. I admit, it's also made me a bit crazy I think (well, I have to blame it on something!). It might be more accurate to say that my choice to employ occasional deceptive cooking practices has taken its toll on my mental health. Keeping secrets, especially from those you love, can mess you up, so you may be happy to know that writing this book has helped to lift a huge weight off me. Now my whole family will know there may be a tomato in their cupcake or a zucchini in their pancake. I hope this mental decline doesn't happen to you, so if you feel the need to be honest, go right ahead. It's likely no one will believe you anyway. I also figured I'd save you from having to learn all the tricks the hard way and share a few with you, so now you'll have more time to eat your delicious creations.

Below I've listed some general, overall tips as well as some food-specific tips:

- I once dropped a whole egg, shell and all, into my food processor as it was blending. For this reason, I always crack my eggs into a small bowl first and then add them to the batter.
- My recipes were only tested with real eggs from my chickens, which are on the large/extra-large size. Small eggs will affect the recipe, so don't be afraid to add an extra egg if you think you need one. I sometimes list the volume of eggs (ie: 1 cup) for this reason.
- As long as the foods are clean and organic, I often don't bother peeling them (unless I don't want the green zucchini skin to discolor the white cupcake). The recipe will designate if the food should be peeled; otherwise, it's really your choice. However, an unpeeled potato may mean a thick batter that would benefit from an extra egg. And always taste the peel for any bitterness before deciding to use it.
- Many of the recipes can be made either in a blender or a food processor. To use a blender, add the eggs, fruit/veggie, nuts (if not using nut flour), and other wet ingredients and blend. Mix the dry ingredients in a bowl then pour the wet into the dry.

- If you want to use your food processor instead of the blender, add the dry ingredients before the eggs or any other ingredients that contain a lot of moisture. Stop it a time or two and stir and scrape down the sides as needed.
- You may substitute blanched, slivered almonds for another nut if you prefer. To de-skin raw almonds, submerge one minute in boiling water, cool, and pinch out of their skins.
- To substitute other nuts for almond flour, add them to the blender with the wet ingredients. About 1¼ cups nuts = 1½ cups almond flour.
- The almond flour I use is finely ground from blanched almonds from one of the brands on my Resources page. If you use another flour that is more coarsely ground, results will differ. You can grind it more fine in your food processor if need be. Do not use nut meal (which contains the skins).
- I use the "dip and sweep" method of measuring flour which means I dip the measuring cup in and level it off with a butter knife, instead of pouring the flour into the cup, which would yield a slightly different measurement.
- If needed, sift sweet potato, coconut flour, and baking powder/soda to remove any lumps.
- While most of these recipes use raw fruits and veggies, I keep baked sweet potatoes and boiled red skin potatoes on hand in my refrigerator for various uses as well. For the sweet potatoes, just place them whole and un-punctured on a cookie sheet and bake them at 325°F for about an hour. Simmer red skin potatoes with their skins on, in water until soft.
- I generally use unsalted butter.
- Grind psyllium husks (don't use the whole seed as results will be affected), and chia seeds to a fine powder in a coffee grinder/Magic Bullet.
- While grinding erythritol will powder it, it still may re-crystalize and have a crunch in some frostings or other low-moisture recipes. If you follow the directions for my frostings, they'll be nice and creamy without a crunch.
- You can substitute for baking powder by mixing 2:1 cream of tartar and baking soda.
- Do not switch baking soda for the baking powder in a recipe where color is important (such as the Red Velvet or Lavender cupcakes)

Bread and Pizza Tips

- Make sure to adequately grease the bottom of the pans for easy removal. I usually use coconut oil, ghee, or palm oil. You can also buy coconut oil cooking spray now.
- The crust may look dark, but it's necessary to ensure that the inside is cooked. Cover with parchment paper or aluminum foil, if desired, to keep it from over-browning.
- For a softer crust, store the bread in a plastic bag so the moisture content can redistribute.
- Don't worry about over-working the dough; there's no gluten to develop.
- If the dough has been sitting out for a while and/or the outside seems dry, spritz it with water before baking.
- Baking pizzas on a stone and/or the bottom rack helps crisp up the crust.
- Liberally grease the pan with olive oil or use a silicone baking sheet instead of parchment paper.

Crusts, Crackers, and Wraps Tips

- Make sure to roll the cracker dough nice and thin and as even as possible.
- Use a silicone baking pad rather than parchment paper because the moisture in the dough or batter can cause the parchment to wrinkle and give you wrinkly crackers and wraps.
- Crackers and wraps can burn quickly, so keep a low oven temperature and a close eye on them.
- After baking, make sure to leave the crackers to dehydrate more in a warm oven to crisp up.
- Always use a crust protector for crust edges.
- For quiches and pies such as pumpkin I find grain-free crusts best fully pre-baked rather than par-baked.

Sweets Tips

Every day it seems a new sweetener comes on the market. Pick a few you like and trust without hidden "natural" ingredients. If you choose a erythritol/monk fruit blend, it will likely be a little sweeter than just plain erythritol. My recipes were tested with pure monk fruit (Lakanto or Pure Monk brands) or liquid stevia (Sweet Leaf or Trader Joe's brands). The liquid needs to be added to the wet ingredients in the blender; however the powder can be added to either the dry or the wet.

- If you don't have paper cupcake liners, coat the cups with coconut oil and dust with coconut flour. I don't suggest silicone baking cups for the cupcakes.
- Most batters should be the consistency of thick pancake batter. Batter consistency will also depend on whether you use the skin or not; the skin will usually make a thicker, stiffer batter.
- If the batter seems too thick, add another egg and blend once more.
- If the batter seems too thin, add an additional tablespoon of coconut flour.
- If you desire more sweetness a few more drops of monk fruit or stevia works great.
- If a recipe calls for a potato/sweet potato, it is usually used raw. It can usually be substituted with a raw summer squash (like a yellow or green zucchini) or even another fruit/veggie, plus an additional tablespoon of coconut flour and a tablespoon of coconut oil.
- Use the toothpick method to check for doneness. Stick the toothpick into the bread or cake, and if it comes out clean, it has finished baking.
- A pinch of guar gum added to frostings increases freezing ability and makes it fluffier.
- If you're counting carbs, ⅔ cup sweet/potato per cupcake recipe = less than 1 tablespoon per cupcake.
- Grain-free pie crusts made without added starch easily absorb moisture, so brushing with an egg and gelatin/agar wash and pre-baking them is essential.
- Using a kitchen scale is quicker and easier than evenly chopping and using a measuring cup.
- Baking powder that has cream of tartar as an ingredient helps maintain the color of the vegetable in the baked good. Adding ½ a teaspoon of cream of tartar to a cake batter helps also, but don't use baking soda as it will affect the color.
- Frost cakes soon after cooling, or wrap in plastic to keep from getting a dry exterior. They all freeze well.

Conversions & Equivalents

	Cup	Ounces	Approx. Grams
Almonds, blanched and slivered	1	5.5	157
Almond Flour, finely ground	1	3.5	99
Coconut, shredded	1	2	57
Coconut, finely shredded	¾	2	57
Walnuts, roughly chopped	1	4	114
Apple, roughly chopped	1	5	142
New/Red Skin Potato, roughly chopped	1	5	142
Sweet Potato/Yam, roughly chopped	1½	7	200
Zucchini/Yellow Squash, roughly chopped	1	5	142

Oven Temperature Equivalent

100°F = 38°C   200°F = 95°C
250°F = 120°C   300°F = 150°C
350°F = 180°C   400°F = 205°C

Equivalents to 1 Cup of Table Sugar

1 cup erythritol/monk fruit blend
1⅓ cup erythritol or IMO sweetener
2 cups date sugar plus extra liquid (depending on recipe)
1–2 teaspoons 100% pure monk fruit—varies with manufacturer and product.
1–2 teaspoons stevia powder or liquid—varies with manufacturer and product.
¾ cup date syrup, maple syrup, or honey, plus 2 teaspoons coconut flour or about 20% less liquid
1 cup xylitol

Almonds

1¼ cups blanched, slivered almonds = 1½ cups flour

Note: The more fiber, fat, and protein in a meal, the slower the digestion and absorption of sugars and carbs, therefore a slower blood sugar elevation.

Part 2:
Real Food Recipes

I dedicate these recipes to
Aurora, Knox, and Bennett, my amazing grandchildren,
and to all the children of the world who are lucky enough to grow up
learning to eat and bake with real whole foods.

CHAPTER 6:

MY FAVORITE BASICS

Tip: Use the pulp for a creamy breakfast cereal, make muffins with it, or stir it into your dog's bowl. This also makes terrific egg nog. Just blend a few eggs into the finished milk and add nutmeg and pure monk fruit or stevia to taste.

NUT MILK AND CREAMER

Don't get me wrong, I actually love fresh cream, however I also enjoy other "milks" as well and like to change it up, too. I know many of you don't do dairy at all, so I've included my favorite cream/milk alternative. I use blanched almonds because I prefer the skins to be removed for easier digestion. You can use this in recipes wherever cream or milk is called for.

Makes about 2 cups cream or 4 cups milk

2–4 cups filtered water
1 cup raw macadamia nuts
1 cup blanched almonds
1 cup unsweetened, shredded coconut
2 large dates (optional)
1 teaspoon vanilla extract or paste (optional)
⅛ teaspoon almond extract (optional)
Pinch of sea salt
Pure monk fruit or preferred sweetener to taste

1. Heat 2 cups of water until very hot.
2. While the water heats, add the rest of the ingredients to your blender.
3. When the water is hot, pour over the blender ingredients. Let rest for 5 minutes.
4. Blend everything together for about a minute.
5. Line a tall bowl with cheese cloth or a nut/juice bag to pour the mixture into and squeeze out the liquid.
6. Adjust sweetness and vanilla flavor to taste.
7. Add more water for a "milk" consistency, or use as is for coffee creamer. Keeps several days in your refrigerator.

Apple Pie Cereal Clusters

These little tidbits are not as hard as granola can be. They're light and crunchy and make a great breakfast cereal or snack. There are two ways to make these—the easy way and the easier way. Use the easier way if you don't want to pull out your food processor. Simply replace the apples with applesauce and the dates with ¼ cup more syrup. The ingredients in the muesli really soak up flavor, so don't be shy with the spices.

Makes about 8 servings

2 chopped apples, or ½ cup applesauce
1 cup soft, pitted dates
¼ cup maple syrup
¼ cup soft butter or coconut oil
2 teaspoons vanilla extract
3 cups muesli mix
1 teaspoon pure monk fruit or stevia (if using liquid, add to the food processor)
1 tablespoon cinnamon
½ teaspoon allspice
½ teaspoon sea salt

1. Preheat the oven to 300°F and line a baking sheet with parchment paper.
2. Blend the apples, dates, maple syrup, butter or coconut oil, and vanilla until almost smooth. I like to leave some bits of apples and dates unblended.
3. Put the muesli into a large bowl and stir in the sweetener and spices.
4. Add the contents of the food processor to the dry ingredients, and use your hands to combine well.
5. Spread evenly onto the baking sheet and bake for about an hour, using a spatula to turn and move around or break up pieces as needed, about 3–4 times.
6. Turn off the oven, crack the door, and let cool until crispy.
7. Store in an airtight container for several weeks.

MUESLI

I like to keep my muesli basic and add fresh fruit to vary the taste when I serve it, because I often use it to make granola clusters. Feel free to add whatever other health promoting goodies you like, then shake it all together in a large glass jar. Shake the jar each time you pour it into your bowl to make sure you get all the goodness. I like to eat it with yogurt and fresh berries or grated apple. Dried fruit like gold raisins, chopped apple, blueberries, or cranberries are also great additions to this recipe—the sky's the limit, really.

Makes 12–16 servings

2 cups shredded coconut
⅔ cup chia seed meal
⅔ cup hemp or other favorite seed
⅔ cup apple fiber (optional), See Resources (page 296)
⅓ cup coconut flour
¼ cup cinnamon
1 teaspoon pure monk fruit
1 teaspoon sea salt
2 cups chopped walnuts
2 cups chopped pecans, macadamias, cashews, or Brazil nuts

1. Mix the shredded coconut, ground chia, seeds, apple fiber, coconut flour, cinnamon, sweetener, and salt in a large bowl.
2. Pulse the nuts in a food processor until they're chopped up.
3. Stir the nuts into the bowl until everything is blended together.

INSTANT NO-OATMEAL PORRIDGE

When we want to warm our bellies on a cold morning, this takes about 2 minutes to make with the muesli you keep on hand. I love it with "my" milk (a few tablespoons of cream with 1 cup of water for me usually) along with a chopped banana and maple syrup.

Makes 2–4 servings

2 cups of water, juice, or milk
1 cup muesli
1 cup blanched almond flour
Pinch of pure monk fruit or stevia

1. Pulse the muesli in your food processor until it's in smaller pieces.
2. Heat water, juice, or milk until almost bubbling. Remove from heat and stir in the muesli, almond flour, and sweetener.
3. Serve with your syrup and fruit of choice.

Easy Raw Jams: Unless we're making a pie, cobbler, or crisp, cooking fruit just seems wrong to me. Sadly, so many people these days don't even know what real, fresh-from-the-organic-vine, ripened fruit tastes like because so much of our produce no longer has flavor, ripened or not, thanks to many modern cultivating practices. One thing's for sure: jams and jellies are traditionally made with copious amounts of sugar and cooked to death, which thoroughly intensifies the flavor into that which we are accustomed to buying. Adding dried fruit to the fresh gives that intensity of the cooked fruit. I love the health benefits of chia seed, but I find I use it enough in other areas so prefer to keep it out of my jams and jellies. Gelatin or agar works great too, but then you must heat at least some of the fruit for the gelatin to set and apparently it won't freeze well. I've discovered that a little ground psyllium husk thickens perfectly when needed. These are base recipes for which you can modify depending upon whether your fruit is fresh or frozen and has lots of juices, sweetness, and flavor or not. When I make jam with our trees' summer fruits, I use much less monk fruit and no extracts, so please, taste, test, and adjust for sweetness and flavor and sprinkle in a little psyllium to thicken, if needed.

Each recipe makes approximately 2–3 cups.

APRICOT/PEACH/PINEAPPLE

12 ounces (about 2 cups) fresh or previously frozen and thawed, sliced peaches, or ½ pineapple
10 ounces dried apricots
3–4 tablespoons honey (preferably Manuka)
2 tablespoons fresh lemon juice
1 teaspoon pure monk fruit powder or stevia
½ teaspoon each vanilla and almond extract
Dash of sea salt

1. Add everything to your blender and blend until smooth.
2. Transfer to jars or containers and refrigerate or freeze (I usually refrigerate one and freeze one).

Tip: To make Fruit Leather, spread the jam thinly on a sheet pan liner and dehydrate at 200 °F for a few hours.

Strawberry/Cherry

. . . .

1 pound fresh or previously frozen strawberries
6 ounces (or about 1¼ cups) raspberries (optional)
2 cups dried cherries
2–4 tablespoons honey or syrup of choice
2 tablespoons fresh lemon juice
½–1 teaspoon pure monk fruit or stevia
½ teaspoon almond extract (optional)
⅛ sea salt

1. Add everything to your food processor and pulse several times to your desired consistency. Or add half of the strawberries and blend smooth, then pulse in the rest of the ingredients.
2. Transfer to jars or containers and refrigerate or freeze (I usually refrigerate one and freeze one).

Blueberry/Plum

. . . .

1 pound fresh or previously frozen blueberries
1 cup dried plums (you can call them prunes)
2–4 tablespoons honey or syrup of choice
2 tablespoons fresh lemon juice
½–1 teaspoon pure monk fruit or stevia
½ teaspoon vanilla (optional)
⅛ sea salt

1. Add everything to your food processor and pulse several times to your desired consistency. Or add half of the strawberries and blend smooth, then pulse in the rest of the ingredients.
2. Transfer to jars or containers and refrigerate or freeze (I usually refrigerate one and freeze one).

RAW APPLESAUCE

This easy recipe tastes like heaven. Oddly, the banana is hardly detectable, especially if it's a bit under-ripened. I usually don't bother peeling my apples either. I doubt I'll ever buy store-bought, cooked-to-death applesauce again.

6 large apples (skins on is fine)
1 just ripe banana
2–4 dates, softened in water or honey/stevia to taste
1 tablespoon lemon juice
¼ teaspoon cinnamon (optional, or more to taste)
Pinch of allspice (optional)

1. Pulse in the food processor until smooth.

Tip: Add ½ cup cranberries for the winter holidays, strawberries for Valentine's Day, or other fruit just to change it up occasionally.

TANGY (FERMENTED) FRUIT CHUTNEY

3–4 peeled, chopped apples, peaches, or ½ chopped pineapple
½ cup each dried chopped apricots, prunes, yellow raisins, cranberries, cherries, pecans
1 sliced leek
Juice of two lemons
¼ cup whey, drained from yogurt or water kefir or kombucha (assures good fermentation)
2 teaspoons sea salt
1 teaspoon cinnamon
⅛ teaspoon red pepper flakes
Water or coconut water to cover

1. In a large bowl, stir together all of the ingredients, except the water.
2. Pack into clean glass jars, leaving an inch or two of space at the top.
3. Cover and rest at room temperature for 2–3 days.
4. Store in the refrigerator for up to a month or freeze.

Serve with roasted meats, beans, quinoa, potatoes or squash, hot cereal, tossed into a smoothie, over ice cream, or just out of the jar.

CRANBERRY CHERRY SAUCE

. . . .

Sometimes not having the right ingredient or even a little mistake can lead to greater things. That's why I encourage you to be fearless in your kitchen. For instance, I just couldn't seem to find fresh cranberries when I needed them, so this yummy version of a classic must-have sauce got a twist.

Makes about 4 cups of sauce

1 thin-skinned juice orange, such as Valencia, chopped and deseeded
2 cups dried cranberries
2 cups pitted fresh cherries (previously frozen is fine)
1 teaspoon pure monk fruit or stevia
1 teaspoon ground cinnamon
½–⅔ teaspoon sea salt
¼ teaspoon ground black pepper
¼ teaspoon ground coriander
A pinch of cloves
¼ cup Port wine or cherry juice
⅓ cup black raisins (optional)
⅓ cup pecans (optional)

1. Add the orange to your food processor and process into small pieces.
2. Add the rest of the ingredients except the wine, raisins, and pecans and blend until chopped into a chunky sauce.
3. Pulse in the wine, raisins, and pecans, and add a bit of water to thin if desired.

Tip: Before serving, the flavors will develop more by letting the sauce rest a few hours, either on the counter or in your refrigerator.

Tip: You can trade the wine/cherry juice for whey and let the chutney rest at room temperature for a day or two then refrigerate.

Tip: I like to set the jars in a cooler and then into the laundry room in case it gets stinky . . . and it will!

Kitchen Sink Cultured Veggies

Keeping kraut or cultured veggies on hand is important. I've found it's an awesome way to get the healing, life-giving properties of the raw vegetables on a regular basis. My dogs (and cats) are probably stranger than yours, but they love a spoonful stirred into their food as much as I do. I use it for soups, sauces, condiments, and salad dressings, so it's easy for us to eat daily. I don't really have a specific recipe for this, I use so many different veggies it often just depends what I have on hand. I like to make enough to last a while, but not so much that it takes me past my patient point. I also don't bother shredding, just rough chop and toss in batches into the food processor because I like the veggies to be chopped small. Here's an example:

Food Processor Ingredients

1 small head cabbage
½ head of cauliflower
1–2 stems of broccoli
½ bunch of celery with leaves
6 carrots with tops (if not too bitter)
1 bunch kale, collard, or beet greens
1 bunch sprouts, such as sunflower or pea
1 bunch parsley or cilantro
1 bunch dill or oregano
About 8 scallions with tops

Blender Ingredients

2 cups of vegetable mix from above
3 cucumbers or ½ bunch of celery
1 cup water
2 tablespoons sea salt
½ cup whey or kraut juice

Peel the carrots and cucumbers. Roughly chop the vegetables and blend in batches in the food processor, then add to a gigantic bowl. Blend the rest of the ingredients in your blender adding water as needed. Toss everything together with your hands until well mixed. Pack into two large clean, glass jars, so the liquid rises above the vegetables, leaving a couple inches of space at the top. Screw on the top. Let set at a comfortable room temperature (about 70–73°F) for 5–7 days.

My Favorite Salsa

. . . .

I'll only use a can if I'm in real a pinch. Here's a good hint though: Italian-style stewed tomatoes are pretty yummy in this. Shhhhhhhh. The men in my household love salsa, and so do I. Really good salsa is so quick and easy to make—it's basically a staple in my kitchen, eaten alone or as a side or stirred into lots of dishes. It's great with plantain chips; just make sure whichever chips you choose are organic.

8–10 Roma tomatoes (or 1–28 ounce can)
2 tomatillos (optional)
2–3 garlic cloves
1–2 jalapeño peppers (depending on the heat desired)
A big handful of cilantro (about ½ cup, packed)
6–7 scallions
Juice of one lime
1 teaspoon sea salt
1 teaspoon dried Mexican oregano or Italian seasoning
½ teaspoon dill weed
¼ cup olive or avocado oil
1–2 tablespoons cultured veggie juice or sauerkraut juice (optional)*

1. Roughly chop all the ingredients and put into your food processor.

2. Pulse several times until finely chopped to the consistency you like.

3. Taste and adjust seasoning.

Note: *If using the fermented veggie juice, let the salsa rest on the counter for a day to begin fermentation. It's a natural preservative.

Variation: Though not "raw," for a deliciously different flavor, roast the veggies (or just the tomatoes) at 350°F on an oiled pan for about 40 minutes before chopping.

Tip: Taste your tomatoes before using them. A bland tomato makes for bland salsa.

Blender BBQ Sauce

. . . .

Easy blender BBQ sauce that tastes like it's cooked all day. Need I say more?

Makes 10–12 cups

2 pounds ripe tomatoes (about 10–12)
1 small yam, or 2 carrots, peeled
1 small onion
1–2 jalapeños (depending on the heat you like)
6 garlic cloves
½ cup dates (about 10)
½ cup coconut aminos, or tamari (*real,*
**   *fermented* soy sauce)**
½ cup honey
⅓ cup apple cider vinegar
1 teaspoon cinnamon
½ teaspoon sea salt
½ teaspoon dry mustard
½ teaspoon smoked paprika

1. Roughly chop the tomatoes, yam/carrots, onion, and peppers and place on a baking sheet. You can roast the garlic if you'd like, but I prefer not to. Roast for about 20 minutes at 400°F.
2. Add the rest of the ingredients to your blender.
3. Once the veggies are roasted, allow them to cool a bit, then add to the blender.
4. Puree until smooth. Add another tomato or a little broth to thin, if necessary.
5. Taste and adjust seasoning.
6. Store in a mason jar in your refrigerator for 10 days, or freeze for up to 6 months.

Quick BBQ Sauce

. . . .

This is a yummy, quick sauce to use if you have ketchup made. Actually, that blender ketchup is so quick and easy you may want to make it specifically for this sauce.

Makes about 2⅓ cups

1 cup homemade ketchup (page 72)
½ cup honey
½ cup coconut aminos or tamari
¼ cup prepared mustard
⅓ cup apple cider vinegar

1. Whisk everything together in a small bowl.
2. Use or store in a mason jar in the refrigerator for two weeks.

CULTURED MAYO

. . . .

I loooove this mayo recipe. I also love avocado oil, but prefer it to be green, cold-pressed, and taste a bit like avocados. So, these oils are a good choice for my mayonnaise.

Makes about 1½ cups

1 whole egg
¾ cup macadamia or sunflower oil
¼ cup MCT oil* or other favorite oil
1 tablespoon apple cider vinegar
1 tablespoon lemon juice
¾ teaspoon sea salt
A pinch of both cayenne and turmeric
1 tablespoon whey liquid (drained from yogurt or sour cream), cultured veggie juice, or a probiotic capsule (optional)

1. Put everything into a wide mouth mason jar in the order listed.
2. Use your immersion blender to blend until whipped and creamy, literally about 30 seconds.
3. If you've added the whey, simply let the mayo sit on your counter for about 8 hours to begin fermentation. This will allow the mayo to keep a little longer in your fridge.

Note: If you don't own an immersion blender yet, use your mini food processor or blender.

* MCT (medium-chain triglyceride) oils are a great energy source and contribute to mental clarity instead of being stored as fat. These oils are altered from their natural state so use only the highest quality such as the one recommended on my Resources page.

Tip: If you use the whey or fermented veggie or sauerkraut juice, let the mayo rest on your counter top all day to start fermentation, it's a natural preservative.

Raw Fermented Ketchup

....

This ketchup recipe is not only easy and quick (my favorite adjectives) but it tastes awesome too! Make sure your tomatoes are flavorful and the sun-dried ones are reddish rather than super dark.

Makes about 4 cups

Ingredients

2 pounds (about 10 large) very ripe Roma tomatoes (or a 28-ounce can)
½ cup sun-dried tomatoes (about 2 ounces, no salt added)
⅔ cup soft, pitted dates (about 10–12 or 2–3 ounces)
½ cup roughly chopped yellow onion
¼ cup fermented vegetable juice, kraut juice, or whey (liquid drained from yogurt)
1 clove of garlic
1 teaspoon anchovy paste, or 1 anchovy
1–2 tablespoons apple cider vinegar
1½ tablespoons sea salt
⅛–¼ teaspoon pure monk fruit or stevia
½ teaspoon cinnamon
⅛ teaspoon cayenne
⅛ teaspoon ground allspice
Pinch of ground cloves

1. Blend everything in your blender on high until smooth and creamy, about 2 minutes, taste, and adjust seasoning if desired.
2. Pour into a glass jar or bowl, cover, and let set on your counter for a day to begin fermentation.
3. Store in the refrigerator 2–3 weeks or freeze.

Note: If your tomatoes are really juicy, you can add 1–2 tablespoons of tomato paste.

Tip: Grate some fresh Horseradish in for a delicious Cocktail Dipping Sauce for Shrimp.

> **PROBIOTIC DRESSINGS:** Make these dressings using whey (the liquid drained from yogurt or sour cream) or the juice from sauerkraut or the fermented veggie recipe on page 65. Of course, you can use store-bought fermented veggies as well; see my Resources page for my favorites. This is another way that makes it easy to get plenty of raw vegetables, probiotics, and healthy fats on a daily basis. When you're not feeling like a salad, drizzle these on simmered veggies, potatoes, or meat. All of these dressings are deliciously creamy, but if you prefer an even thicker dressing, add a tablespoon of chia seeds or a handful of sunflower seeds to thicken them up.

Caesar Dressing

1 egg
1 cup olive oil
2 teaspoons anchovy paste
2 tablespoons whey or lemon juice
1 teaspoon Dijon mustard
1 teaspoon Worcestershire sauce or coconut aminos
1 garlic clove, minced
Sea salt and cracked black pepper to taste
¼ cup grated Parmesan or blanched almond flour

1. Put everything into a glass mason jar and use your immersion blender to blend until smooth and creamy.
2. If using whey, let it rest on your counter for a day to begin fermentation.

Honey Herb Dressing

³/₄ cup fermented vegetables (page 65, or store bought)
4 tablespoons honey, preferably Manuka/raw (see Resources, page 296)
½ cup macadamia nut oil
1–2 teaspoons Italian seasoning or a handful of your favorite fresh herbs
Sea salt and pepper to taste

1. Put everything into your blender and blend until smooth and creamy.

Note: The amount of honey and salt you use will depend upon the flavor of your fermented veggies.

Tip: Switch the whey for a probiotic juice such as sauerkraut, coconut kefir, or kombucha.

FRENCH DRESSING

½ cup fermented vegetables
2 large tomatoes, quartered
½ cup MCT oil* or olive oil
A couple of slices of onion
½ cup raw sunflower seeds
3–4 tablespoons honey, preferably Manuka/raw
1½ tablespoon apple cider vinegar
2 teaspoons paprika or smoked paprika
1–2 teaspoons sea salt (depending upon the saltiness of your fermented veggies)
½ teaspoon black pepper

1. Blend everything in your blender until smooth and creamy, taste and adjust seasonings, adding stevia or monk fruit, if desired.

*MCT (medium-chain triglyceride) oils are a great energy source and contribute to mental clarity instead of being stored as fat. These oils are altered from their natural state so use only the highest quality such as the one recommended on my Resources page (296).

AVOCADO RANCH DRESSING

½ cup sauerkraut
A couple slices of white onion, or 1 garlic clove
1 avocado
⅓ cup homemade mayo (page 70)
½–1 teaspoon dried or 1 tablespoon freshly minced dill and oregano
½–1 teaspoon dried or 1 tablespoon freshly minced tarragon, parsley or basil (optional)
Sea salt and pepper to taste

1. Blend the sauerkraut, onion (or garlic), and avocado in your blender until smooth.
2. Pulse in the mayo and herbs.
3. Chill for a few hours.

Tip: No sauerkraut on hand? Swap it for 2 tablespoons lemon juice and 1 medium peeled zucchini

Quick Raw (or Not) Marinara

· ·

Sometimes our schedule or time available becomes too big of a factor on how we eat—well, you'll have to think of another excuse now, because it takes only minutes for this raw version. Or, if you prefer, you can toss it in a slow-cooker while you gossip with the neighbors. If your sun-dried tomatoes are dark, the sauce will be dark. That's good for a "Bolognese" sauce over meatballs, but if you like to keep it a bright reddish marinara, it's best to use bright red sun-dried tomatoes (or substitute tomato paste instead). Double the herbs if using fresh instead of dried.

Makes about 4 cups of sauce

10–12 fresh Roma tomatoes (about 2 pounds)
1 cup softened sun-dried tomatoes (about ½ cup chopped) or 2 tablespoons tomato paste
2 medium peeled carrots and/or ½ medium beet or a small yam
1 zucchini
½ medium onion
1 garlic clove
¼ cup virgin olive oil
2 tablespoons dry wine (or use 1 tablespoon wine vinegar)
3 tablespoons Italian seasoning or 1 tablespoon each oregano, rosemary, and basil
1–2 teaspoons sea salt
⅛–¼ teaspoon red pepper flakes
2 tablespoons ground chia seeds (optional)
Broth or water to thin as needed

1. Roughly chop the vegetables and add to your blender with the olive oil and wine and blend until smooth.
2. Add the herbs and blend briefly. Taste the sauce, adjust seasoning to your liking and add the ground chia to thicken, if desired.
3. Toss into hot pasta or steamed veggies/red potatoes, or use as a dipping sauce.
4. For a hotter sauce, gently warm on the stove top.
5. For a thicker, cooked sauce, simmer until desired consistency.

Tip: If you like your sauce chunkier, save a few tomatoes and a little zucchini to add after you've blended the rest smooth. Stir in some finely grated Parmesan and use for pizza sauce.

Tip: Whenever you're roasting meat, throw some vegetables in with it, then use the veggies and meat juices to blend into a gravy. Leftover mixed veggies, potatoes, or sweet potatoes, work really well here too, but we don't always have leftovers to use so I'll just use raw. If you blend it long enough, the raw veggies cook right in the blender for that real gravy taste.

GRAVY, PESTOS & SAUCES: This is not just a cook (or un-cook) book full of easy-to-follow recipes. This is a book I hope will encourage you to be brave in the kitchen. It's not always about perfect planning or needing to run to the store to follow every recipe to a T. Sometimes a substitution can create your own masterpiece! Don't be afraid to try new ingredients, especially when it comes to raw soups, dressings, and sauces, because so many veggies and herbs blend together beautifully for a delicious, creative dish. It's so boring to follow just another pesto recipe with basil, garlic, and olive oil when it can be recreated so many ways. Use your favorite herbs, nuts, and oils. Try beet greens, arugula, or Swiss chard. Leave the garlic out and try fresh turmeric or ginger. Sometimes you've just gotta live a little on the wild side. To get you started, here are some ideas . . .

Lazy Gal's Blender Gravy

Yup, I admit, I can be a bit on the lazy side, so de-glazing pans, scraping brown bits, making a flour roux, and whisking the lumps from refined starches just don't happen in my kitchen anymore. But that's okay because this gravy tastes like I made it that old-fashioned way.

Makes about 2 cups

1 cup stock, veggie or bone broth
1 small yellow or white sweet potato (approximately 7–8 ounces)
1 carrot, peeled
1 celery stalk
½ small onion
¼ cup butter
Salt and pepper to taste
Garlic powder and your favorite herbs (thyme, sage, and so on) (optional)

1. Heat the broth in a small saucepan until almost boiling.
2. While the broth heats, rough chop the vegetables and add everything else to your blender. No need to peel the sweet potato so long as the skin is not bitter.
3. Pour the broth into the blender, let rest a minute, and blend on high until smooth and velvety. Adjust the seasonings, or add more liquid if needed. If you like thicker gravy, toss in a little coconut, sweet potato, or almond flour, or ground chia seeds instead of a starch.

Note: The color of broth you use will affect the color of the gravy. For Southern "Red Eye" gravy, try using coffee instead of stock and adding a generous shot of hot sauce.

Sweet and Spicy Orange Pesto

Who says pesto has to be green? And who says it has to be served over pasta? How about with veggies, potatoes, or as a cracker spread? Why not combine it with mayo for a sandwich spread? Stir it into soups, salad dressings, or top pizzas with it. And rather than raw, I often use roasted and salted sunflower seeds because I'm a rebel.

Makes about 3 cups

1 small peeled yam
1 medium red or orange bell pepper
2 carrots
½ cup sunflower seeds, pine nuts, or cashews
1 two-inch piece of turmeric or 1 teaspoon ground
½ teaspoon red pepper flakes
1 thin-skinned juice orange
1 or more cups olive or avocado oil
Sea salt and pepper to taste

1. Chop and add everything into your food processor and blend until smooth or chunky, to a consistency you prefer.

Green Pesto

I'll admit that the classic recipe for pesto: basil, olive oil, pine nuts, and Parmesan is a simple and nourishing summer treat. But why stop there? Remember to be brave, it's your kitchen!

Makes about 3 cups

Greens from the tops of 1 bunch of carrots (taste to make sure they are not *too* bitter)
2 big handfuls of spinach
1 medium zucchini
1 bunch of basil
4 big sprigs fresh oregano or your favorite herbs
½ medium onion
½ cup raw sunflower seeds or walnuts
1–3 garlic cloves (optional)
1 teaspoon sea salt
½ teaspoon black pepper
1 or more cups olive or macadamia nut oil, + more to top

1. Add everything into your food processor and blend until achieving your desired consistency.

Tip: Store in a glass container and top with more oil.

CREAMY RAW ALFREDO SAUCE

· ·

The raw sweet potato is good for the tummy and this makes for a refreshing variation of the old classic.

Makes about 2 cups

2 yellow summer squash (or peeled zucchini), about 12 ounces
1 small yellow or white sweet potato, peeled (about 7 ounces or 1½ cups, roughly chopped)
¼ cup chopped onion (about 2 ounces)
1 garlic clove (optional)
1 cup heavy cream, or ³/₄ cup nut milk
2–4 tablespoons butter, ghee, or macadamia nut oil (optional, use if not using cream)
Broth or water for thinning, only if needed
½–1 cup grated Asiago or Parmesan cheese (or nutritional yeast or almond flour as desired)
1 teaspoon sea salt
Pepper to taste

1. Add everything to your blender and blend on high until smooth and creamy.
2. Warm on the stove top, stirring constantly just until hot (use your finger to test), be careful not to overheat or it will no longer be raw.
3. Toss with hot pasta or gnocchi.

RAW DIPPING OR PIZZA SAUCE

· ·

3 Roma tomatoes
½ cup chopped sun-dried tomatoes, softened in water
2 tablespoons red wine vinegar
1 tablespoon olive oil
2 teaspoons dried oregano
1 teaspoon dried rosemary
1 teaspoon sea salt

1. Blend everything together in a small food processor.
2. Thin to desired consistency with water or carrot juice.

Tip: For a crispy coating, dredge the pre-cooked "meat" in egg, dip in almond flour, and fry in desired oil/fat. Almonds burn easily, so I like to cook the "meat" through first. Re-crisp leftovers in the oven at 375°F for about 10 minutes.

No-Chicken Strips

These days, I find I need more vegetarian options in my household. I was shocked when I went looking for chicken substitutes. It seems everything contains tons of soy or wheat gluten, even in the recipes I found. I can't eat chickpeas either, so I went back to what made sense to me. This also makes a yummy patty on a bun and little stir-fry pieces for other "No-Chicken" dishes.

1½ cups roughly chopped cauliflower, about 7–8 ounces
1½ cups roughly chopped yellow sweet potato
1½ cup almond, cashew, or other nut flour
2 eggs
¼ cup coconut flour
4 tablespoons psyllium husk powder
3 tablespoons melted butter or ghee
1½ teaspoons sea salt
¼ teaspoon garlic powder or any other seasoning desired (optional)

1. Puree the cauliflower and sweet potato in your food processor to very fine bits.
2. Add the rest of the ingredients and blend for a good minute, stopping to scrape sides at least once.
3. It will be a thick, sticky batter. Remove the blade and turn into a bowl.
4. Let it rest a few minutes, then knead it together with a rubber spatula.
5. With damp hands, shape into desired shapes (strips, patties, nuggets, etc.).
6. Fry in ghee or coconut oil on medium-high heat for a few minutes on each side in a lightly oiled skillet.

Note: For "stir-fry pieces" pull off small, random pieces of dough and drop in boiling water for about three minutes. Transfer to a baking sheet with a cooling rack and dry in a 325°F oven until no longer moist, about 10 minutes. Use in casseroles, taco filling, Asian dishes, etc.

GROUND NO-MEAT

This recipe makes life a little easier because the meat eaters even like it. Heck, if you don't tell them it's not meat they may not even notice! I usually double this batch because I like to keep some in my freezer or fridge to have on hand for burgers, etc. This recipe will make a nice sized "meatloaf" or 12–16 good sized meatballs. It's also great filling for tacos or tostadas, or just about any place you'd use ground beef. If the beet makes it too pink for you, just use less, or use all yam instead.

2-ounce package of dried shitaki mushrooms or
   8 ounces fresh mushrooms*
½ small beet with skin, about 2 ounces
1 small yam with skin, about 4 ounces
1 cup walnuts or pecans
2 large eggs
1 tablespoon tomato paste
3 tablespoons coconut aminos, or tamari
1 can black beans, rinsed and drained
2 teaspoons psyllium husk powder, or 2
   tablespoons ground chia seeds
1 cup grain-free bread crumbs, or cooked/
   soaked quinoa, or ⅔ cup almond flour
1 teaspoon sea salt and pepper to taste
Optional: onion, garlic, herbs

Meatloaf glaze

¼ cup maple syrup
1 tablespoon tomato paste
1 tablespoon coconut aminos
1 teaspoon medicinal mushroom powder
   (optional)

1. Add the mushrooms to your food processor and process until fine and powdery. Chop the beet and yam, and add these with the nuts. If using fresh mushrooms, add them to the food processor along with the other vegetables and nuts and process until finely minced.
2. Add the eggs, tomato paste, coconut aminos, and beans, and blend until the beans are chopped.
3. Add the psyllium or chia seeds and bread crumbs or almond flour and pulse several times until the consistency is similar to ground beef.
4. Taste and adjust seasoning to your taste.
5. Bake times will vary. At 350°F approximate times for meatballs and burger patties is 25–35 minutes; meatloaf should be approximately 50 minutes; if crumbled and spread on a sheet pan for taco filling, 30 minutes.
6. To store, wrap in plastic wrap and store in the freezer or refrigerator.
7. *For the Glaze*, stir ingredients together in a small bowl and brush over meatloaf halfway through baking.

*Note: I always keep dried shitaki mushrooms on hand in my pantry. If you use fresh mushrooms, add a tablespoon of coconut flour to the mix because there's more water in them.

Tip: If you use medicinal mushroom powder, add a tablespoon for extra flavor and nutrition.

Carrot Yam Soup

Orange is my hub's favorite color. Halloween is my favorite holiday (no gift shopping or wrapping, lots of crazy food, and adults get to act like children). This is a fun autumn soup. Feel free to spice it up with a dash of cayenne and stir in a little cooked quinoa or white rice if you're feeling dangerous.

Serves 6

Ingredients

4 cups broth of choice
4 carrots, peeled
1 small yam, peeled
2 apples
2 celery stalks
½ small onion
A few slices of red bell pepper
¼ cup butter or cream
1 teaspoon sage
2 teaspoons curry powder
Sea salt and pepper to taste

1. Warm the broth in a small saucepan until hot to the touch.
2. Roughly chop the vegetables (and apples) and add to the blender along with the butter or cream and spices.
3. Pour the broth into the blender and blend until smooth, creamy, and hot.

CREAMY BROCCOLI SOUP

. . . .

I like raw broccoli, but the flavor just doesn't transfer to the favorite comfort soup most of us like. For this reason, I cook the broccoli until tender and keep the rest of the ingredients raw.

6–8 servings

About 1 bunch (3–4 heads) of broccoli + their stems (about 1 pound)
Water to cover broccoli, 4–6 cups
1½ cups roughly chopped cauliflower, or peeled yellow sweet potato (about 7 ounces)
2 celery stalks
¼ cup diced onion
1 teaspoon dried dill
1 teaspoon ground turmeric, or a fresh 2–inch piece
2 teaspoons sea salt
1 teaspoon black pepper
2 big handfuls of spinach
A small handful of fresh parsley, chopped
1 cup heavy cream or 6 ounces cheddar cheese, cut into ½ inch pieces (optional)

1. Chop the broccoli into equal sized pieces, including the stems, and put into a medium-sized pot, cover with water, and cook until tender, about 5–7 minutes.
2. While the broccoli is cooking, add the rest of the ingredients to your blender, except the parsley.
3. When the broccoli is tender, use a slotted spoon to transfer to a large bowl. Set aside a few florets to add to the bowls when serving.
4. Pour enough of the cooking water or broth over the contents of the blender so that it blends up nice and smooth.
5. Add the broccoli and cheese, if using, and blend again. Do this in a couple of batches if necessary.
6. Return the soup to the pan to heat and adjust seasoning to your taste. Add enough of the cooking water to get the consistency you like.
7. Add the parsley and the florets you set aside to each serving.

Quick Tomato Bisque

Don't forget tomatoes are a fruit. I know science says that cooking the tomatoes and carrots releases more of the carotenoids but I think a high-speed blender does a pretty good job too. Either way, I think I could live on fresh, juicy, ripe tomatoes. Juicy, ripe tomatoes and cheese. Ripe tomatoes, cheese, and baguettes. Okay, tomatoes, cheese, baguettes, and wine. Done.

Serves 4

8–10 lovely, ripe, Roma tomatoes, divided
1–2 carrots, peeled (optional)
1 garlic clove
¼ cup olive oil
1 teaspoon sea salt
1 tablespoon dried oregano or Italian seasoning
¼ teaspoon red pepper flakes
¼ cup heavy cream or milk of choice (optional)

1. Set aside 1–2 tomatoes to add at the end for a chunkier texture, if desired.
2. Roughly chop the tomatoes and carrots, toss in your blender with the garlic, olive oil, and salt, and blend on high until smooth.
3. Chop and add the rest of the tomatoes, seasoning, and cream, if using, and pulse a few times.
4. Warm on the stove top until hot to the touch.

Raw Summer Squash Soup with Dill

This recipe is so quick and easy I almost feel guilty calling it a "recipe," but I make it so often I couldn't leave it out. It's refreshing cold in the summer, or simmer up some sliced squash to add to the soup base for a heartier comfort meal. I guess that would then be considered semi-raw instead of raw, but let's not nit-pick, right? Sometimes I toss a handful of spinach or another green in too. Remember to have fun experimenting!

Serves 4

2–4 summer squash, crookneck or zucchini
4 cups broth (veggie or bone)
2 celery stalks
A couple pieces or about ¼ small onion
A few sprigs fresh dill or 2 teaspoons dried dill
Sea salt and pepper to taste
4 tablespoons butter or ghee (optional)

1. Cut up the squash and toss everything into the blender and blend until smooth.
2. Serve warmed or cold.

Tip: For a refreshing change if you serve this cold, substitute a cucumber for half the squash or add a diced cucumber to the soup after it's blended.

Tip: Add a sprinkling of chia seeds, ground psyllium, or sweet potato flour if your tomatoes are super juicy.

Tip: Add a dose of MCT oil or a scoop of collagen powder if you have them on hand. However, I've tried many of the "tricks" that supposedly help to keep a soft and creamy ice cream and haven't found much difference from adding gelatin, glycerin, or vodka to this.

Vanilla Custard Ice Cream

Is my household the only one that views vanilla ice cream in the freezer as a basic need for survival? Creamy homemade ice cream (especially if you choose to do a non-dairy version) can be hard to achieve, mostly because our home freezers just don't freeze it quick enough to keep the ice crystals really small. But I was on a mission to figure out a way around this obstacle. Even though ice cream churners are easy to use, being the lazy gal I am, I sometimes need a recipe that's still great without churning. I don't use plantains that often because, as I said, I'm a bit lazy and they can be a pain in the patootie to peel. For the love of delicious, nutritious ice cream I must get over it. The eggs add flavor and texture; the dates, plantain, or sweet potato, add fluff and keep the ice cream from melting quickly; and the syrup and guar gum keeps it creamier.

2½ cups cold cream and/or full-fat coconut milk or cream
2 eggs + 2 egg yolks
3 large soft, peeled and pitted dates, or 2 tablespoons date paste
A small piece of yellow sweet potato or barely ripe plantain or banana (about 1 ounce)
⅓ cup syrup of choice
½ teaspoon pure monk fruit or stevia
1–2 tablespoons vanilla extract
1 teaspoon almond extract (optional)
A pinch of sea salt
¼–½ teaspoon guar gum (optional)

1. Add all of the ingredients and blend until smooth and fluffy.
2. Transfer to an airtight container and freeze or, use your ice cream maker until it's a soft serve consistency, then transfer to an air-tight container and freeze.

Note: I use raw eggs because I believe they're safe and nutritious, but you can cook the eggs with the cream (if you must), stirring constantly until thickened, strain if necessary, then chill mixture before continuing.

Fresh Fruit Soft (or Frozen) Serve

. . . .

Keeping with my philosophy that you can't go wrong with fresh, organic whole foods, especially fruit, go ahead and throw abandon to the wind! Vary your choices at the market or use what you have on hand. The likelihood of it not tasting great is slim to none. This recipe is the basic recipe I use, typically just switching out the diced mango for anything from berries to grapefruit. The juicier the fruit is, the more banana you may want to throw in, otherwise it's more like a sorbet. I'm sorry, but if that's a mistake, it's okay with me. If you eat fresh eggs, you can toss one in too.

Makes about 2½ cups

1 banana
2 cups diced mango
1 cup chilled coconut cream (the solid part of the coconut milk at the top of the can)
2 tablespoons MCT or coconut oil (optional)
⅔ teaspoon pure monk fruit or stevia

1. For an immediate soft-serve consistency, have the fruit frozen. Add all of the ingredients to your blender or your food processor and blend until smooth.

Note: If you use room temperature or chilled fruit, you'll have more of a smoothie consistency, but you can always toss it in your ice cream maker and freeze as directed.

Hot Fudge Sauce

. . . .

When I was just a lass (oh brother, would you rather I say "little gal"?), my favorite treat was a Banana Royal Sundae from Farrell's Ice Cream Parlor. Vanilla ice cream, bananas, walnuts, hot chocolate sauce, whipped cream, and a cherry, of course. Now that I'm all growed up, I occasionally have this for dinner, except I make it myself, and I make my husband serve it to me.

Makes about 2½ cups

4 ounces 100% chocolate (such as baking chocolate)
½ cup butter
½ cup syrup of choice
1 teaspoon pure monk fruit or stevia
1 teaspoon vanilla extract
½ teaspoon almond extract or instant espresso crystals (optional)
½ cup water or cream
Pinch of sea salt

1. Melt the chocolate with the butter and syrup in a small pan on the stove top.
2. Stir in the rest of the ingredients.
3. Store in a glass jar in your fridge for a month.

Tip: Add more water or cream for a thinner consistency. For a "hot fudge" sauce that remains thick, when heated, use cream rather than water.

Caramel Sauce

Dates make an amazing caramel sauce and they blend so smoothly they aren't even detectable (you can press them through a strainer if you don't have a powerful blender). You can leave this sauce raw, but for real gooey, deep caramel flavor and texture I recommend the cooked version. Dates bring so much whole food goodness and such delicious sweet flavor that sometimes I stir a spoonful into my morning coffee.

Makes about 1½ cups

¼ cup butter
½ cup cream or coconut milk
1 cup soft, pitted dates (preferably Medjool), about 5 ounces
½ cup syrup of choice
1 teaspoon vanilla extract (optional)
Pinch of sea salt or as much as ½ a teaspoon for a "salted caramel" taste

1. Melt the butter with the cream in a small saucepan.
2. If your dates are not soft, add them to the pan, cover and let rest for 30 minutes. Otherwise, just add the dates directly to your blender.
3. Add the contents of the pan and the syrup to the blender and blend until very smooth.
4. Keep raw or pour the sauce back into the saucepan (straining it, if desired).
5. Cover and simmer for 10 minutes, checking and stirring as necessary.
6. Let cool somewhat then stir in the extract and salt. Store in a glass jar in your fridge for up to 2 weeks.

Note: This makes a thick caramel. If you want a pourable sauce, add more syrup or cream.

Chapter 7:

BREADS, BUNS & BISCUITS

When I first began to omit grains from my life, bread was the most difficult to stop eating. With no one in my family having obvious reactions to gluten at the time, I kept trying to eat a little bread here and there. Then, I graduated to thinking, *I'll just eat gluten-free breads*, because I thought gluten was the villain. Wrong. All that refined starch in those gluten-free breads wreaked havoc on my health and my weight (particularly my mid-section). What?! Life without a piece of good ol' bread now and again? That wasn't going to work. So, I got to work and lo and behold: delicious and simple bread recipes made without grains, processed starches, or yeast. Taking yeast out of the equation means we no longer must wait hours for a loaf of bread. I like that almost as much as knowing I can eat bread anytime now. Psyllium husk is a necessary ingredient in these recipes and using the brand I recommend in Resources will assure your best results—I grind it to a powder in my coffee grinder. And, for a really nice loaf of bread, use the right size bread pan. The disposable ones in the baking aisle will do.

Big Soft Pretzels

. . . .

During the years we spent in New York City, my oldest son Josh loved nothing more than to taste as much street vendor food as possible. Pretzels and knishes slathered in mustard topped his list in those days, but nowadays my Big Soft Pretzels fit the bill. Josh's wife, Charity, shares my passion for alternative baking and my first grandchild, Aurora, shares her dad's passion for these soft, chewy, and satisfying snacks!

Makes 6–8 pretzels

Dry Ingredients

⅔ cup almond flour
3 tablespoons psyllium husk powder
¼ cup coconut flour
1 teaspoon baking powder
³/₄ teaspoon sea salt
¼ teaspoon baking soda

Blender Ingredients

1 cup peeled, roughly chopped zucchini
3 large eggs
2 tablespoons apple cider vinegar

Toppings

1 large egg (or egg white) for brushing
Coarse sea salt

1. Preheat oven to 400°F.
2. Whisk together the dry ingredients and set aside.
3. Blend the wet ingredients in your blender until smooth.
4. Pour the wet ingredients into the dry and whisk briskly, then stir and fold the batter together.
5. Let the batter set up a minute or two, to become more dough-like, then knead it with your hands for another minute. It will become denser and slightly sticky.
6. Scoop about ¼–⅓ cup of dough and place on a sheet of waxed paper.
7. Use damp hands to roll each portion into a rope about 12–13 inches long and ½-inch wide. It needs to be thin enough so that when it bakes, it puffs into a pretzel shape.
8. Roll into a pretzel shape and smooth with dampened hands.
9. Brush generously with egg and sprinkle with coarse sea salt.
10. Transfer each pretzel onto a parchment-lined cookie sheet and bake for about 18–20 minutes, or until a deep golden brown.

Tip: If you've not shaped pretzels before, shape and bake one as a test before baking them all.

CHALLAH BREAD

. . . .

Because I'm such a lazy gal, I usually roll this dough into balls and toss them into a 5 x 8-inch loaf pan to get the "challah" bread look. But for those of you with patience and a knack for braiding, this dough will work for that too (as you can see in the picture). I actually did a three-strand braid for you! I don't know how to do a traditional six strand braid (I guess I didn't learn because I never had to braid any of my boys' hair). If braiding bread dough into fancy Challah loaves is a fun pastime for you, please send me a picture so I can see what a person with this type of patience looks like.

Makes 1 loaf, about 16 slices

Dry Ingredients

½ cup coconut flour
1¼ cups almond flour
¼ cup psyllium husk powder
1 rounded tablespoon baking powder
1 teaspoon sea salt
Pinch of turmeric (optional, for extra color)

Blender Ingredients

5 large eggs
1 cup roughly chopped yellow squash or apple
   (about 5 ounces)
$1/3$ cup water
2 tablespoons honey

Topping

Egg wash for brushing

1. Preheat oven to 375°F
2. Sift the coconut flour, if needed. In a medium-sized bowl, whisk together the dry ingredients.
3. Blend the wet ingredients in your blender until smooth.
4. Add the wet ingredients to the dry ingredients and whisk until the mixture begins to thicken. Let the batter rest a few minutes while it continues to thicken.
5. Use your fingers or a rubber spatula to mix and knead the dough for a couple of minutes. It will be somewhat sticky. If it's too sticky, knead in 1 more tablespoon of coconut flour.
6. Use damp hands to divide the dough into three sections and roll out each section to 12–13 inches.
7. Lay them next to each other on a lined sheet pan so they're laying sort of in a triangle shape and squeeze together the ends that come together.
8. Begin to braid one strand over the center strand just as you would a regular braid. Use water to help smooth the dough.
9. Bake for 1 hour; tent with foil about half way through.
10. Brush all over the top with whisked egg 5 minutes before removing from the oven.
11. Cool in the pan for 5–10 minutes, remove with potholders, and finish cooling on a rack.

Note: If you don't have the time to braid the dough simply brush a regular-sized (8 x 5 x 2½-inch) loaf pan with clarified butter, ghee, coconut, or nut oil, then roll sections of dough into large balls and place into the loaf pan. Once all the dough is in the pan, gently press down on the top to shape it more "bread-like" and bake as directed.

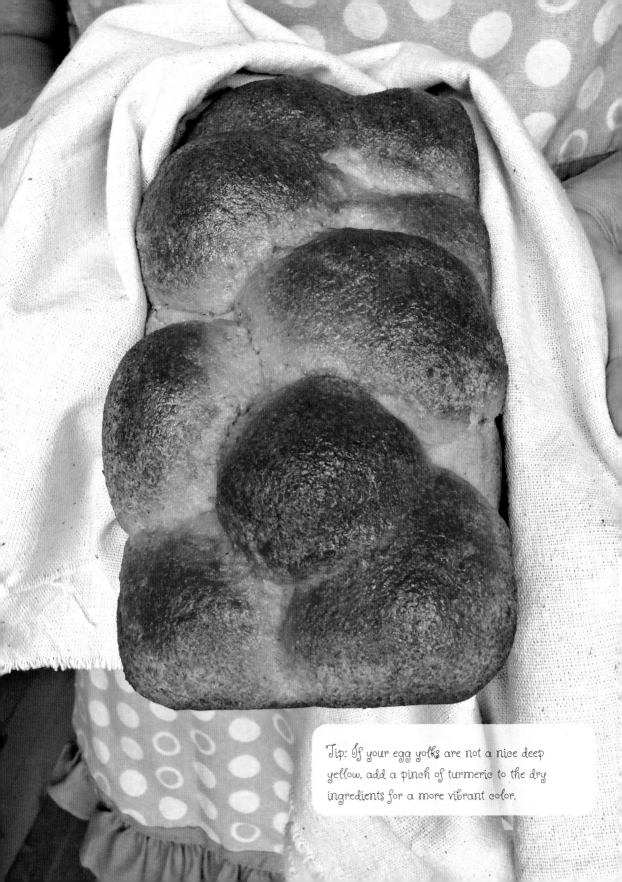

Tip: If your egg yolks are not a nice deep yellow, add a pinch of turmeric to the dry ingredients for a more vibrant color.

Cinnamon Raisin Bread

. . . .

I like to lay several slices of this bread on a cookie sheet and toast them in my oven and eat them with tons of butter. I know it's hard to believe it could even get better than that, but sometimes I get really crazy and add a few slices of banana on top of the toast and drizzle with a little honey, then put it under the broiler just until the bananas start to sweat. Ooooooh, my heavens!

Makes 1 loaf, about 16 slices

Dry Ingredients

³/₄ cup coconut flour
²/₃ cup almond flour
3 tablespoons psyllium husk powder
1 teaspoon sea salt
2 teaspoons baking powder
²/₃ cup gold or black raisins
1 tablespoon cinnamon

Blender Ingredients

5 large eggs
1 cups roughly chopped apple (about 1 medium/large, 4–5 ounces)
½ cups walnuts, pecans, Brazil nuts, hazelnuts, or a mixture of any, about 2 ounces
½ cup water
2 tablespoons honey

Additional Ingredients

¼ cup almond flour
1 tablespoon cinnamon
⅛ teaspoon pure monk fruit or stevia powder

1. Preheat your oven to 375°F and line a loaf pan with parchment paper or brush with coconut or nut oil.
2. Sift the coconut flour, if needed. In a medium-sized bowl, whisk together the dry ingredients.
3. Blend the wet ingredients in your blender until smooth.
4. Pour the wet ingredients into the dry ingredients. Whisk briskly then let the batter rest a few minutes while it continues to thicken.
5. Use damp hands or a rubber spatula to knead the batter for another minute then turn onto waxed paper and pat into a rectangle-shape, about 7 x 10-inches.
6. Stir together the "Additional Ingredients" and sprinkle over the dough, leaving an inch around all sides.
7. Start at the short side (opposite of how you would roll cinnamon rolls) and roll into a loaf.
8. Set into the prepared pan and smooth the top with a damp hand if necessary.
9. Place in your oven on the center rack and bake for 40 minutes. Cover with parchment paper or foil and continue to bake about 50 more minutes.
10. Cool in the pan for 5–10 minutes, then remove with potholders and finish cooling on a rack.

Note: The disposable paper or aluminum loaf pans in most local grocery stores work great for grain-free breads because they're narrow with high sides to help the bread rise. I use Fat Daddio's 7³/₄ x 3³/₄ x 2³/₄-inch pan, which is available on my website.

Tip: If you don't care about seeing the pretty cinnamon "swirls" in the sliced bread, you can omit the "Additional Ingredients" and just shape into a loaf and bake.

Corn (or No-Corn) Bread

. . . .

If you're like me and love a sweet cornbread, then this recipe is for you. If not, simply omit the honey and monk fruit, and it's savory but still delish. I 'm sure there are many dishes that accompany cornbread well, but my brain always thinks Chili Beans. Chili and Cornbread is like Peanut Butter and Jelly, or like Jack 'n Coke as my hubby would say. This bread also makes a great stuffing.

Makes 1 (10-inch) pan, about 9–12 pieces

Dry Ingredients

2 cups almond flour
2 tablespoons coconut flour
1 tablespoon baking powder or teaspoon baking
    soda
1¼ teaspoons sea salt

Additional Ingredients

¼ cup butter
Salt, cracked black pepper, and garlic powder to taste
⅔ cups fresh or frozen corn (optional)

Blender Ingredients

4 large eggs
1 cup fresh or frozen corn or roughly chopped
    yellow sweet potato
2 roughly chopped apples (about 9 ounces)
1 cup shredded coconut (about 2 ounces)
⅓ cup honey (optional)
1 tablespoon lemon juice
⅓ teaspoon stevia or pure monk fruit (optional)

1. Preheat oven to 375°F and add the butter to a 10-inch cast-iron skillet or casserole dish.
2. Sprinkle with salt, pepper, and garlic powder, if desired, and warm the pan in the oven until the butter begins to look toasty.
3. Stir together the dry ingredients and set aside.
4. Blend the wet ingredients in your blender until smooth.
5. Stir the wet ingredients into the dry and combine well.
6. Stir in the additional corn, if using, and pour batter into the pan with the melted butter. The butter may roll up the sides and onto the top; that's okay.
7. Bake at 375°F for 40 minutes or until a toothpick inserted in the center comes out clean.
8. Cover with aluminum foil partway through as it becomes brown.

Note: Feel free to stir in different ingredients, like diced jalapeños, shredded cheese, crumbled bacon, or even a few olives.

Everything Good for You Bagels

Bagels are another fond memory from our years in New York City. My husband had his favorite shops to grab a cream cheese and smoked salmon fix, sandwiched with a soft, warm bagel. Even back then I guess I shied away a bit from loads of heavy bread, but it's great to know I don't have to now. Bring on the salmon and cream cheese. Yes, these taste and toast up like real bagels without the need to boil first. But if that's your thing, don't let me stop you, these will hold up.

Makes 6–8 bagels

Dry Ingredients

1 cup almond or other nut flour
¼ cup psyllium husk powder
¼ cup coconut flour
1 teaspoon baking soda
1 teaspoon sea salt
¼ teaspoon garlic powder or onion powder (optional)

Blender Ingredients

1 cup roughly chopped white or yellow sweet potato (about 5 ounces)
4 large eggs
2 tablespoons apple cider vinegar
2 tablespoons honey (optional)

Toppings

2 tablespoons each of your favorite seeds like chia, pumpkin, sesame, or sunflower
Coarse sea salt and cracked black pepper to taste
1 large egg or egg white for brushing

1. Preheat oven to 425°F.
2. Whisk together the dry ingredients.
3. Blend the wet ingredients in your blender until smooth.
4. Pour the wet into the dry and whisk briskly, then stir and fold the batter together.
5. Let it set up a minute or two, then use your fingers to knead it another 1–2 minutes until it becomes a slightly sticky dough.
6. Portion the dough into 6–8 sections and use damp hands to roll each portion into a rope about 7 inches long and an inch wide.
7. Roll into a circle and pinch together the ends, smoothing and turning each bagel over, shaping to look neat.
8. Brush generously with egg or egg white and sprinkle with toppings.
9. Transfer each bagel onto a parchment-lined cookie sheet and bake for about 18 minutes, or until a deep golden brown.

Focaccia Bread

....

Oh, Foccacia, oh how I love you. When I serve this at a dinner party, I just let my friends think I worked all day. For some reason, the little finger pokes seem to impress novice focaccia makers. Or maybe it's the pools of melted butter or olive oil settled in these little divots. We have tons of rosemary around our property, and like the many grapes in the area, it grows well in our sandy soil, made up of plenty of decomposed granite. It kind of grows like weeds, which appeals to my lazy nature. While I used rosemary here, you really can't go wrong with your favorite herbs.

Makes about 12 pieces

Dry Ingredients

1 cup almond flour
6 tablespoons coconut flour
2 tablespoons psyllium husk powder
½ teaspoon baking soda
½ teaspoon sea salt
¼ teaspoon garlic powder

Blender Ingredients

1 cup roughly chopped yellow summer squash
   or peeled zucchini (4- 5 ounces)
3 large eggs
½ cup water
1 tablespoon lemon juice

Toppings

3–4 tablespoons olive oil
1 teaspoon rosemary
1 teaspoon thyme
1 minced garlic clove, or ¼ teaspoon garlic
   powder
⅛ teaspoon black pepper
Pinch of sea salt

1. Preheat the oven to 375°F.
2. Generously oil a baking sheet with olive oil.
3. In a medium-sized bowl, whisk together the dry ingredients.
4. Blend the wet ingredients in your blender until smooth.
5. Whisk the wet ingredients into the dry. As it thickens, stir and fold together.
6. Let the batter set up for a few minutes to absorb the liquids and then knead it with your fingers for about a minute.
7. Turn the dough onto the prepared baking pan and pat into a rectangle about 8 x 10 inches. It should be about $^3/_4$-inch thick.
8. Use your fingertips to press little dimples all over the dough.
9. Pour the olive oil over the top and sprinkle on the herbs.
10. Bake for about 28–30 minutes, until the top is a deep golden brown.

Garlic Cheese Drop Biscuits

. . . .

Ahem . . . I'm sorry, but . . . garlic, cheese, and biscuit? Need I say more? Oh, yes, butter! While I've lived in California most of my life, I must confess that I was born in Mississippi on an Air Force base and lived there until I was two, when my parents moved the family back to their native California home. My husband and I also spent two years outside of Charleston, South Carolina, where I was introduced to Red Eye Gravy. Just Google that if you don't have a recipe, because dunking these babies in that gravy is divine. However, these cheesy morsels really need no help at all.

Makes 8–10 large biscuits

Dry Ingredients

1½ cups almond flour or other nut flour
3 tablespoons coconut flour
2 tablespoons psyllium husk powder
1 rounded teaspoon baking powder
1 teaspoon sea salt
¼ teaspoon baking soda
1 cup shredded sharp cheddar cheese (about 3 ounces)

Blender Ingredients

2 large eggs
½ cup roughly chopped yam (about 2–3 ounces)
³/₄ cup water
¼ cup sour cream

Topping

⅛ teaspoon each salt and garlic powder
3 tablespoons melted butter

1. Preheat oven to 400°F and generously butter a baking pan. A sheet pan works fine, but the biscuits won't rise as high, so I like to use a 9 x 9-inch square pan that perfectly fits 9 biscuits.
2. In a medium-sized bowl, whisk together the dry ingredients and set aside.
3. In your blender, blend the wet ingredients until smooth.
4. Whisk the wet ingredients into the dry ingredients; the leavening will make it very bubbly.
5. Let the batter set up a minute or two then use your hands or a rubber spatula to stir and fold the dough over itself, sort of kneading it several times until stiffened.
6. Use an ice cream scooper to drop dollops of dough into the prepared baking pan. Press the tops down with a damp palm for a more "biscuit-look."
7. Sprinkle the top with the salt and garlic powder and bake for 30 minutes until they become golden brown.
8. Brush the baked biscuits with the melted butter when they come out of the oven.

Hamburger & Hot Dog Buns

. . . .

We have a few restaurants in town that serve grass-fed burgers, but the only buns they have are wheat or starchy gluten-free thingies. So, I always bring our buns with us because we have the best buns in town (hee-hee)! Some restaurants will gladly use our bread and put the burgers together for us and others don't want to take outside bread into their kitchen (not sure what they think it might do to their kitchen), so if that's the case, we'll just switch it out at the table. These buns hold together great and are soft and bun-like, just like they're supposed to be. These are what I call QHED buns (quick, healthy, easy, and delicious) and they make our barbecues so much more fun now.

Makes 8 buns

Dry Ingredients

1 cup almond flour or other nut flour
³/₄ cup coconut flour
¼ cup egg white powder
¼ cup psyllium husk powder
1 teaspoon sea salt
1 teaspoon baking powder
½ teaspoon baking soda

Wet Ingredients

1½ cups water
1 large egg
2 tablespoons applesauce
1 tablespoon apple cider vinegar

1. Preheat your oven to 400°F and line a baking sheet with a baking liner or liberally brush the pan with coconut oil or ghee.
2. Whisk/sift together the dry ingredients to remove any lumps.
3. Whisk together the wet ingredients in another bowl.
4. Pour the wet ingredients into the dry ingredients and whisk briskly, then stir and fold until the batter is evenly moistened.
5. Let the batter rest a few minutes until it becomes more like dough than a batter, then use your fingers or a rubber spatula to knead and fold the dough for 1–2 minutes.
6. Use a large scooper and measure out portions of dough about ¹/₃ cup in size. With damp hands, gently shape into balls for hamburger buns, or elongated shapes for hot dog buns.
7. Place on the prepared baking sheet and press down gently with a dampened palm to flatten.
8. Bake for about 25 minutes or until golden brown.
9. Cool a few minutes, and then transfer to a rack to finish cooling.

IRISH POTATO BREAD

....

Hmmm, it's not easy to say this, but I think this is my favorite bread in this book. I looove the old-world taste of caraway and the rustic look of the loaf. Seriously, I hardly noticed the raw cheese, although it makes the perfect accompaniment. My husband, who we lovingly refer to as "Animal" in these parts, is of Irish descent, and our second son, Jeremy, and his bride Drea spent their honeymoon traveling through the Irish countryside. I've never visited Ireland, so I was clueless when the kids told me there was a very poor selection of fresh produce there. I'd love to visit, but I couldn't live there long with minimal fresh produce. I must say, though, this bread paired with some Guinness stew? That's gold at the end of the rainbow!

Makes 1 (9-inch) round loaf

Dry Ingredients

⅔ cup almond flour
⅔ cup coconut flour
¼ cup egg white powder
3 tablespoons psyllium husk powder
1½ teaspoons baking soda
¾ teaspoon sea salt
½ teaspoon caraway seeds (optional)

Blender Ingredients

2 cups roughly chopped white or yellow sweet potatoes
2 large eggs
¾ cup water
2 tablespoons apple cider vinegar
1 teaspoon caraway seeds

1. Preheat your oven to 400°F and line a baking sheet with parchment paper.
2. In a medium bowl, whisk together the dry ingredients and set aside.
3. Blend the wet ingredients in your blender on high until smooth, about 45 seconds.
4. Pour the wet ingredients into the dry and whisk briskly, then stir and fold as it thickens.
5. Let the batter set 5 minutes until it becomes more dough-like.
6. Use your hands or a rubber spatula to knead and fold the dough for about a minute.
7. Use damp hands to shape the dough into a ball and place on the prepared baking sheet.
8. Dampen your hands again to shape it into a round loaf and smooth the surface.
9. Dust with coconut flour and use a sharp knife to core the top of the dough with an X.
10. Bake for 60–70 minutes. Cover with aluminum foil towards the end if it begins to over-brown.
11. Cool on a wire rack.

Quick Blender Sheet Bread

. . . .

This recipe first came to be a few years back when I needed to have bread as quickly as possible. You know, for those times when somebody in your household absolutely must have a grilled cheese or tuna sammy and you realize you don't have any bread. That's why I always keep some in the freezer (all the breads freeze really well, btw). This recipe is fun because it's so quick and crazy how tasty and bread-like it is.

Makes 12 slices

Dry Ingredients

2 cups blanched almond or other nut flour*
¼ cup coconut flour
1 rounded tablespoon gelatin
1 teaspoon baking soda
1 teaspoon sea salt

Blender Ingredients

6 large eggs
2 cups rough chopped, summer squash
    or apple (about 10 ounces)
⅓ cup water
1 tablespoon lemon juice

> *Tip: If you use apple, add a teaspoon of cinnamon and a handful of raisins for fun.*

1. Preheat your oven to 350°F. Brush the edges of a 12½ x 17 x 1–inch rimmed cookie sheet with coconut oil or ghee and lay a Silpat on the bottom.
2. In a medium-sized bowl, whisk together the dry ingredients and set aside.
3. Add the wet ingredients to your blender and blend on high until smooth.
4. Pour the wet into the dry and stir well to combine.
5. With an off-set spatula or pie server, spread the batter equally to cover the cookie sheet. It will become a thin layer.
6. Bake for about 25–30 minutes, until just beginning to brown.
7. Cool, and run a knife around edges if necessary. Then place a second cookie sheet on top of the bread and invert onto the underside of the second cookie sheet.
8. Peel off the parchment paper and use a pizza cutter or knife to cut it into the size squares you desire. I usually do 12 squares.

Note: You can substitute the fruit for yellow or white sweet potato plus 2 more tablespoons of water.

*Note: If you're out of almond flour, you can omit it and add 1½ cups of any nuts to the wet ingredients in your blender.

Tip: You may use a smaller-sized cookie sheet for thicker bread; just bake a little longer.

Rustic Loaf, Baguettes, or Rolls

Sweet potato is my go-to for these breads because I prefer the flavor over regular potatoes since we don't need to cook them first. There is just nothing to compare with rustic bread sopping up extra sauce on your plate. Try slicing this, smearing garlic butter and herbs on it, then toasting in the oven a bit. You won't be sorry.

Makes 1 (4 x 10-inch) loaf, or 2 baguettes, or about 12 rolls

Dry Ingredients

2 cups fine almond flour
½ cup coconut flour
3 tablespoons psyllium husk powder
1 teaspoon baking soda
1¼ teaspoons sea salt

Blender Ingredients

1 cup roughly chopped white sweet potato
   (about 5 ounces)
2 eggs
3 egg whites
1 cup + 2 tablespoons water
2 tablespoons apple cider vinegar

1. Preheat your oven to 400°F.
2. Line a sheet pan with parchment paper. Or, if you own a French loaf or baguette pan, generously coat them with coconut oil, ghee, or olive oil.
3. In a medium-sized bowl, whisk together the dry ingredients.
4. Blend the wet ingredients in your blender until smooth.
5. Pour the wet ingredients into the dry and stir and fold the batter, then let it set up a couple of minutes until it is more dough-like.
6. Knead the dough for a minute. Use damp hands to roll, shape, and smooth the dough into a "French-bread-looking" loaf or divide in half for two smaller baguettes. Use a knife to score the top of the loaf. If you don't score it, it may naturally split on top, which is also nice.
7. Place in the oven and bake for 1 hour for 2 baguettes, or 1 hour 15 minutes for a larger loaf. The crust should be browned and firm.
8. Dust with potato or coconut flour, if desired.
9. Storing in a plastic bag will soften the crust.

For Dinner Rolls
Scoop out large spoonfuls of dough, and using a light touch and damp hands, shape into egg-shaped balls and place into a buttered 9-inch round cake pan with edges nearly touching. Bake for about 25 minutes, until the rolls are firm and spring back when touched.

Tip: If you choose to leave the skin on the potato, taste it to make sure it's not bitter.

White Sandwich Bread

. . . .

After my quick Sheet Bread, this was the first "real" bread recipe I developed. Once you see how easy baking these breads are and you smell the heavenly scent as it wafts from your oven, you will always want to bake bread. This is the best bread for toast, or your kid's PB&J or grilled cheese, or your husband's anchovy and mustard sandwich. Okay, probably just my husband's. The size bread pan you use will have a lot to do with the shape and rise of the loaf breads in this section. The disposable paper or aluminum loaf pans in most local grocery stores work great for grain-free breads because it is narrow with high sides to help the bread rise. I use Fat Daddio's 7 ³/₄ x 3 ³/₄ x 2 ³/₄-inch pan, which is also available on our website. If you choose to use a glass pan you have on hand, the loaf will still turn out good, but it will be wider and not as tall. I don't recommend using one much larger than the size I suggest.

Makes 1 loaf, about 16 slices

Dry Ingredients

2 cups almond flour
²/₃ cup coconut flour
3 tablespoons psyllium husk powder
1 tablespoon baking powder
1 rounded teaspoon sea salt

Blender Ingredients

1 cup egg whites (about 5 large)
½ cup applesauce
³/₄ cup water
3 tablespoons apple cider vinegar

1. Preheat your oven to 400°F.
2. Brush a bread pan with coconut or nut oil or line with parchment paper, if desired.
3. Sift the coconut flour, if needed. In a medium-sized bowl, whisk together the dry ingredients.
4. Whisk together the wet ingredients until frothy.
5. Add the wet ingredients to the dry ingredients and whisk until beginning to thicken. Let the batter rest a few minutes while it continues to thicken.
6. Use your fingers to knead the dough for about a minute, then roll it into a loaf shape (sort of a small football shape) to fit inside your pan.
7. Place in your oven on the center rack and bake for 1 hour and 15–20 minutes.
8. Tent with foil if it begins to brown too much.
9. Cool in the pan for 5–10 minutes, then remove with potholders and finish cooling on a rack.

Note: Make sure your psyllium is only the light-colored husk or your bread will be darker, even purplish if your brand contains the seed. See the Resources for the brands I suggest (page 296).

Note: If you don't have applesauce, put the wet ingredients in the blender with 1 roughly chopped apple (about 3–4 ounces).

Tip: Don't forget that your doggies and kitties love those yolks. They're also great in your smoothies, ice creams, and salad dressings.

Whole-Grain-NOT! Sandwich Bread

For some weird reason we just think bread is healthier if it's darker in color. It must be from the old slogan "eat your whole grains" we have instilled in us. When my husband and I started our bread company, we picked the slogan "Silly people . . . grains are for the birds!" Right?! So, now you can keep our baking mixes in the cupboard for a quick fix, or when you're having a particularly "lazy day" and don't feel like spending any time in the kitchen. Either way, it's now possible to always have a loaf of Real Bread on hand when you need some. This bread looks suspiciously like pumpernickel bread, which often uses onion, caraway, and molasses. Hey, I won't stop you from experimenting.

Makes 1 loaf, about 16 slices

Dry Ingredients

⅔ cup coconut flour
3 tablespoons psyllium husk powder
1 teaspoon sea salt
1 teaspoon baking soda

Blender Ingredients

5 large eggs
1 cup roughly chopped zucchini (about 1 medium, 4–5 ounces)
1½ cups walnuts, pecans, Brazil nuts, hazelnuts, or a mixture of any
⅓ cup water
2 tablespoons honey or molasses

1. Preheat your oven to 375°F.
2. Brush a bread pan with coconut or nut oil or line with parchment paper.
3. Sift the coconut flour, if needed. In a medium-sized bowl, whisk together the dry ingredients.
4. Blend the wet ingredients in your blender until smooth.
5. Pour the wet ingredients into the dry ingredients. Whisk briskly then let the batter rest a few minutes while it continues to thicken.
6. Knead the dough with your fingers for about a minute.
7. Use damp hands to pat or roll it into a loaf shape (sort of a small football shape) to fit inside your pan. You can also just scrape the dough into the prepared pan, piling it higher in the middle. Then smooth the top with wet hands.
8. Place in your oven and bake for 1 hour and 25–30 minutes. Tent with foil, if it begins to brown too much.
9. Cool in the pan for 5–10 minutes, remove with potholders, and finish cooling on a rack.

Note: The 7¾ x 3¾ x 2¾ -inch pan by Fat Daddio's is the loaf pan I use, which you can purchase on my website. The disposable paper or aluminum loaf pans in most local grocery stores is almost exactly that size so they also work great for grain-free breads.

Tip: For a lighter bread (sort of whole wheat-looking) use honey rather than molasses, cut the amount of nuts in half, and add two more tablespoons of coconut flour.

CHAPTER 8:

BREAKFAST & BRUNCH

During the work week my breakfasts usually consist of coffee, fresh juices, and smoothies. When the weekend rolls around, however, it's another story. Who doesn't love the smells of a home-cooked breakfast mingling with fresh brewed coffee on a lazy Sunday morning? Now, the best part is enjoying it guiltlessly without starting the day with sugar and all those carby flours and starches. I say a gal oughta be able to enjoy some biscuits, muffins, and waffles without sacrificing her girlish figure. And the guys oughta be able to enjoy some doughnuts and cinnamon rolls before, after, or even during their workouts. Move over bacon. It's also fun to experiment with substituting different fruits and veggies in the recipes. Some bananas in the pancakes or cherries in the chocolate doughnuts work great.

Apple Spice Muffins

....

The smell of apple muffins baking in the morning can only be trumped by bread baking in the afternoon. There's nothing better than having your very own fruit trees. I can't say it's been easy though! Some years the winter chill here isn't long and cold enough for our stone fruit trees to much produce fruit, and that can mean a sad summer for me. On the good years, we struggle with the squirrels making off with loads of fruit. Before I understood "the ways of country life," I actually thought we had thieves who would steal our fruit in the middle of the night. Well, actually, we did, it's just that they were squirrel thieves. Incredibly organized little critters, they could wipe out a tree in one night! This is when we had to put our foot down to our dogs: No more sleeping inside in the summertime.

Makes 8 muffins

Dry Ingredients

2 cups almond flour
¼ cup coconut flour
1 tablespoon egg white powder (optional)
1 teaspoon baking soda
½ teaspoon ground cinnamon
½ teaspoon sea salt

Blender Ingredients

4 large eggs
1 cup applesauce or 2 chopped apples (about 9–10 ounces)
¼ cup honey
2 teaspoons vanilla extract
⅔ teaspoon pure monk fruit or stevia

Crumb Topping

½ cup chopped pecans
2 tablespoons honey
3 tablespoons cold butter
Pinch of allspice

1. Preheat the oven to 350°F.
2. Line muffin pan with cupcake liners and set aside. Blend together the Crumb Topping ingredients with your fingers, or a pastry blender, into a crumble and set aside.
3. In a medium-sized bowl, whisk together the dry ingredients.
4. Whisk (use your blender if using fresh apple) together the wet ingredients.
5. Pour the wet ingredients into the dry and whisk to combine.
6. Using an ice cream scoop, fill the cupcake liners almost full.
7. Sprinkle with a tablespoon of the crumb topping.
8. Bake about 30–35 minutes, or until a toothpick inserted comes out clean—cover with aluminum foil when they begin to brown.
9. Cool in pan for 15 minutes, then remove to finish cooling on a rack or paper towels to prevent any sogginess.

BANANA NUT BREAD

The smell of banana bread baking in the morning or in the afternoon is pretty awesome, wouldn't you agree? I never enjoyed baking so much until I started baking this "whole food" way. That's because I just couldn't enjoy eating something I knew wasn't 100% beneficial to myself or my family's health. Now, baking is so much fun! My kitchen smells great, the food tastes amazing, and everyone's happy. Who wants some banana bread now?

Makes 1 (8 x 5 x 3-inch) loaf

Dry Ingredients

2 cups almond flour
¼ cup coconut flour
1 teaspoon psyllium husk powder* (optional)
1 teaspoon baking soda

Extras

Butter for pan
1 cup chopped walnuts or pecans

Blender Ingredients

4 large eggs
2½ cups very ripe bananas, about 5 medium sized
1 tablespoon vanilla extract
1 tablespoon lemon juice
½ teaspoon sea salt
¼ teaspoon pure monk fruit or stevia

1. Preheat oven to 350°F and butter an 8 x 5 x 3-inch loaf pan, or line it with parchment paper.
2. In a medium-sized bowl, whisk together the dry ingredients.
3. Mash the banana with a fork and blend together with the rest of the wet ingredients, or use your blender until smooth.
4. Pour the wet ingredients into the dry and whisk to combine. Add in chopped walnuts or pecans.
5. Pour into the buttered loaf pan.
6. Bake for about 60–65 minutes until a toothpick comes out clean.
7. Cover loosely with foil after about 45 minutes (when it's browned).

> *Tip: The psyllium powder adds a little extra structure.

BRUNCH PUFFS

. . . .

Cream puffs for breakfast? Well, why not? I love them filled with whipped cream, but you can fill them with your imagination! Try fruit, scrambled eggs, chicken or lobster salad, last night's leftovers, pepperoni, sauce, and cheese . . . the universe is your oyster! Sometimes I add a few drops of stevia in the wet ingredients and omit the erythritol, or just leave the sweetener out, depending on what I'm stuffing these with. They're so simple and look great on a brunch buffet table. Of course, you can always fill them with pastry cream and drizzle with chocolate for a fancy-ish dessert.

Makes about 6–12 depending on size you want

Dry Ingredients

3 tablespoons almond flour
2 tablespoons psyllium husk powder
2 tablespoons coconut flour
2 teaspoons baking powder
½ teaspoon sea salt

Blender Ingredients

2 large eggs
6 tablespoons water

1. Preheat the oven to 400°F and line a baking sheet with parchment paper.
2. Whisk the dry ingredients together in a medium bowl.
3. In a separate bowl, whisk the wet ingredients together.
4. Whisk the wet ingredients into the dry ingredients. As the batter thickens, stir and fold together.
5. Let the batter rest for a few minutes. It will thicken into a dough.
6. Knead together with your hands a minute, until it becomes a firm, shiny, sticky dough.
7. Use a small ice cream scoop to measure portions of dough, about 1½–2 tablespoons each.
8. With damp hands roll each into an egg-shaped ball and stand on end on prepared baking sheet.
9. Bake at 400°F for 20 minutes, then turn the oven down to 350°F and bake until deep brown and firm to the touch, 10–20 minutes, depending upon the size. If you remove them from the oven too soon, they will collapse.
10. Cool on racks. Once cool, use a serrated knife to cut the top off. Gently scrape the doughy interior out and set aside for bread crumbs or a snack for your doggy.
11. Fill with a savory filling like cream cheese and salmon, tuna/egg salad, or sweetened whipped cream, pastry cream, jam, or fresh fruit.

Note: I recommend testing one puff before baking them all. If you find your puff isn't puffing enough, knead in a little more water and try again.

California Flapjacks

When I was little, my mother would occasionally add corn to her pancake batter (usually made with Bisquick!) and cook them in butter in her skillet. Oh, I loved those yummy "corn fritter pancakes" as she called them. I must admit I love these California Flapjacks even more. They taste just as great as Mom's without *those not-so-good ingredients*. The edges get crispy and soften in maple syrup, mmmm.

Makes 8–10 3- or 4-inch flapjacks

Dry Ingredients

1¼ cups almond or cashew flour
1½ teaspoons psyllium powder, or 1 tablespoon
    coconut flour*
½ teaspoon baking soda
½ teaspoon sea salt

Blender Ingredients

1½ cup fresh or frozen corn, divided
3 large eggs
¼ cup sour cream
1 tablespoon honey or maple syrup
Ghee or clarified butter for frying

1. In a medium bowl, stir together the dry ingredients.
2. Blend 1 cup of the corn with the rest of the wet ingredients in your blender until smooth.
3. Stir the wet ingredients into the dry ingredients, then stir in the rest of the corn.
4. Heat a cast-iron skillet over medium heat until hot.
5. Add a few tablespoons of ghee into the skillet and when it sizzles, add dollops of the batter.
6. Cook about 3 minutes per side, until browning and edges crispy.

Maple Crème Fraiche or Sour Cream

1/3 cup crème fraiche or sour cream
1 tablespoon maple syrup

1. Stir together and spoon on top of the flapjacks.
2. Serve with more maple syrup.

*Note: The psyllium slightly bulks and binds these, but if you don't have it on hand, use coconut flour.

Devil's Food Cake Doughnuts

. . . .

Living out in the country, one's love of doughnuts isn't easily satisfied with a walk down the street. Unless you happen to be my neighbor, stopping by after smelling these blowing in the country wind. Husbands, big kids, and little kids have no idea these are packed full of goodness. We've just gotta keep some things a secret.

Makes 6 large or 12 small

Coconut oil or spray, for greasing

Dry Ingredients

⅔ cup coconut flour
⅓ cup cocoa powder (preferably Dutch processed)
½ teaspoon sea salt
½ teaspoon baking soda
Pinch of cayenne (optional)

Blender Ingredients

4 large eggs
⅔ cup peeled, roughly chopped beet (3–4 ounces)
1 cup packed beet greens or baby spinach (2 ounces)
1½ tablespoons vanilla extract
1½ teaspoons almond extract
1 teaspoon pure monk fruit or stevia

1. Preheat oven to 350°F.
2. Grease or spray six large doughnut molds, or twelve small molds, with coconut oil or spray. Set aside.
3. Whisk the dry ingredients together in a medium-sized bowl.
4. Blend together the wet ingredients until smooth.
5. Stir the wet ingredients into the dry until combined.
6. Transfer the batter into a plastic zip-lock or pastry bag. Snip the corner and squeeze the batter into the molds and bake for 15–18 minutes.
7. Cool in the pans for a few minutes before turning out onto a rack to finish cooling.
8. Choose one of the glazes below and dip each doughnut in the glaze.

Sugarless Chocolate Glaze

1 tablespoon syrup of choice
1 tablespoon melted butter
1 tablespoon cocoa powder
1 teaspoon sweet potato flour
½ teaspoon pure monk fruit or stevia
½ teaspoon each vanilla and almond extract
Pinch of sea salt
Pinch of cayenne (optional)

1. Stir together until smooth.

Chocolate Chip Glaze

½ cup chocolate chips
1 tablespoon butter
2 tablespoons water

1. Stir over low heat until melted together.

Tip: You can substitute the veggies out for ½ cup of pureed pumpkin if your blender is on the blink. Blend beet powder and erythritol for pink sprinkle topping.

Fluffy Pancakes & Waffles

. . . .

I love pancakes and eggs for dinner because I rarely eat breakfast enough to enjoy these regularly. When I do eat breakfast, these pancakes are often my choice. I think it's because once the thought occurs, these delicious (make-me-feel-good-no-matter-what) morsels can appear in mere minutes with very little effort. There's just something about pancakes. Oh, yes, pancakes, butter, and maple syrup. Or maybe pancakes, sour cream, and jam. How about pancakes, strawberries, and whipped cream? Getting hungry again . . .

Makes approximately 10 (3- to 4-inch) pancakes or 8 (4-inch) waffles

3–4 tablespoons melted butter, ghee, nut or coconut oil, divided
3 large eggs
1 cup roughly chopped, peeled yellow/white sweet potato (about 5 ounces)
²⁄₃ cup roughly chopped apple or yellow summer squash or peeled zucchini (about 3 ounces)
1 tablespoon lemon juice
1 tablespoon vanilla extract
¹⁄₃ teaspoon sea salt
1½ cups almond flour or other nut flour
2 teaspoons baking powder (or ½ teaspoon baking soda plus 1 teaspoon cream of tartar)
¹⁄₈ teaspoon pure monk fruit or stevia (optional)

1. Add 1 tablespoon of the fat and the rest of the ingredients in the order listed, to your blender and blend until smooth.
2. I like to pour the batter into a bowl and use a measuring cup to put spoonfuls (to make 3–4-inch pancakes) onto a hot, buttered (using your remaining ghee/coconut oil) skillet and cook about 2 minutes per side.

For Waffles

1. Add 2 tablespoons of coconut oil or melted butter to the batter.
2. Brush waffle maker with coconut or nut oil.
3. Heat thoroughly or until the light turns off.
4. Ladle batter into waffle maker, being careful not to overfill, leaving room to close the lid.
5. Close lid and cook until steam stops escaping, and lid lifts easily, about 5 minutes.

Tip: You can also substitute another veggie or fruit (or ⅓ cup applesauce, pumpkin, or mashed banana) if you'd like. Just add another tablespoon of coconut flour if the batter is too thin. Also, feel free to add a splash of your favorite sweetener to the batter if you'd like to.

Annabelle Lee | 142

Tip: For a slightly chewier pancake texture, reduce the almond flour to 1 cup and add 1 teaspoon of psyllium husk powder to the ingredient list.

Golden Crepes with Mascarpone & Fruit

....

My husband's favorite time of year is fall, but living in the southern California countryside, we miss the autumn colors that we experienced during the years we lived back East. Our property has a few maple and fruit trees, but otherwise the trees are evergreens. Alas, we simply cannot have everything, so when I'm really troubled about that, a fruit-filled crepe can help to ease the pain. For that reason, I often keep some crepes in my fridge or freezer for when I need them. Besides fruit, they're also great filled with creamed chicken, shrimp, or veggies—or you can even use them for enchiladas. Use a crepe pan or non-stick skillet for the best results.

Makes 10–12 crepes

Ghee, butter, or coconut oil for greasing

Dry Ingredients

½ cup almond flour
1 tablespoon psyllium husk powder
Pinch of sea salt

Wet Ingredients

4 large eggs
⅓–½ cup heavy cream or coconut milk
1 tablespoon lemon juice
Optional, for sweet fillings: 1 tablespoon vanilla extract, ⅛ teaspoon pure monk fruit or stevia

1. In a medium-sized bowl, whisk together the dry ingredients.
2. In a small bowl, whisk together the wet ingredients.
3. Whisk the wet ingredients into the dry ingredients.
4. Heat a non-stick skillet, preferably a crepe pan, over medium heat until hot. Brush the pan with ghee, butter, or coconut oil.
5. Use a ladle or large spoon to scoop and pour 2–3 tablespoons of crepe batter onto the hot skillet.
6. Quickly use the back of the spoon to spread the batter into thin, round crepes, 6–8 inches in diameter.
7. Cook until the top begins to dry out and the underside is browning.
8. Carefully flip and cook another minute.

To Serve

1. Stir together ½ cup of mascarpone cheese with 2 tablespoons each cream or sour cream, lemon juice, and jam.
2. Spread on the crepes and add berries or sliced fruit.
3. Top with thinned jam or a drizzle of honey.

Tip: You can also spread the batter onto a Silpat-lined cookie sheet and bake at 325°F for about 12 minutes. If you use two cookie sheets, you can bake several crepes at one time.

Not-Too-Naughty Fried Doughnuts

. . . .

I very rarely fry much of anything these days, however doughnuts are so worth it. Yum! I would be telling a lie if I led you to believe I never set foot in a doughnut shop. We have one in town that makes the most amazing, warm, glazed twist doughnuts on this planet. I deal with this by not thinking about them; sometimes this involves meditation, self-hypnosis, and other techniques of mind control. Or, sometimes, I simply whip these up and eat them quick before others come and get them. So, now with this recipe, you too can pass on that sneaky trip to the doughnut shop every Saturday morning.

Makes about 8–12 doughnuts and 8–12 doughnut holes (depending on the size you make)

Dry Ingredients

1½ cups almond flour
6 tablespoons coconut flour
2 tablespoons psyllium husk powder
¼ teaspoon baking soda
2 teaspoons baking powder
¼ teaspoon salt

Blender Ingredients

4 large eggs
⅔ cup sour cream
¼ cup water
2 teaspoons vanilla extract
⅔ teaspoon pure monk fruit or stevia

Coconut oil for frying (use a triple filtered brand if you don't want a coconut flavor)

1. Brush two sheets of waxed paper with coconut oil and set aside.
2. Whisk the dry ingredients together in a medium bowl.
3. In a separate bowl, whisk the wet ingredients together.
4. Pour the wet ingredients into the dry ingredients and combine thoroughly.
5. Let the batter rest a minute to become more dough-like, then knead it together for a minute.
6. In a large, heavy bottom pan, heat 3–4 inches of coconut oil or ghee to about 350°F.
7. Roll the dough out between the two sheets of paper to about ½-inch thickness. Cut with a doughnut cutter (like a cookie cutter).
8. Use damp hands to roll the center sections into balls.
9. Fry both the doughnuts and doughnut "holes" in the hot oil and cook until golden brown, about 2–3 minutes per side.
10. Remove with a slotted spoon to drain on paper towels.
11. Sprinkle with erythritol/monk fruit, drizzle with jam, or dip in a glaze once they're cool.

Note: Sometimes I use a deep small pot instead of a large one because it greatly reduces the amount of oil I have to use. This makes me stand at the stove a bit longer because I can only fry 2 at a time, but I don't mind if it saves me from using up all my expensive oil.

Tip: If you don't have a doughnut cutter, simply roll sections of dough into a "rope" about 5 inches in length and pinch the ends together to form doughnuts.

Sour Cream Biscuits

· ·

It was pretty difficult to decide whether these biscuits should be pictured with jam, gravy, or just gobs of butter. As you see, the jam won out (just barely). In my household, biscuits and gravy are also a huge favorite for a weekend breakfast or an evening meal. Whatever time of day or whatever topping you choose, I promise these soft, fluffy biscuits won't disappoint.

Makes about 8 large biscuits

Dry Ingredients

1 cup almond or other nut flour
¼ cup coconut flour
¼ cup egg white powder
2 tablespoons psyllium husk powder
1 tablespoon baking powder
½ teaspoon sea salt

Blender Ingredients

1 large egg
¹/₃ cup applesauce, or ½ a large apple (about 2 ounces)
½ cup sour cream or yogurt
½ cup water

Topping

2 tablespoons melted butter for brushing

1. Preheat oven to 400°F and butter an 8-inch round cake or springform pan and set aside.
2. In a medium-sized bowl, whisk together the dry ingredients, sifting as necessary, to remove lumps.
3. In a small bowl, whisk together the wet ingredients (if using apple, use your blender).
4. Whisk the wet ingredients into the dry ingredients, then let the batter set for about 5 minutes.
5. Use a large ice cream scoop to place mounds of dough into the buttered pan. They will look like "drop biscuits." Keep them close together so they can help each other rise instead of spreading out.
6. Use wet fingers to gently smooth the tops.
7. Bake for 20–25 minutes, or until they become golden brown.
8. Brush the baked biscuits with melted butter when they come out of the oven.

Cinnamon Rolls

While testing this recipe, I made several batches (I know, darn, somebody had to eat them!). We had so many cinnamon rolls, I think half the town got to taste test. What I found during all that testing? That it's actually hard to make a bad cinnamon roll, because even if it doesn't look perfect, it still tastes like a gooey piece of heaven! My baking mix also makes delicious cinnamon rolls—call me crazy, but I think whipping these up from scratch is more fun; I guess I must not be lazy all the time.

Makes 12 rolls

Dry Ingredients

2 cups almond flour
¼ cup coconut flour
3 tablespoons psyllium husk powder
2 teaspoons baking powder
½ teaspoon sea salt

Blender Ingredients

3 large eggs
1 cup roughly chopped, peeled zucchini, about 4–5 ounces
½ cup water
2 teaspoons vanilla extract
⅛ teaspoon pure monk fruit or stevia

Filling

½ cup soft butter
¼ cup erythritol/monk fruit blend or date sugar (or granulated sweetener of choice)
¼ cup cinnamon
⅓ teaspoon pure monk fruit or stevia

1. Preheat your oven to 375°F and butter the bottom and sides of a 10-inch round cake pan or 9 x 11-inch casserole dish or a couple of pie pans.
2. In a medium-sized bowl, whisk together the dry ingredients, sifting as necessary.
3. Puree the wet ingredients in your blender until smooth.
4. Pour the wet ingredients into the dry ingredients and whisk until it begins to thicken. Let the batter set up a few minutes.
5. Use your fingers to sort of knead the dough for about one minute, until becomes a bit sticky.
6. Transfer to a baking sheet or waxed paper that has been sprinkled with water.
7. Gently press down to create sort of a flat log shape, dampen the top, and cover with another sheet of waxed paper.
8. Use a rolling pin or your hands to press or roll it into a rectangle shape about 8 x 13 inches.
9. Remove the top sheet of waxed paper and generously butter the entire dough, leaving about ½ an inch of the edge so the dough can attach to itself once it is rolled into a log.
10. Stir together the cinnamon and sweetener in a small bowl and sprinkle over the butter. If using liquid rather than powdered monk fruit or stevia here, stir it into the soft butter first.
11. Pick up the edges of the bottom sheet of waxed paper that is nearest you and begin to fold up over the edge of the dough, and continue rolling the dough over snuggly until it is in a nice little log shape.
12. Use a pastry cutter or spatula to cut the log into 10–12 pieces.
13. Use the pastry cutter to scoop each piece up and place into the prepared baking pan. Nestle them close together to help each other rise. If necessary, dip the cutter in water between cuts.
14. Bake for about 25 minutes, until golden brown.
15. While the rolls cool a little, make the frosting and frost while still warm.

continued on page 152

Frosting

This is one of the rare instances when I've been known to use powdered sugar with a little bit of water, but when I'm being the good me, I'll whip up the glaze below:

4 tablespoons soft butter
1 teaspoon sweet potato flour (the whole ground flour, not the starch)
Water, heavy cream, or coconut milk to your desired consistency
⅛–¼ teaspoon pure monk fruit or stevia

Tip: You can also slather on the cream cheese frosting from page 238

1. Whisk together to your desired consistency.

2. Smear or drizzle on top of the warm rolls.

CHAPTER 9: .

CRACKERS & WRAPS

Because crackers are a go-to snack of mine, I always try to keep some ready at hand for a quick bite, maybe with a slice of raw cheese, or to replace chips for dipping. If they soften in storage, just crisp them up again on a cookie sheet in the oven for a few minutes. I tested these recipes using gelatin powder, but if you're strictly vegetarian, agar should be a good substitute. Our local store sells a spring roll with avocado, veggies, sprouts, and shrimp wrapped in a traditional rice wrap. Unfortunately, rice has become so contaminated in recent years that I avoid it when eating out. These tortillas and wraps are so quick and easy to make that I rarely need to purchase them anymore. There are so many goodies to stuff in these wraps, from scrambled eggs to smoked salmon, they've come a long way since the bean-and-cheese-burrito-days, but that's still one of my favorites.

Tip: For best results, invest in some baking liners (see my Resources, page 296) rather than using parchment paper for baking these crackers and wraps because the paper will wrinkle from the moisture.

No-Need-For-Cheese Snack Crackers

. . . .

My son Jake always loved those little Goldfish® crackers, so this was the first grain-free cracker I ever made. Since he stands about 6'4" now, he no longer asks for the cute fish shape for these tasty, crunchy bites. And don't tell anyone, but I've even used baby food carrots in place of the pumpkin before. Anyhow, I was so delighted with the outcome when I made these that I started experimenting with more recipes and look what's happened—I've gone and created a whole cookbook. Who knows what I'd be doing if it weren't for Jake and this cracker.

Makes 1 (12 x 17-inch) cookie sheet full (approximately 120 1-inch crackers)

Ingredients

2 cups roughly chopped carrots, or ½ cup pumpkin puree
½ cup butter
2½ cups almond or cashew flour
2 teaspoons sea salt
½ teaspoon garlic powder or 1 fresh clove, mashed into a paste
½ teaspoon turmeric
½ teaspoon onion powder
⅛ teaspoon cayenne powder (more to taste)
2 tablespoons coconut flour
1 tablespoon gelatin

1. Preheat oven to 325°F.
2. If using fresh carrots, puree them into a fine meal in your food processor.
3. Whisk together the rest of the ingredients, add the carrots or pumpkin, and combine well.
4. Roll out the dough between two layers of waxed paper or baking mats that have been lightly brushed with ghee or oil, to about $1/16$–⅛-inch thickness.
5. Bake between the parchment paper layers for about 6–8 minutes.
6. Peel off the top layer of parchment paper and cut into squares.
7. If desired, use a wooden skewer to gently poke a hole in the middle of each square.
8. Return to the oven and bake until the edges start to brown, about another 6 minutes.
9. Turn off the oven, crack the door open, and let rest for about 30 minutes, until crispy.

> Tip: You can add ⅓ cup nutritional yeast for extra cheese flavor.

Savory Butter Crackers

. . . .

I love this cracker because it's simple and tasty and goes with just about anything. Take your time when rolling out the dough, so it's thin enough and as even as possible. This way each cracker will be consistent. Make sure you rest them in the warm oven so they can fully crisp up.

Makes 1 (17 x 12-inch) cookie sheet

Ingredients

10 ounces white or yellow sweet potato (about 2 cups, roughly chopped)
1³/₄ cups almond, cashew, or macadamia nut (or 2 cups nut flour)
½ cup butter
1 tablespoon gelatin
1½ teaspoons sea salt
Egg for brushing

1. Preheat the oven to 350°F.
2. Brush two baking liners or two sheets of parchment paper with butter, ghee, or oil.
3. Fitted with the S blade, puree the sweet potato in your food processor until very fine.
4. Add the rest of the ingredients (except the egg) and puree until smooth and pasty.
5. Divide the dough in half and roll or press each half out to ¹/₁₆ inch between the two sheets of paper. Take your time to roll it evenly.
6. Remove the top layer of paper and use a pastry cutter or spatula to cut into squares or rectangles. If the top paper sticks, simply transfer the dough with the paper to a baking sheet and bake with the paper on for about 8 minutes, then cut into squares.
7. Remove any browned edges and poke a pattern on top with a fork.
8. Whip the egg with a fork until frothy, brush it on the crackers, and sprinkle with additional sea salt.
9. Return to the oven and continue to bake until they're beginning to brown.
10. Turn off the oven, crack open the door, and let rest about 30 minutes until crackers become crispy.
11. Store in an airtight container.
12. If the crackers soften over time, re-crisp them in the oven at 300˚F for about 5–7 minutes.

Note: If you want to make these in your blender instead of the food processor: Use nut flour rather than whole nuts. Melt the butter and blend with the sweet potato in your blender until smooth, then stir together in a bowl with the rest of the ingredients.

Veggie Seed Crackers

....

My husband and I live on a piece of country acreage that we share with occasional renters in a few unique, tiny homes on the property. Most of our guests have been a bit "unique," as well, which is probably why they were drawn to our quirky, little place. We've had a balloon pilot who left to sail around the world, a horse trainer, a film student from Belguim working on his PhD for Yale, a paramedic, and even a couple who met here, moved away, married, had a baby, and moved back. I can't say it's ever boring. One renter Luke, and his family, has a cheesecake company that specializes in savory cheesecakes that happen to be delicious with these crackers. I usually make these crackers with rosemary (which grows here really well) or tarragon (one of my favorite herbs in pot-pie, green beans, and salad dressings). But feel free to have fun and use your favorite herbs.

Makes approximately 18–24 crackers

Ingredients

1 medium/small zucchini (about 6–7 ounces)
¼ cup chopped onion
¼ cup chopped red bell pepper
1½ cups pumpkin seeds, raw or lightly roasted
¼ cup chia seeds
2 cloves chopped garlic
1 sprig fresh tarragon or rosemary leaves, or your favorite herb
1 tablespoon olive oil
1 teaspoon sea salt
½ teaspoon black pepper
Course sea salt for sprinkling

1. Preheat the oven to 325°F and grease a lined baking sheet with olive oil.
2. Process the vegetables until finely chopped.
3. Reserve ½ cup pumpkin seeds. Add the rest of the ingredients and process briefly, for the seeds to be chopped up a bit.
4. Add the rest of the pumpkin seeds and pulse 2–3 times.
5. Use a small ice cream scooper or drop by heaping tablespoons onto the prepared baking sheet as you would drop cookie dough.
6. Use a flat-bottomed glass to press each mound into a thin cracker, dipping the bottom in water after each press and sprinkle with more sea salt, if desired.
7. Bake for 12–15 minutes.
8. Remove from oven and use a spatula to gently flip each cracker, return to oven, and bake another 12–15 minutes or just until the edges are beginning to brown.
9. Turn off the oven, and remove any crackers that are obviously browning and crisp.
10. Crack open the door and let the remaining crackers rest until the they are all crispy.
11. Store in an airtight container. These are also freezable!

Note: You can also dehydrate these crackers in a 200°F oven until crisp, 2–3 hours.

Easy "Flour" Tortillas

. . . .

Instead of standing around frying up tortillas, I prefer to use two cookie sheets to bake four of these at the same time, while I do something else—mop the floor, or pull some weeds . . . or possibly have a little glass of wine and put my feet up. Once they're made, you can always reheat them in your frying pan, if you wish, or heck, go ahead and slap some good cheese on them, fold over, and fry in some ghee.

Makes 6 (6-inch) tortillas

Ingredients

Oil, for baking sheet
½ cup almond or cashew flour
2 tablespoons coconut flour
2 tablespoons psyllium husk powder
½ teaspoon sea salt
³/₄ cup water

1. Preheat the oven to 350°F.
2. Oil a baking sheet or use a silicone baking liner.
3. Whisk together the dry ingredients in a small bowl.
4. Whisk in the water.
5. Let the batter rest a few minutes until it becomes thicker.
6. Use an ice cream scoop to portion out the dough.
7. Roll each dough ball into tortillas between two sheets of waxed paper, or use a tortilla press if you have one. Oil or sprinkle the waxed paper with water between dough balls.
8. Bake for about 10–12 minutes, just as the edges begin to brown.

FRESH CORN OR NO-CORN TORTILLAS

· ·

Fresh (organic and non-GMO, of course) corn is not a grain, but a vegetable in my book. So, if you don't have trouble digesting it, I say "enjoy it!" I'm sure growing up so close to Mexico and cultivating a deep love for the food has definitely impacted my taste buds. You can even fry up these tortillas in coconut oil, ghee, or lard on occasion . . . they're the perfect platform for your tostada.

Makes about 8 (6-inch) tortillas

Ingredients

Ghee or oil, for the pan
2 cups fresh or frozen corn, or 1⅔ cups roughly chopped yellow sweet potato (about 7–8 ounces)
½ cup water or fresh veggie juice (beet, carrot, kale, etc.) for a beautiful color
⅔ teaspoon sea salt
1 tablespoon psyllium husk powder
2 tablespoons coconut flour

1. Preheat your oven to 350°F.
2. Line a baking sheet with a baking liner (parchment paper may wrinkle because of the moisture) or generously brush a sheet pan with ghee or oil.
3. Blend the vegetable and water until smooth.
4. Transfer to a bowl, sprinkle the dry ingredients on top, and whisk briskly.
5. Use an ice cream scooper to put 4 scoops of batter onto each prepared cookie sheet.
6. Use an offset spatula to spread the batter into thin tortilla rounds, about $1/_{16}$– ⅛-inch thickness.
7. Bake until golden brown, about 10–11 minutes.

Spicy Salsa Wraps

....

Refried beans, avocado, diced tomatoes, and raw cheese are my favorite fillings in this wrap. Oh, and grilled fish is really good in these, too. When my son Jeremy was little, he loved to toddle around chewing on pickled okra wrapped in a napkin. He called them "O-O's" and I think it cultivated his love of rather unique burrito fillings, such as kimchi. But then, I could probably list a few dozen other goodies to wrap these around, just not sure I'd choose pickled okra.

Makes 6–8 (8-inch) wraps

Ingredients

1 cup roughly chopped yam or sweet potato (about 5 ounces)
2 large eggs (optional, but they make a sturdier wrap)
⅔ cup salsa
1 tablespoon avocado or olive oil
¼ teaspoon sea salt (use a bit more if you use both the eggs)
1 tablespoon psyllium husk powder

1. Preheat your oven to 350°F.
2. Blend the sweet potato (and eggs, if using) with half the salsa in your blender until nice and smooth.
3. Add the rest of the salsa, oil, and salt and pulse a few times.
4. Pour into a bowl, sprinkle psyllium over the top, and whisk to combine. Let the batter sit a minute.
5. Use a baking liner or sheet pan and measure two portions of batter onto the pan.
6. Use a spatula to spread the batter into thin, round wraps. Bake for about 10–12 minutes.
7. If you use two cookie sheets, you can bake four tortillas at once, on two oven racks.

Gordita Wraps

....

The guys in my family really like large burritos, so I needed a wrap that would hold up to all their burrito fillings and then some. These wraps are perfect for when you want to really pack them with lots of beans, cheese, veggies, salsa, meat if you like, and guacamole. Go ahead and "man-handle" them, no need to be dainty. If you choose not to peel the veggie because you're a lazy gal, make sure it's organic and has no bitter taste. You can also use a plantain here, and if you do, have fun peeling it!

Makes 4 (10-inch) tortillas

Butter, ghee, or oil, for the pan

Dry Ingredients

½ cup almond flour
2 tablespoons coconut flour
1 tablespoon unflavored gelatin
2 tablespoons psyllium husk powder
½ teaspoon sea salt

Blender Ingredients

1 cup roughly chopped and peeled white sweet potato or other root veggie (about 5–6 ounces)
2 eggs
¼ cup water

1. Preheat your oven to 350°F.
2. Line a baking sheet with a baking liner (parchment paper may wrinkle because of the moisture) and brush with butter, ghee, or oil.
3. Whisk together the dry ingredients in a medium-sized bowl and set aside.
4. Blend the wet ingredients in your blender until nice and smooth, with no chunks left.
5. Whisk the wet ingredients into the dry.
6. Measure two portions of batter onto the sheet pan.
7. Use an offset spatula (dampen if necessary) to spread the batter into thin, round tortillas about 10 inches in diameter. Try to spread as even a thickness as you can to prevent thin spots that will brown and crisp in the oven.
8. Bake for about 12 minutes or just when edges are beginning to turn golden.

Note: If the batter is too thick to spread easily, whisk in another tablespoon of water.

Tip: If you use two cookie sheets, you can bake four tortillas at once, on two oven racks.

Masa Flour Corn Tortillas

....

Masa flour is generally more digestible than dried corn because it's been soaked in lime. So, those of you who can't eat corn, are likely able to eat masa. Growing up in San Diego helped to cultivate an early and life-long love of Mexican food in me. There's just nothing quite like the taste of real Mexican masa, so I had to include this recipe.

Makes 12 (6 – 8-inch) tortillas

Ingredients

2 cups warm water
2 tablespoons avocado oil, olive oil, ghee, or melted butter/lard
2 cups organic masa flour
1 tablespoon psyllium husk powder

1. Stir together the warm water and oil in a bowl.

2. In another bowl, whisk together the masa and ground psyllium husk.

3. Whisk the wet ingredients into the dry ingredients until the dough holds together well.

4. Use an ice cream scoop to divide the dough into 12 equal pieces and roll each into a ball.

5. Use a tortilla press or rolling pin to roll out each ball between 2 sheets of waxed paper, peel off the top layer, and invert onto an ungreased cast-iron skillet.

6. After a minute, peel off the rest of the waxed paper, flip and cook on the other side, about another 1–2 minutes.

Note: I add the psyllium to this recipe because it helps keep the tortillas from cracking when folded. You can substitute gelatin if you'd like, but you may need to reduce the water a bit.

Pesto Wraps

There have been years when I just couldn't quite get it together and my gardening abilities were one of the many things that suffered. I could always count on my basil and tomato plants to come through though, no matter how much I neglected them. Our summers can get pretty darn hot and dry in these parts, so simply missing a watering day can be disastrous. Our plants always appreciate any extra well water (or occasional summer storm) that comes their way. I love using the fresh basil from my garden to make these delicious wraps.

Makes 6 (8-inch) wraps

Ingredients

1 cup roughly chopped zucchini or summer squash (about 5 ounces)
1 garlic clove
1 tablespoon fresh lemon juice
1 tablespoon olive oil + extra for the pan
2 large eggs (optional, but makes a sturdier wrap)
1 big handful of fresh basil
1 tablespoon psyllium husk powder
1 tablespoon coconut flour
½ teaspoon sea salt

1. Preheat your oven to 350°F and use a silicone baking mat or generously oil a sheet pan.
2. Blend the zucchini, garlic, lemon, oil, and egg (if using) in your blender until nice and smooth.
3. Add the basil and blend briefly.
4. Pour into a bowl.
5. Stir together and briskly whisk in the psyllium powder, coconut flour, and salt.
6. Let the batter rest a minute.
7. Measure two portions of batter onto the pan.
8. Use an offset spatula to spread the batter into thin, round tortillas.
9. Bake for about 10–12 minutes, just until the edges start to brown.
10. If you use two cookie sheets, you can bake four wraps at once, on two oven racks.

Note: You can substitute ¼ cup pesto sauce for the basil, garlic, and olive oil.

Tip: If you have a Silpat liner for your cookie sheet, it works great. If you don't have a baking liner, I suggest liberally greasing the pan rather than using parchment paper. Parchment doesn't work well here because this is a wet batter that causes it to wrinkle.

Plantain Flour Tortillas

. . . .

I realize many grain-free bakers aren't yet using plantain flour, but I prefer it over cassava flour because it's much more a human food than cassava (which is toxic prior to processing). I love working with fresh plantains, but peeling them doesn't excite me, so the flour is next best thing. I love the flour, but the flavor of the brand I've been testing with is a bit strong, so I like to cut it a with the mildness of blanched almond flour.

Makes about 6 (8-inch) tortillas

Ingredients

½ cup blanched almond flour
¼ cup plantain flour
1 tablespoon psyllium husk powder
½ sea salt
½ cup water

1. Stir together the dry ingredients.
2. Stir in the water and use your fingers if need be until it's a well combined dough.
3. Measure into equal-sized balls (I use an ice-cream scooper) and roll out between two pieces of parchment or waxed paper.
4. Fry in a small amount of oil for few minutes on each side or, for a sturdy tortilla that works well for tostadas, bake at 350°F for about 12 minutes.

Tip: For a larger, more "flour" like tortilla,
add more water when baking.

Spinach Wraps

. . . .

If I made these and sold them back in the day, I know Popeye would've kept me in business. They're so much more versatile than that ol' can of spinach he used to pour down his throat. He had the right idea though, because those muscles he got from that spinach must've been what kept Olive Oyl around. My family loves tuna or chicken salad in these wraps, but they also make great holiday wraps. Try them sliced into bite-sized pieces with cream cheese and red peppers for Christmas time, or with salmon spread and black olives for Halloween appetizers.

Makes about 6 (8-inch) wraps

Ingredients

1 roughly chopped zucchini (about 4–5 ounces)
½ cup packed spinach, or one big handful
2 large eggs
⅔ teaspoon sea salt
1 tablespoon lemon juice
1 tablespoon coconut flour
1 tablespoon psyllium husk powder

1. Preheat your oven to 350°F.
2. Blend everything except the psyllium husk powder and coconut flour in your blender until nice and smooth and pour into a bowl.
3. Stir together the coconut flour and psyllium husk, whisk into the batter, and let rest a minute.
4. Use a baking liner or lightly butter or oil a cookie sheet and measure two portions of batter onto a baking sheet.
5. Use an offset spatula to spread batter into thin wraps.
6. Bake for about 10–12 minutes.
7. If you use two cookie sheets, you can bake four tortillas at once, on two even racks.

Veggie Wraps

. . . .

You can try all different kinds of vegetables in these wraps, in all different colors, like bright orange carrots or dark green kale. I used beets, carrots, and zucchini for one. I know you'll have fun experimenting with your favorite veggies. Once you start cooking this way, it really opens your mind to all the possibilities. I can't be the only nut out there who sees wraps, cookies, and cupcakes when I look at veggies.

Makes 6–8 wraps

Ingredients

1½ cups roughly chopped veggies like beets, squash, carrots, broccoli, and kale (about 7–8 ounces)
2 large eggs, or ¼ –¹/₃ cup water (depending upon the liquid in the veggies you use)
1 tablespoon fresh lemon juice
1 tablespoon psyllium husk powder
1 tablespoon coconut flour
²/₃ teaspoon sea salt
½ teaspoon of your favorite herb (optional, I used tarragon and black pepper for this one)

1. Preheat your oven to 350°F and line a sheet pan with a silicone liner or brush the pan with oil.
2. Blend everything in your blender until nice and smooth and pour into a bowl.
3. Measure two portions of batter onto the cookie sheet.
4. Use an offset spatula to spread batter into thin, round or rectangle wraps.
5. Bake for about 10–12 minutes.
6. If you use two cookie sheets, you can bake four tortillas at once, on two oven racks.

Tip: If you have a Silpat liner for your cookie sheet, it works great. Parchment paper doesn't work well for wraps because it wrinkles when it gets too wet.

Chapter 10:

LEGUMES, PASTA, PIZZA & MORE

I'm a big proponent of consuming raw foods, but I'm not big on making dishes like raw lasagna, mainly because it just takes a bit too much planning and time to prepare foods that way (and remember, I'm a lazy gal). I rely mostly on my juices and smoothies during the day and raw soups, sauces, salad dressings with healthful, cold pressed oils (avocado, olive, pumpkin, or macadamia nut), and condiments in the evening. When I don't get enough of these raw foods, my body truly feels it. So, while the recipes to follow are good for you, don't forget to add a raw sauce or a fermented condiment alongside. In a hurry? Just slice up some tomato, cucumber, and avocado. Also, some of these recipes call for ground beef, so I would highly recommend asking your meat department to grind a fresh chuck roast or other cut you like, so you know your ground meat only comes from one cow. Or, just use my recipe for Ground No-Meat on page 86.

BEANS/LEGUMES/PULSES: A funny thing happened to me on the way to writing this book. I woke up one morning and thought to myself, Why do I consume animals? Okay, I get it, there's a long list of "whys"; like, short ribs, hamburgers, or slow-roasted anything. However, once I started really looking into their little faces and getting to know them as the incredible creatures they are, I decided that unless I'm in dire need, there's really not a good enough reason for meat to be a large part of my diet. So, I really upped my hearty, plant-sourced meals and cut meat waaay back. This is why you will notice there's not a lot of meat dishes in this book. I still eat some fish (sorry, fishies!) and I may have mentioned that bacon might pass my lips on occasion (and if it does, I never tell Chuckles, my pig).

Now, where was I? Ah, yes, legumes. Some of the longest-lived societies in the world consume legumes/beans on a regular basis. I've included a few of my favorite bean recipes because beans are nice and filling and anything yummy and filling that's linked to living longer seems like a good thing to me. Eating beans with fermented veggies can help with digesting them. These recipes call for jarred or canned beans, quicker and easier for the typical household, but by all means feel free to double the recipes and make a big batch using dried beans. Soaking dry beans in salt water prior to cooking helps them stay intact, which makes lovely looking beans.

BAKED BBQ BEANS

The easy, homemade BBQ sauce on page 68 really give these beans a great depth of flavor. Don't be lazy and use store-bought, please (pick another day for laziness because we all need balance in life!). These recipes are so good they don't even need bacon; however, I know how many of you feel about bacon, and if you just can't live without, go ahead and cook it up and use the drippings instead of the butter.

Serves 4–6

Ingredients

2 (14-ounce) jars or cans of navy or pink beans
4 tablespoons butter
1 medium yellow onion, chopped
½ medium bell pepper, any color, chopped
2 garlic cloves, minced
2½ cups BBQ sauce (page 68)
1 tablespoon mustard, or 1 teaspoon turmeric
**Splash of hot sauce or pinch of cayenne, if
    desired**
1 teaspoon sea salt

1. Rinse and drain the beans.
2. In a cast-iron skillet, sauté the vegetables in the butter until soft.
3. Stir in the beans and the rest of the ingredients. If the BBQ sauce is thick, add ½ cup (or more, if necessary) of broth, coffee, or water.
4. Transfer skillet to the oven and bake at 350°F until bubbling, about 50 minutes.

Drunken Cowboy Beans with Meat (or, No-Meat) Balls

. . . .

I usually toss everything in my slow-cooker and let it do its job for a few hours on low. But you can also toss these in the oven or just make them right on the stove top if you prefer. Again, don't let me stop you from adding bacon if you must, just sauté it with the onions and garlic and cut the amount of butter in half. Use my homemade ketchup recipe on page 72 because it's so easy to make. You should never be without!

Serves 6–8

Ingredients

½ cup (1 stick) butter, divided
1–2 diced or sliced jalapeños (depending on the heat you like)
About 10–12 diced scallions
3 garlic cloves, minced
1 rounded tablespoon chili powder
2 teaspoons smoked paprika
1 teaspoon cumin
1 teaspoon thyme
2 teaspoons sea salt and black pepper to taste
$^1/_3$ cup whiskey (optional, but you need to change the name of this recipe if you don't use it)
1 (14-ounce) can each navy beans, black beans, pinto beans, kidney/adzuki beans
1 (14-ounce) can of fire-roasted tomatoes with juices
1 cup ketchup (page 72)
½ cup molasses
$^1/_3$ cup maple syrup
3 tablespoons balsamic or apple cider vinegar

1. In a Dutch oven, or large pot, add half the butter and sauté the jalapeños and scallions until limp.
2. Add the garlic and spices and cook another 30 seconds.
3. Add the whiskey and stir until it deglazes the pan.
4. Add the rest of the ingredients and combine well.
5. Cook uncovered over medium-low heat until some of the liquid has evaporated and the beans are tender. This can be done in the slow-cooker, oven, or on the stove top.
6. Stir in the rest of the butter, adjust seasoning, and serve to your cow people.

For Meatballs

Add 1 cup of bread crumbs, an egg, and ¼ cup heavy cream to 1 pound of seasoned ground beef and roll into meatballs. Or, make balls with the Ground No-Meat recipe on page 86 and bake at 350°F for about 20–25 minutes.

White Beans or Black-eyed Peas and Greens

. . . .

While I'm a big proponent of eating raw foods, some veggies are just plain better eaten cooked. That's why smoothies, soups, and condiments are great when salads become tiresome. Heartier greens like kale, collards, chard, or beet greens can be difficult on some people with tummy flora not quite diverse enough to break them down properly. They're also higher in oxalates than other veggies, which can bind with calcium in the blood and form crystals, causing kidney stones as well as other issues. However, we shouldn't have calcium floating around in our blood either, and if we get enough vitamin K_2 from fermented veggies, it will escort the calcium into our cells where it belongs (don't forget that sauerkraut and other fermented veggies go great alongside beans). No matter, I like well-cooked greens and I toss the cooking water along with most of the oxalic acid before serving, so everyone can enjoy them. Feel free to toss in a ham hock or turkey leg, but this easy dish is really delicious without.

Ingredients

About 4 bunches of mixed greens such as kale, chard, beet tops, or collards
Water to cover the greens
1–2 tablespoon sea salt
1 onion (optional)
2 garlic cloves (optional)
4 tablespoons butter, divided
4 cups broth (bone or veggie)
2 (14-ounce) cans/jars of white beans or black-eyed peas, rinsed and drained
Red pepper flakes and cracked black pepper to taste

1. Rinse and remove tough stems from the greens, roughly chop them, and add to a large pot.
2. Cover the greens with enough water to submerse them, add 1–2 tablespoons of sea salt, so the water tastes like the sea.
3. Cook until desired tenderness, 10–30 minutes, depending upon your preference.
4. Strain the cooking water (use it to water your plants).
5. If using onion and garlic, chop and sauté in half of the butter, until limp.
6. Add the broth and the greens back into the pot.
7. Stir in the beans or peas, remaining butter, and pepper.

Lentil & Mushroom Ragout with Roasted Vegetables & Spaghetti Squash

. . . .

Blame it on my lack of knife skills, but I find no joy in cutting a squash in half to bake it. Sometimes I'll buy the bags of pre-peeled and chopped butternut squash, but when I see a recipe that tells me to peel and chop a squash, I usually run. These types of squash are amazing baked whole, thank goodness, so that's what we do here in my kitchen.

Ingredients

1 spaghetti squash (optional)
1 or 2 medium sized beets
1 or 2 medium sized yams
4 tablespoons olive oil, divided
8 ounces sliced mixed or wild mushrooms
1 small onion or leek, roughly chopped
5 garlic cloves, roughly chopped
4 cups broth
1 cup dry white wine
1 cup lentils, preferably sprouted
2 teaspoons rosemary
2 teaspoons thyme
Sea salt and pepper to taste
¼ cup butter

1. Roast the squash whole in a 350°F oven until a knife pierces through tender flesh, about an hour.
2. Roughly chop the beet and yam, toss in 2 tablespoons of the olive oil, and bake alongside the squash until tender, about 20 minutes.
3. In a large pot, sauté the mushrooms, onion, and garlic in the remaining olive oil, until tender.
4. Add the broth, wine, lentils, and seasoning, cover and simmer until lentils are tender to your liking, 20–40 minutes.
5. Remove lid and stir in the butter.
6. Once the squash is cool enough to handle, slice in half, remove the seeds, and use a fork to fluff up the noodley strands of squash.
7. Serve the lentils over the spaghetti squash and top with the roasted vegetables.

Split Peas and Carrots

. . . .

Hearty dishes are one sure way to avoid the old starchy, grainy standbys you've been used to. A thick split pea soup or stew is one of my family's favorite stick-to-the ribs dishes, especially my oldest son, Josh. The spices and butter keep the soup super flavorful, even if you opt to keep it meatless and forgo the traditional ham hock. If you're a pig mama (like me), you can respect the ham and toss in a smoked turkey leg, if you're feeding meat lovers. And the lazy gal in me usually uses a bag of the little carrots, saving me the peeling and chopping time. I always have them in the fridge because they're one of my dogs' favorite crunchy treats.

Ingredients

2 cups split, green peas (sorted and rinsed)
6 cups bone or veggie broth
4–5 peeled and roughly chopped carrots
1 cup chopped onion or leek
1 cup chopped celery
1 tablespoon dried tarragon
2 teaspoons dried oregano
2 teaspoons dried sage
1 teaspoon dried dill
⅛ teaspoon red pepper flakes
1 teaspoon sea salt
1–2 tablespoons fresh lemon juice
4 tablespoons butter
Smoked ham shank or turkey leg (optional)

1. Put everything in a big pot, cover, and cook on the stove top for about 45 minutes or in your slow cooker on low for 8–10 hours, or on high 5–7 hours.
2. Remove the meat, if using, shred, and return to pot. Adjust seasonings and serve.

CHICKEN & BONE BROTH *OR* VEGGIE BROTH & DUMPLINGS

Sometimes we need flexible options for comforting dishes that usually call for meat, because many of us have vegetarians in the family or we may be squelching our carnivorous tendencies a bit ourselves. And, we simply must treat ourselves to grain-free dumplings no matter our meat-eating preferences. If you have a pressure cooker, this recipe can be made in a fraction of the time it takes in a slow cooker, a Dutch oven, or on the stove for that matter. I like how slow cooking wafts that amazing soup aroma throughout the house. Topped with these dumplings, this makes for a perfect Sunday-kind-of-dinner. Using the bones of free-range chickens instead of tossing them in the trash supplies your body with a hefty dose of minerals and collagen. I often make the bone broth and veggie broth recipes just for sipping on during the day as well as for during a fasting period.

Makes 8–10 servings

Ingredients for chicken and bone broth

1 whole chicken
10–12 cups water, divided
1½ tablespoons sea salt
¼ cup apple cider vinegar

1. Place the chicken, whole or cut up, into your slow cooker with the sea salt and add enough water so that it is halfway up the sides of the chicken, about 5–6 cups.
2. Cover and cook on the low setting overnight until the chicken is very tender (about 8–10 hours).
3. In the morning, remove the chicken to cool on a platter.
4. Remove the meat from the bones and return the bones to the broth in the slow cooker. Add the apple cider vinegar and the remaining 5–6 cups of water.
5. Place the chicken meat in a sealed container and refrigerate while you let the bones continue to cook in the broth (12 - 24 hours). Periodically, you may need to add a little more water to keep the bones submerged.
6. About one hour or two prior to your dinner, remove the bones from the slow cooker. They should be soft enough that your dogs can enjoy them (once cooled) without concerns of splintering.
7. At this point you should have approximately 10 cups of liquid. Strain the broth into a large stock pot to remove any remaining small bones or cartilage pieces.

For Veggie Broth

Many vegetables promote collagen production, so I consider this veggie broth a vegetarian's equivalent to consuming bone broth. This is a delicious, healing broth, but feel free to experiment, and if you don't have everything on hand, use what you have—it's hard to go wrong. If you prefer, strain it for pure broth and puree the veggies into a dip or cracker spread.

Veggie Broth Ingredients

10 cups salted water

6 celery stalks, with leaves

6 whole carrots (with whole tops, remove before serving)

1 whole yellow onion, unpeeled and cut in half

3 cups of any of your favorite roughly chopped vegetables such as yams, parsnips, chard, kale, spinach, asparagus, green beans, mushrooms, leeks, golden beets, etc.

2 teaspoons each of dried dill, tarragon, or thyme

1 handful of freshly chopped cilantro and parsley

Handful seaweed like kombu, nori, or dulse, if desired

1 tablespoon of spirulina or smashed garlic, if desired

1 tablespoon turmeric

A good pinch of ground cloves

½ cup butter, macadamia nut oil, or olive oil

Sea salt, pepper, and lemon juice, to taste

Dumpling Ingredients

2 cups roughly chopped white or yellow sweet potato or cauliflower (approximately 10 ounces)

1 cup almond flour

2 eggs

1 rounded tablespoon psyllium husk powder

2 tablespoons coconut flour

1 teaspoon sea salt

⅛ teaspoon garlic powder

¼ teaspoon baking powder

⅓ cup minced, fresh parsley

¼ cup minced onion or leek (optional)

1. Roughly chop the onion, celery, and carrots, and any other veggies, and add to the broth.
2. Stir in the herbs, seaweed, and any other ingredients.
3. Bring to a simmer and cook uncovered for an hour or more on the stove top, or covered all day in your slow cooker. Cover if the water gets too low.
4. Stir in the fat, salt, pepper, and lemon juice at the end of cooking.

Note: Unless I'm fasting I don't strain the broth because I love the soft vegetables. When I strain it, I usually use the veggies to make a dip or creamy vegetable soup for anyone in my household that's not fasting.

While the soup simmers, make the dumplings.

1. Fill a medium-sized pot ⅔ full of lightly salted water and let come to a boil.
2. In the food processor, fitted with the S blade, puree the potato, almond flour, and eggs for 2–3 minutes, until the dough resembles fluffy oatmeal.
3. In a small bowl, stir together the psyllium, coconut flour, sea salt, garlic powder, and baking powder. Add this mixture to the top of the food processor, while it's running.
4. Blend 30 seconds, until it becomes dough-like. Scrape the sides and blend another 30 seconds.
5. Pulse in the parsley and onion or leek, if using.
6. Remove the blade and pile the dough onto a surface. Use your fingers to knead the dough for about a minute, as it will get tighter and slightly stickier.

continued on page 193

7. Use an ice cream scoop to measure approximately 2 tablespoons of dough into your hands. Smooth and shape them into dumpling balls.
8. Drop the dumplings into simmering water and continue to simmer, uncovered, for about 6 minutes. You may notice the dumplings "oozing" a bit. This is just the psyllium (which binds like gluten) and is normal.
9. With a slotted spoon, remove the dumplings and add directly to your soup.
10. Serve with more chopped fresh herbs like parsley.

Notes and Tips:
- The bone broth can also be made in a stock pot on your stove top if you start it in the morning and let it cook through the day.
- The dumplings can be cooked directly in the soup also, the old-fashioned way. I've found that simmering them in water first (or baking, covered for about 30 minutes) keeps a prettier, clearer soup broth.
- All slow cookers are not created equal, so whether you cook on a low or high setting will be based on your cooker.

Eggplant Carbonara

. . . .

Like potatoes, eggplant is one of those vegetables that just doesn't quite work raw. If you ever invite me for dinner and you ask what I'd like, I would suggest you make eggplant, and as long as it's cooked, I'll be in heaven! I'll even eat it battered and fried (and you know I try not to fry much)! Our local Indian restaurant even cooks it into a baby food-like mush and I still think it's amazing. For the eggplant lover or not, this dish is killer, with or without the traditional bacon or pancetta. As you may remember, my pig Chuckles has greatly contributed to reforming my bacon-eating habits, so this is pictured without the bacon.

Makes 4–6 servings

Ingredients

2 medium eggplants
Juice of one lemon
1–2 teaspoons sea salt
½ pound bacon or pancetta (optional)
1–2 tablespoons butter or olive oil (if you use pancetta)
3 egg yolks
½ cup heavy cream
½ cup blanched almond flour or freshly grated Parmesan cheese
Salt and pepper to taste

1. Peel each eggplant and slice them thinly, lengthwise (about ⅛–¼-inch thick).
2. Stack three or four of them and slice into fettuccini noodle shape (about ¼–½-inch width).
3. Place the eggplant "noodles"' into a colander and squeeze the lemon juice over them.
4. Sprinkle generously with salt and toss with your hands to evenly coat. Set aside.
5. If using, cut the bacon into bite-sized pieces and sauté over medium heat, until starting to crisp. Reserve drippings. If using pancetta, sauté with olive oil or butter. Turn off heat.
6. In a large bowl, beat the egg yolks with the cream and almond flour (or Parmesan).
7. Add bacon and drippings and salt and pepper to taste. Set this aside while you cook the "noodles."
8. Rinse the eggplant "noodles" with water and gently roll them in a clean kitchen towel to remove excess water.
9. Toss the "noodles" into the pan the bacon was cooked in, add a couple teaspoons of olive oil or butter, and stir-fry the eggplant over medium heat for about 5 minutes or until limp. You can also cover and steam them a bit.
10. Add the eggplant to the bacon and egg mixture and toss to coat evenly. Serve with additional Parmesan or almond flour and lots of fresh cracked pepper.

> *Tip: If your eggs don't come from your own clean chickens, wash the eggs before you crack them to remove possible contaminants.*

Quick Farmhouse Stuffing

. . . .

Hubby's favorite holiday is Thanksgiving, and this stuffing is always on the table in mass quantities, so you'll want to double this recipe for a crowd. If we're lucky enough to have leftovers, I like to use it in my Thanksgiving pot-pie recipe—that is, if somebody hasn't already eaten it for breakfast. One year, as I sat on the couch de-boning the turkey in the early-morning-after-Thanksgiving and while others slept, I sipped coffee and had my eye between the turkey and the morning news channel (gotta watch that hogwash sometimes, right?). Suddenly, a little furry paw swiped a chunk of turkey off the platter that rested on my lap! Startled, I looked up to see a mama raccoon rush out the open French doors. With me still blurry-eyed, only one cup of coffee down, she pulled that off so easily I couldn't believe it! She was the same mama that enjoyed the contents of our trash cans on a regular basis and also destroyed our laundry room (like a heavy metal band at the Hilton), which housed the cat food. Oh well, she was a good mama, I suppose.

Serves 6–8

Ingredients

2 large carrots
2 celery stalks
1 yellow onion (optional)
2 cups broth (veggie, chicken, bone, etc.)
½ cup each: dried cranberries, gold raisins, and chopped pecans
1 teaspoon each dried parsley, sage, and thyme (or 1 tablespoon each of fresh)
1 teaspoon black pepper
6 cups crumbled grain free cornbread and/or bread (use food processor to pulse into large crumbs)
Sea salt to taste
2 large eggs
¼ cup broth or nut milk

1. Roughly chop the vegetables.
2. Add the vegetables and the broth to your blender and blend on the lowest setting, until vegetables are chopped into small pieces.
3. Pour the blender contents into a stock pot and cover; simmer until tender, about 5 minutes.
4. Add the dried fruit, nuts, and herbs to the broth.
5. Stir in the bread, cover, and allow the bread time to absorb the liquid, stirring occasionally, and adding more broth if necessary.
6. Taste, add salt, and adjust seasoning.
7. In a small bowl, whisk together the eggs and additional ¼ cup broth or nut milk and stir into the stuffing.
8. Enjoy as is, or turn into a large buttered casserole dish or cast-iron skillet and bake for about 40 minutes or until golden brown on the top.

Note: If using any bread recipe from this book, this stuffing is best without the addition of butter.

Tip: Cornbread crumbles well. If you use bread or a mixture of cornbread and bread, make sure you trim off the crusts (doggies love the crusts) and cut or crumble the sandwich bread up into small pieces to assure it softens in the broth. Also, you can freeze this for a couple months before baking it. Just increase your baking time and tent with foil, if necessary.

Gnocchi, Any Way You Want It: I first tasted gnocchi at an amazing Italian restaurant while living in New York City. It has always been my favorite pasta, so I'm thankful it translates into grain-free ingredients so well. Gnocchi is my go-to pasta now; it's quick and easy to make and hits the pasta spot. I included a few variations to see if it doesn't just become your favorite also. It boils up in a few minutes the traditional way, but I prefer to bake it because it comes out looking prettier, and that's important, right? However, if looks just don't matter to you, go ahead and toss them in a pot of water or some thin marinara sauce about 3–4 minutes. They'll even thicken the sauce up for you too. And if your lazy heart just doesn't want to peel the sweet potato, remember to taste the skin to make sure it's not bitter. If it's a good organic potato, there shouldn't be a problem. I don't use regular potatoes here because I'm not fond of the taste of a slightly under-cooked potato, whereas a slightly under-cooked sweet potato tastes great. Speaking of potatoes, it's important we not limit the beloved gnocchi and think out of the box a bit to see its ultimate potential. Just imagine the color and taste possibilities when you think vegetables! Talk about a sneaky way to get more veggies down the family's hatch. Broccoli, beet, carrot, and cauliflower are some of my gnocchi faves.

Each gnocchi recipe serves 6–8

Sweet Yam Gnocchi with Brown Butter & Sage

Ingredients

2 medium orange yams or 2½ cups roughly
    chopped
1 cup almond flour
1 egg
1 teaspoon sea salt

2 tablespoons psyllium husk powder
2 tablespoons coconut flour
Pinch of nutmeg (optional)
½ cup butter
2 tablespoons maple syrup (optional)
½ teaspoon ground sage + fresh sage leaves for
    garnish

1. Add yams to your food processor, along with almond flour, egg, and salt, and puree for a couple minutes, until well blended. Scrape the sides as needed.
2. Add psyllium, coconut flour, and nutmeg (if using) through the top. Blend another minute and scoop onto a smooth surface. Use your fingers to knead/massage the dough a minute.
3. Divide into four sections. If the dough seems too sticky, knead in a little coconut flour, 1 tablespoon at a time, just until you obtain a workable consistency.
4. With your hands, roll each section into a long rope, about an inch in width.
5. If desired, dip a fork in water and run the back of the tines down the length of the rope (this helps the gnocchi hold the sauce). I find it easier to do it this way rather than the traditional method of cutting first and running each cut piece over the fork.
6. Using a pastry cutter, a spatula, or fat knife, cut the rope into ½-inch gnocchi pieces.
7. Melt the butter in a large skillet, add the syrup, sage, and gnocchi, and roll them around a little.
8. Position the gnocchi in a single layer, cover, and bake at 350°F for 20 minutes.

Note: I use my food processor, but any of the gnocchis can also be made in the blender instead, by blending the vegetable with the egg, then stirring it into a bowl with the rest of the ingredients.

Gnocchi with Brussels & Squash

Ingredients

1 butternut squash
12 ounces yellow sweet or white sweet potato (about 2½ cups roughly chopped)
1 cup almond flour
1 egg
1 teaspoon sea salt + more to taste
2 tablespoons psyllium husk powder
2 tablespoons coconut flour
3–4 tablespoons olive oil
1 pound Brussels sprouts
Black pepper to taste

1. Place the whole squash on a baking sheet in a 350°F oven for about an hour, or until a knife easily pierces all the way through the dense part. Let cool a bit before slicing in half and removing the pith and seeds.

2. While the squash bakes, make the gnocchi: Use your food processor, fitted with the S blade, puree potatoes, almond flour, egg, and salt into a batter for a couple of minutes, until well blended (it will look similar to a fluffy, cooked oatmeal). Stop to scrape the sides 2–3 times or as needed.

3. Add the psyllium husk and coconut flour through the top while blending.

4. Blend another minute to a smooth batter and scoop out onto waxed or parchment paper.

5. Use your fingers to knead/massage the dough a minute.

6. Divide the dough into four sections. If the dough seems too sticky to work with, knead a little coconut flour in, 1 tablespoon at a time, just until you obtain a workable consistency.

7. With your hands, roll each section into a long rope, about an inch in width.

8. Dip a fork in olive oil and run the back of the tines down the length of the rope (this helps the gnocchi hold the sauce). I find it easier to do it this way rather than the traditional method of cutting first and running each cut piece over the fork.

9. Using a pastry cutter, a spatula, or fat knife, cut the rope into ½-inch gnocchi pieces.

10. Sprinkle with some olive oil and roll them around a little.

11. Add more olive oil to a large skillet with a cover. Toss in the gnocchi in a single layer, sprinkle a couple of tablespoons of water over the gnocchi, cover, and bake at 350°F for 20 minutes.

12. Turn the oven up to 400°F. Cut the stems off the Brussels sprouts, remove the outer leaves, and put them in a bowl. Cut the heart of the sprout in half, and place on a baking sheet. Toss in olive oil, salt, pepper, and roast them in the oven at for about 15 minutes. Toss the leaves in olive oil and add to the hearts, bake for a few minutes more, until the leaves begin to crisp.

13. To serve, toss the gnocchi, Brussels sprouts, and scoops of the squash in a big bowl. Top with more olive oil, cracked black pepper, and Parmesan, if desired.

Cauliflower Gnocchi with Spicy Marinara

Believe it or not, the cauliflower flavor is barely detectable here. However, if you have a true cauliflower hater in your household, feel free to use white or yellow sweet potatoes here instead.

Ingredients

12 ounces roughly chopped cauliflower (about half a head) or russet potatoes, peeled (about two)
1¼ cups almond flour
1 egg
1 teaspoon sea salt
2 tablespoons psyllium husk powder
2 tablespoons coconut flour
2 tablespoons olive oil
Grated Parmesan (optional)

Sauce Ingredients

1 (28-ounce) can Roma tomatoes, or 8–10 fresh tomatoes
¼ cup chopped onion
1–2 garlic cloves
1 teaspoon sea salt
1–2 teaspoons dried oregano or Italian seasoning
A big pinch of red pepper flakes
Splash of wine vinegar

1. Put the cauliflower or potato in your food processor, fitted with the S blade, and puree to small pieces.
2. Add the almond flour, egg, and salt, and puree into a batter for a minute or two, until well blended. Stop to scrape the sides as needed.
3. Add the psyllium husk and coconut flour through the top while blending.
4. Blend another minute to a smooth batter and scoop out onto a smooth surface.
5. Use your fingers to knead/massage the dough a minute.
6. Divide the dough into four sections. If the dough seems too sticky to work with, knead in a little coconut flour, 1 tablespoon at a time, just until you obtain a workable consistency.
7. With your hands, roll each section into a long rope, about an inch in width.
8. If desired, dip a fork in water and run the back of the tines down the length of the rope (this helps the gnocchi hold the sauce). I find it easier to do it this way rather than the traditional method of cutting first and running each cut piece over the fork.
9. Using a pastry cutter, a spatula, or fat knife, cut the rope into ½-inch gnocchi pieces.
10. Add the olive oil to a large skillet with a lid, add the gnocchi in a single layer, cover, and bake at 350°F for 20 minutes.

While the gnocchi bakes, make the sauce:

1. Blend everything in your blender.
2. Pour into a pot and simmer for 10 minutes.
3. Serve with the gnocchi and grated Parmesan.

Tip: For a thicker sauce, toss the baked gnocchi into the pot for the last 2-3 minutes of simmering, the psyllium in the gnocchi will slightly thicken the sauce. Or, stir in a tablespoon of tomato paste.

Broccoli Gnocchi with Cheesy Pumpkin Sauce

Ingredients

12 ounces (or 2½ cups) roughly
   chopped broccoli
1 cup almond flour
1 egg
1 teaspoon sea salt
2 tablespoons psyllium husk powder
2 tablespoons coconut flour
2 tablespoons olive oil

Sauce Ingredients

½ cup nutritional yeast (optional)
½ cup grated white cheese, your choice
   (optional, definitely use if not using
   nutritional yeast)
1 teaspoon psyllium husk powder
1 teaspoon sea salt
1 teaspoon ground turmeric
½ teaspoon paprika
1 cup pumpkin puree
½ cup each heavy cream and broth or 1 cup nut
   milk
1 teaspoon apple cider vinegar

1. Put the broccoli into your food processor, fitted with the S blade, and puree to small pieces.
2. Add the almond flour, egg, and salt, and puree into a batter for a minute or two, until well blended. Stop to scrape the sides as needed.
3. Add the psyllium husk and coconut flour through the top while blending.
4. Blend another minute to a smooth batter and scoop out onto a smooth surface or onto waxed or parchment paper.
5. Use your fingers to knead/massage the dough a minute.
6. Divide the dough into four sections. If the dough seems too sticky to work with, knead in a little coconut flour, 1 tablespoon at a time, just until you obtain a workable consistency.
7. With your hands, roll each section into a long rope, about an inch in width.
8. If desired, dip a fork in water and run the back of the tines down the length of the rope (this helps the gnocchi hold the sauce). I find it easier to do it this way rather than the traditional method of cutting first and running each cut piece over the fork.
9. Using a pastry cutter, a spatula, or fat knife, cut the rope into ½-inch gnocchi pieces.
10. Add the olive oil to a large skillet with a lid, add the gnocchi in a single layer, cover, and bake at 350°F for 20 minutes.

Make the sauce while the gnocchi bakes:

1. In a small bowl, combine nutritional yeast, cheese, psyllium husk, and seasonings, and set aside.
2. In a small sauce pan, stir and warm the pumpkin puree and cream/broth/nut milk with the vinegar.
3. When hot, whisk in the nutritional yeast/cheese mixture and stir until smooth.
4. Serve with or stir into the gnocchi.

Tip: This sauce is also great stirred into sweet potato fries or grain-free macaroni and baked till bubbly!

Gnocchi with Creamy Spinach Sauce

. . . .

I love those thin-skinned red potatoes, but they have to be cooked first or their flavor profile doesn't work in this type of cooking. This is why I always use the sweet potato. Did you know that the sweet potato isn't even in the same family as the potato? It's actually part of the morning glory family. If you choose not to peel it, make sure you taste the skin first. If it's at all bitter, you'll want to bust out the peeler.

Ingredients

12 ounces white or yellow sweet potato (or 2½ cups roughly chopped)
1 cup almond flour
1 egg
1 teaspoon sea salt
A sprig or about 1 tablespoon fresh, chopped rosemary (optional)
2 tablespoons psyllium husk powder
2 tablespoons coconut flour
½ teaspoon each sea salt and black pepper
2 tablespoons butter

Sauce Ingredients

2 tablespoons butter
1 cup cream or nut milk (optional)
5-ounce package of fresh spinach
Sea salt and cracked pepper to taste
⅛ teaspoon ground nutmeg

1. Put the potato in your food processor, fitted with the S blade, along with the almond flour, egg, and salt, and puree into a batter for a couple of minutes, until well blended. Stop to scrape the sides as needed.
2. Add the rosemary, psyllium husk, and coconut flour through the top while blending.
3. Blend another minute to a smooth batter and scoop out onto a smooth surface or onto parchment paper.
4. Use your fingers to knead/massage the dough a minute.
5. Divide the dough into four sections. If the dough seems too sticky to work with, knead in a little coconut flour, 1 tablespoon at a time, just until you obtain a workable consistency.
6. With your hands, roll each section into a long rope, about an inch in width.
7. If desired, dip a fork in water and run the back of the tines down the length of the rope (this helps the gnocchi hold the sauce). I find it easier to do it this way rather than the traditional method of cutting first and running each cut piece over the fork.
8. Using a pastry cutter, a spatula, or fat knife, cut the rope into ½-inch gnocchi pieces.
9. Melt the butter in a large skillet with a lid, add the gnocchi, and roll them around a little.
10. Position the gnocchi in a single layer, cover, and bake at 350°F for 20 minutes.

While the gnocchi bakes, make the sauce:

1. Add the butter and cream to a saucepan with a lid.
2. Add the spinach, cover, and let come to a simmer until the spinach is wilted, about 5 minutes. If you use nut milk, sprinkle a little coconut or almond or sweet potato flour in to help thicken the sauce.
3. Add the salt, pepper, and nutmeg, and stir.
4. Toss with the gnocchi and serve with fresh grated nutmeg, if desired.

Lasagna with Olives

. . . .

This is a lengthy recipe, but once you read it over you'll see how easy it is. Preparing any lasagna is a labor of love, especially making the fresh pasta. While we can purchase grain-free pasta these days, I prefer mine for several reasons: The ingredients are always on hand, it's far more budget-friendly, and it has NO extracted starch. This brings to mind one last NYC Italian restaurant story. Did you know that Al Lewis, who played Grampa from the old TV show the Munsters opened an Italian restaurant on Bleeker Street a few years ago? Okay, quite a few years ago . . . hmm, never mind, let's just say, back in the day. It was called, guess what? Grampa's! I must say he made some killer meatballs and had some mean recipes for an old vampire guy.

Serves 6–8

Pasta Ingredients

Olive oil, for the pan
12 ounces white or yellow, sweet or new potato
    (about 2½ cups rough chopped)
1 cup almond flour
1 egg
3 tablespoons psyllium husk powder
2 tablespoons coconut flour
1 teaspoon sea salt

Sauce Ingredients

6–8 lovely, ripe, roughly chopped Roma
    tomatoes, or 1 (28-ounce) can with juices
¼ cup olive oil
1 carrot, peeled (optional)
1 garlic clove
1 tablespoon dried oregano or Italian seasoning
¼ teaspoon red pepper flakes
1 teaspoon sea salt

1. Lightly brush an 8 x 8 x 2-inch pan or 6 x 10 x 2-inch pan with olive oil and set aside.
2. In the food processor, fitted with the S blade, puree the potato, almond flour, and egg into a batter, scraping as needed. It will take 2–3 minutes and will look similar to fluffy oatmeal.
3. Mix together the psyllium husk powder, coconut flour, and salt.
4. Add to the food processor, and blend another minute.
5. Remove the dough to a piece of parchment paper and knead it into a ball, then cut into three equal sections.
6. Roll each section between two sheets of parchment or waxed paper that have been sprinkled with water. You can do this ahead or as you place each layer in the pan (see assembly instructions below).
7. For the sauce, toss everything in your blender or food processor and pulse/blend it to a chunky sauce consistency.

Cheese and Olive Filling

2 cups grated mozzarella cheese, divided
8 ounces cream cheese or strained ricotta
8–10 Kalamata olives, rough chopped
1 egg
2 tablespoons minced fresh parsley
½ teaspoon black pepper

continued on page 210

1. Reserve 1 cup of the mozzarella cheese for topping.
2. Using a fork, blend the ingredients together in a medium bowl.

Meat Lasagna Ingredients

½ pound ground meat or Ground No-Meat (page 86), or 6–8 leftover meatballs or meatloaf
½ teaspoon sea salt
½ teaspoon pepper
½ teaspoon crushed fennel
½ teaspoon marjoram
½ teaspoon thyme
½ teaspoon sage
½ teaspoon allspice

1. If not using leftovers, sauté the meat just until it's no longer pink.
2. Stir together the herbs and spices in a small bowl and sprinkle over the meat.

To Assemble:

1. Preheat your oven to 350°F.
2. Put a few tablespoons of sauce in the bottom of your lasagna pan.
3. Place your first layer of the pasta on top of the sauce.
4. Spread half of the cream cheese mixture over the pasta.
5. If using meat, top with a little more than half of the meat, then a few tablespoons of sauce drizzled over the meat.
6. Repeat this for each layer, finishing with the last layer of pasta.
7. Pour as much of the sauce over the top and sides as the pan will hold.
8. Bake until it is bubbling, about 40 minutes.
9. Remove from oven, top with the rest of the mozzarella, and return to the oven until it's melted. If the cheese releases extra moisture on top, wait until the liquid evaporates and the cheese just begins to brown.
10. Remove from oven and let the lasagna cool and set up for 10–15 minutes before cutting.
11. Serve with the remaining raw sauce on the side, or, you may simmer it for a few minutes on your stove top, if you prefer it be cooked.

Meat (or No-Meat) & Mushroom Hand Pies

Put one of these in someone's lunchbox and see what happens. If they're as popular in your town as they are around these parts, you may just start yourself a thriving business. I don't know if you'd make much money, but I'll bet it would keep you busy! The spices are really fragrant and festive. I've made mini ones for holiday party hors d'oeuvres and they always disappear quickly. Grain-free pastry can be delicate to work with, so I admit that these are a bit of a labor of love, but worth every minute in my opinion.

Makes about 8 (2½ x 4-inch) pies

Dough Ingredients

Melted butter for brushing
1½ cups (about 7 ounces) roughly chopped
  yellow or white sweet potato
2 tablespoons butter
2 tablespoons gelatin powder
⅔ teaspoon sea salt
½ teaspoon baking soda
3 cups almond flour
1 egg for brushing

Filling Ingredients

½ pound Ground No-Meat (page 86), or ground
  meat (it's best if your butcher will grind it
  fresh for you)
⅔ cup diced mushrooms
1 carrot, peeled and diced
½ cup diced onion
1 garlic clove, minced
2 teaspoons grated orange peel
½ teaspoon cinnamon
½ teaspoon allspice
½ teaspoon nutmeg
½ teaspoon sea salt
½ teaspoon pepper
2 teaspoons chia seed, or ½ teaspoon psyllium
  husk powder
1 tablespoon balsamic or apple cider vinegar
1 tablespoon honey

1. Preheat oven to 350°F.
2. Brush two sheets of waxed paper with melted butter.
3. Add the sweet potato to your food processor, and process to very small pieces.
4. Add the butter, gelatin, salt, and baking soda and process until smooth.
5. Add the almond flour and process until it comes together into a smooth ball. Stop to scrape the sides if necessary.
6. Whisk the egg and set aside.
7. For the filling, in a large skillet, add the meat, mushrooms, carrot, onion, garlic, and orange peel, and cook over medium heat.
8. Cook until the mushrooms and onion are soft, and the meat loses its color, breaking the meat up with a fork as it simmers. While the meat simmers, stir together the spices and chia/psyllium, and sprinkle over the meat mixture.
9. Stir together the vinegar and honey and drizzle over the meat, stirring to incorporate.
10. Turn off the heat. The mixture should be very moist, but not runny. If it seems too moist, sprinkle on a tablespoon of coconut or sweet potato flour and stir. Set aside to cool.

continued on page 213

To assemble:

1. Preheat your oven to 350°F.
2. Separate the pie dough into 8–10 sections, rolling each into a ball.
3. Roll each ball of dough between two sheets of buttered parchment paper.
4. Place a few tablespoons of the meat mixture on one side and use a spatula or the parchment paper to help fold the other side over the top.
5. Press down the edges with your fingers and seal with fork tines.
6. Repeat until the crust and meat mixture is all used. Place pies on a parchment-lined cookie sheet and brush all over the tops with whisked egg.
7. Bake in a 350°F oven for about 30 minutes, until they're a nice golden brown.

Tip: These are easier to make if you keep them on the smaller side and they're great served with whole grain mustard and cultured vegetables.

MY MOTHER'S SPANISH RICE

. . . .

My mom had a handful of dishes she rotated throughout the month. Dad wasn't always easy to please, so she learned early on how to keep dinnertime less stressful, and that was to serve what he liked. Usually it had something to do with meat and potatoes, so this was one of the rare dishes that only used a modest amount of bacon in it. Even though I still eat white rice sometimes, I prefer to use sweet potatoes in this recipe and rarely use bacon in it these days. but I must say, this is every bit as delicious as the one Mom served, and I know she'd agree.

Serves 4–5

Ingredients

1 large white or yellow sweet potato (about 2 pounds), or 1 smallish head of cauliflower
2 tablespoons butter, ghee, red palm oil, or olive oil, + 2–3 tablespoons (unless using bacon)
½ medium bell pepper, any color
1 celery stalk, chopped
½ medium yellow onion, chopped
3–4 garlic cloves, minced
1 (14-ounce) can chopped or stewed tomatoes, drained (or 4 fresh, chopped)
2 teaspoons Italian seasoning or oregano
½ teaspoon smoked paprika (optional)
½ teaspoon turmeric
1 teaspoon sea salt
½ teaspoon ground black pepper

Additional Optional Ingredients

¼ pound bacon or large link sausage, cut into 1–inch pieces and sautéed, reserving its fat in the pan
½ pound shrimp or other (shell) fish
2 cups cooked, roughly chopped vegetables such as cubed butternut squash or broccoli

1. Peel and roughly chop the sweet potato or cauliflower (sometimes I use half of each).
2. Add to your food processor, fitted with the S blade. Pulse several times until it is finely chopped and resembles rice. If your food processor is smaller you will have to do this in 2–3 batches.
3. Add the butter, bell pepper, celery, onion, and garlic to the pan and sauté the vegetables until soft.
4. If not using bacon, add the additional 3 tablespoons of butter or oil to the pan; when it's hot add the "rice" and toss/stir until coated in the oil.
5. Add the seasonings and tomatoes and sauté a few minutes, tossing and stirring until al dente.
6. Cook about 1 minute more, cover, and turn off the heat. Let rest until the "rice" is to your desired tenderness.

Tip: When I double this recipe for a crowd, I use my wok for the extra room it provides.

Pizza, California Country-Style

. . . .

Years ago, a "new" restaurant opened near our home in the suburbs of San Diego. It was called California Pizza Kitchen, and it was there that I first had a chopped salad on top of pizza crust. So many years later, I still think that was true genius. It's also quick, healthy, easy, and delicious, my favorite adjectives. You can toss your favorite salad on this crust, or make this tasty version of a BLT with avocado.

Makes 1 (12-inch round) pizza

Crust Dry Ingredients

1¼ cups blanched almond flour, or other nut flour
¼ cup coconut flour
1½ tablespoons gelatin, or agar powder
¾ teaspoon sea salt

Blender Ingredients

1½ cups (about 7–8 ounces) chopped summer squash*
2 large eggs
2 tablespoons olive oil

1. Position your oven rack to the lowest setting and preheat the oven to 350°F.
2. Liberally brush your pizza pan and two sheets of waxed paper with olive oil and set aside.
3. Measure the dry ingredients into a large bowl and set aside.
4. Blend the squash, eggs, and olive oil in your blender until smooth.
5. Stir the contents of the blender into the flour blend until it becomes a dough.
6. Roll the dough out between the waxed paper, allowing it to be thicker around the edges for a crust and invert it into the pan.
7. Bake until it's a light, golden brown, about 25 minutes.
8. Top with the "salad" topping below.

*If you want to use another other favorite veggie, please do—however you may need to adjust the amount of coconut flour you use according to the juiciness of the vegetable you choose. Also, sometimes I omit the gelatin and add 1 cup of grated mozzarella to the crust.

Tip: If you eat organic cornmeal, a sprinkling of it on the oiled pan or on the crust before inverting it onto the pan gives a nice texture and crunch. I even like to press it into the crust a bit.

continued on page 218

Salad Topping Ingredients

6 ounces uncured bacon (optional)
¼ cup homemade mayo (page 70)
2 large Roma tomatoes
2 medium Haas avocados
2 small or 1 large head of romaine hearts
1 cup fresh basil leaves torn into pieces
1 handful arugula
½ cup shredded Parmesan cheese or nutritional yeast
Sea salt and pepper to taste
1½ teaspoons dried oregano and ½ teaspoon garlic powder (both optional)

1. Cut the bacon into bite-sized pieces and sauté in a cast-iron skillet until crisp. Add the bacon and drippings to a large bowl.
2. Add the mayo to a medium-sized bowl and stir in the oregano and garlic powder, if using.
3. Chop the tomatoes, avocados, and romaine hearts into bite-sized pieces and add to the bowl.
4. Add the basil, arugula, and Parmesan.
5. Add salt and pepper to taste and toss to coat.
6. Pour this salad mixture on top of the pizza crust and serve.

Note: Substitute 3 tablespoons virgin olive oil and 2 tablespoons fresh lemon juice for the mayo if necessary.

Pizza, Deep Dish-Style

. . . .

To me, this is a cold-weather meal, but my family loves it anytime of the year. There's just something about guys and pizza, at least around my house. When my husband and I were first married, we lived in the Los Angeles area for a short time. We used to get deep dish pizza at a nearby place called Numero Uno. We often had the same waiter, a real tall guy with an outgoing, humorous personality who would occasionally tell us that we'd see him on TV someday. He was right! Brad Garrett went on to play Robert in the sitcom Everybody Loves Raymond, *and many other roles. Before he became the well-known actor, he was just a funny guy who served a great pizza. Personally, I think that was a pretty important job.*

Serves 8

Ingredients

Oil for the pan
8 ounces yellow or white sweet potato (about 1⅔ cups rough chopped)
2 eggs
1⅔ cups almond flour
2 tablespoons coconut flour
2 tablespoons gelatin powder, or agar powder
1 teaspoon sea salt
2–3 tablespoons cornmeal (optional)

Filling Ingredients

2 tablespoons olive oil
1 pound Italian sausage or leftover meatballs/meatloaf made from the Ground No-Meat on page 86
8 ounces sliced mushrooms
1 medium onion, chopped (approximately ⅔ cup)
3 garlic cloves, or ½ teaspoon garlic powder
6–8 fresh Roma tomatoes, or 1 (28-ounce) can diced tomatoes, drained
1 (2-ounce) jar sliced black olives, drained
1 tablespoon dried oregano or Italian seasoning
1½ teaspoons sea salt
½ teaspoon ground fennel seed
¼ teaspoon red pepper flakes
2 tablespoons tomato paste
2 cups shredded mozzarella cheese, divided
½ cup fresh grated Parmesan cheese

1. Adjust the oven rack to the lowest setting and preheat the oven to 350°F.
2. Liberally brush the bottom and sides of a cast-iron skillet, approximately 10 × 10 × 2 inches, or a similar sized casserole dish, with olive oil and set aside.
3. Puree the potato to small pieces in your food processor.

continued on page 220

4. Add the eggs and almond flour and blend a couple of minutes until it resembles fluffy oatmeal.

5. Add the coconut flour, gelatin, and salt and blend a few seconds more.

6. The dough will roll out between two sheets of parchment paper, but I prefer to just press it into the pan. About half the dough should fit the bottom and the other half should be pressed up the sides.

7. Sprinkle the cornmeal (if using) onto the bottom of the crust and press it into the crust. (I like this for a little interesting texture). Bake on the lower rack for about 20 minutes, until starting to turn golden.

8. While the crust par-bakes, make the filling: Sauté the sausage, mushrooms, onion, and garlic in the olive oil. Add the tomatoes and cook until the tomatoes break down and release some of their water.

9. Add the herbs and olives and cook a few minutes more to let some of the liquid evaporate. Stir in the tomato paste.

10. Sprinkle half of the mozzarella cheese on the bottom of the crust. Add the meat filling and bake on the lowest rack for about 30 minutes, until filling is bubbly and crust is golden brown.

11. Remove from oven, top with the remaining cheese and return to the oven for a few minutes until melted.

Note: I used my No-Meat Meatloaf for this pizza. If you use ground meat or sausage and want it to stay more compact like the picture, sprinkle in a couple of teaspoons of psyllium or whisk an egg and stir into cooled mixture before filling the crust.

Tip: I find it easier to make the crust in my food processor, but you can also blend the potato with the eggs in the blender, pour into a bowl, and stir in the rest of the ingredients. Of course you can shorten the time and ingredient list and open a jar of ready-made marinara sauce instead of the tomatoes and herbs!

Pizza with Pepperoni Sauce

The guys absolutely love this pizza. So do the kids. Funny how alike they can be. I'm just kidding, but don't pretend you don't know what I'm talking about (unless you're a guy). If you're a guy, just calm down a minute (where's your sense of humor?). I can say this stuff because I've spent most of my life being very outnumbered when it came to expressing my "woman's point of view." However, that's never stopped me from expressing it.

Makes 1 (11 x 15-inch) pizza

Olive oil for the pan
Crust

Dry Ingredients

2 cups almond or cashew flour
¼ cup coconut flour
1 cup grated mozzarella, or 2 tablespoons gelatin
1¼ teaspoons sea salt
Garlic powder and other seasonings (optional)

Blender Ingredients

10 ounces (or about 2 cups) rough chopped white or yellow sweet potato
3 large eggs
3 tablespoons olive oil

1. Position your oven rack to the lowest setting and preheat the oven to 375°F.
2. Liberally brush a cookie sheet or pizza pan with olive oil and set aside.
3. Measure the dry ingredients into a large bowl and set aside.
4. Blend the sweet potatoes, eggs, and olive oil in your blender until smooth.
5. Stir this mixture into the dry ingredients until it becomes a smooth a dough. Add more coconut flour if necessary.
6. Roll or press the dough out between two sheets of parchment or waxed paper. Allow it to be thicker around the edges to form a nice crust edge.
7. Bake until light and golden brown, about 20 minutes.
8. Remove from the oven and turn up the heat to 375°F.
9. Top with sauce and toppings and pop back in the until they're heated through, about 5–10 minutes.

Sauce

Raw Dipping Sauce from page 82 *or:*
    3 ounces sliced pepperoni
    ½ can crushed tomatoes
    1 tablespoon red wine vinegar
    1 tablespoon olive oil
    1 tablespoon Italian seasoning
    ¼ teaspoon crushed fennel seed
    ¼ cup grated Parmesan cheese

Toppings

2 cups shredded mozzarella cheese
3 ounces sliced pepperoni

1. Chop the pepperoni into small pieces and stir into the rest of the ingredients.

Tip: I like to brush the crust with a whisked egg right before it comes out of the oven to create a barrier between the crust and sauce.

Chapter 11:

. . . .

SWEETS

. . . .

Give me a blender and I'll make you a cake. Remember when I said, "throw out what you think you know about baking"? Well, I meant it. By the time this book is in your hot little hands there will probably be even more sweetener choices on the shelves. Right now my favorites are liquid, pure leaf stevia and 100% pure monk fruit. I used to use erythritol more often, which is a good sweetener, but the pure monk fruit and stevia work well and taste great in these recipes and seem to have a broader appeal in various "health circles." Feel free to switch out your favorite sweeteners, but you may need to make small adjustments to the recipe. When a recipe calls for syrup, the type of syrup you use is your choice. Obviously, the flavors and blood sugar affects all differ and so do our tastes. See my suggestions on page 47 for help. Cutting sugar from my diet (sans the rare occasion) has been a process, but with the sweeteners available today, even my family can't tell the difference, and their bodies will forever benefit.

Cakes and Cupcakes

AnnaBanana Vanilla Cake

. . . .

Don't let the name of this cake fool you because it tastes more like vanilla than banana, but the fresh banana is what gives it a little extra oomph! My big brother used to call me AnnaBanana . . . a lot. He knew that would entice me to chase him around the house swatting wildly at him, because I disliked being called a banana. Now, I miss that name. It's a much better name than some others I've been called since then. Really, this cake should be called Steve's Vanilla Cake, because I made it in his honor and I know he would love it. You can use plantain here if you'd like to—just don't call it AnnaBanna Cake.

Makes 1 (8-inch round) or 1 (7-inch springform) or 2 (6-inch round) cakes or 12 cupcakes

Coconut oil for the pan

Dry Ingredients

1 cup almond flour
½ cup coconut flour
2 tablespoons egg white powder
1 tablespoon baking powder
½ teaspoon sea salt

Blender Ingredients

4 large eggs
1 just ripe banana or small plantain (about 6 ounces), or ½ cup of applesauce
1¹/₃ cups heavy cream or full-fat coconut milk
¹/₃ cup of your favorite syrup sweetener (I use VitaFiber syrup in this cake)
2 tablespoons vanilla extract, paste, or powder
½ teaspoon almond extract
1 teaspoon stevia or pure monk fruit

1. Preheat oven to 350°F and brush your cake pan(s) with coconut oil.
2. Cut a round of parchment paper to fit into the bottoms of the pans (this assures easy removal).
3. In a medium-sized bowl, whisk together the dry ingredients and set aside.
4. Blend the blender ingredients until smooth.
5. Whisk the contents of the blender into the dry ingredients.
6. Bake about 30–40 minutes, until a toothpick inserted in the middle comes out clean. Cover, as needed, with aluminum foil or parchment paper to prevent excess browning.
7. The cake is done when the center is firm to the touch and a toothpick inserted comes out clean. Make sure it's cooked through.
8. Cool in pans about 15 minutes, then remove from pans and finish cooling, right-side up, on cooling racks. Cool completely before frosting.

continued on page 228

Fluffy Vanilla Frosting

1½ tablespoons plantain flour*
⅔ cup heavy cream, room temperature
¼ cup of your favorite syrup sweetener
¹/₃ cup egg white powder
½ cup soft palm shortening or butter
¼–¹/₃ teaspoon stevia or pure monk fruit sweetener
1 tablespoon vanilla extract, paste, or powder
½ teaspoon almond extract (optional)

1. In a small saucepan, whisk the plantain flour into the cream.
2. Whisk over medium heat until it becomes a thick paste.
3. Remove from heat and whisk in the syrup and egg white powder.
4. Transfer to a mixing bowl, and cool to room temperature.
5. Use your handheld mixer to whip in the palm shortening or butter, sweetener, and extracts.
6. Whip until fluffy, chilling if necessary.

*Substitution for plantain flour: a 3-inch section of a barely ripe banana + 1 tablespoon sweet potato flour:

1. Blend the banana with the cream, syrup, egg white powder, and sweet potato flour in the blender until smooth.
2. Transfer to a small, tall bowl, add the soft shortening or butter and use your handheld mixer until smooth and combined.
3. Add the sweetener and extracts and whip until fluffy, chilling if necessary.

Tip: If your palm shortening is not very soft, whip it smooth before adding to the mixture.

Coconut Cake

. . . .

My mother was a true southern California gal, born and raised here, even right down to attending Hollywood High. I, however, was born on a Mississippi Air Force base and arrived in SoCal at the ripe old age of two. I also spent a few years in Charleston, South Carolina. All this means is that I believe I am enough of a "southern belle" to bake (and eat!) an amazing coconut cake. By the way, I say "hogwash" to all the whipping egg whites separately and extra bowls and work. See if you don't agree.

Makes 1 (8-inch round) or 1 (7-inch springform) or 2 (6-inch round) cakes, or 12 cupcakes

Coconut oil for the pan

Dry Ingredients

¾ cup coconut flour
¹⁄₃ cup egg white powder
1 tablespoon baking powder
½ teaspoon sea salt

Blender Ingredients

4 large egg whites
2 cups peeled and chopped summer squash or apple (about 10 ounces)
¾ cup coconut milk (or about half a can)
²⁄₃ cup shredded coconut
1 teaspoon stevia or pure monk fruit
2 teaspoons fresh lemon juice
2 teaspoons vanilla extract
2 teaspoons coconut extract
1 teaspoon almond extract

1. Preheat oven to 350°F and brush your cake pan(s) with coconut oil.
2. Cut a round of parchment paper to fit into the bottoms of the pans (this assures easy removal).
3. In a medium-sized bowl, sift together the dry ingredients and set aside.
4. Blend the blender ingredients until smooth (the coconut will not blend completely smooth).
5. Whisk the contents of the blender into the dry ingredients. The batter will become sort of thick and fluffy.
6. Bake about 30–40 minutes, until a toothpick inserted in the middle comes out clean. Cover, as needed, with aluminum foil or parchment paper to prevent excess browning.
7. The cake is done when the center is firm to the touch and a toothpick inserted comes out clean. Make sure it is cooked through thoroughly.
8. Cool in pans about 15 minutes, then remove from pans and finish cooling on cooling racks. Cool completely before frosting.

continued on page 231

Coconut Cream Frosting

½ cup dried coconut milk powder
1 tablespoon sweet potato flour
½ cup palm shortening
1 cup room temperature coconut cream (or heavy cream)
¼–⅓ teaspoon stevia or pure monk fruit sweetener
1 teaspoon coconut extract (optional)

1. In a small bowl, sift together the coconut milk powder and sweet potato flour so there are no lumps and set aside.
2. In a separate bowl, use your handheld mixer to whip the palm shortening until smooth and creamy.
3. Blend in the cream in three additions. Add the sweetener and extract.
4. Sprinkle in the coconut milk powder/flour mixture and whip until fluffy.
5. Frost and sprinkle the frosted cake with shredded coconut, if desired.

Tip: Here's some ideas to use the leftover egg yolks, if you don't use egg whites in the carton: Make custard and spread between the cake layers instead of frosting. You can also put them in your smoothies, make ice cream or mayo, or stir them into your dog's food. You may also use the whole eggs in the cake, but it will make a more yellowish cake instead of white.

BLACKOUT CAKE

. . . .

The only thing better than gooey chocolate cake is good-for-you gooey chocolate cake with amazing choco-late frosting. I made this one in a 7-inch springform pan (the one used to make cheesecakes). The diameter is slightly smaller than your regular cake pan, but the sides are higher, so it makes it easier to be impressive in the kitchen. That's because it only takes two layers to make a beautiful four-layer cake. So, if you've got a crowd, double the recipe, bake them together, cool, then with a long, serrated bread knife slice each layer in half (or a string will work, too). Frost, and prepare to be aaah-maaaz-ing!

Makes 1 (8-inch round) cake or 1 (7-inch springform) cake or 2 (6-inch round), or 12 cupcakes

Cooking spray

Dry Ingredients

⅔ cup coconut flour
½ cup cocoa powder, preferably Dutch
    processed*
1½ teaspoons baking powder
⅔ teaspoon sea salt
1½ teaspoons pure monk fruit or stevia

Blender Ingredients

5 large eggs
¾ cup chopped sweet potato or yam, any color
    (about 4 ounces)
1½ cups chopped zucchini (1 medium, or about
    7 ounces)
½ cup melted shortening or butter
½ cup of your favorite syrup sweetener
1 tablespoon vanilla extract
1 teaspoon almond extract (optional)

1. Position your oven rack to the middle portion of oven and preheat it to 350°F.
2. Spray your cake pan with cooking spray and cut a piece of parchment paper to fit into the bottom of the pan.
3. In a medium bowl, whisk together the dry ingredients and set aside.
4. In your blender, blend together the wet ingredients until smooth.
5. Whisk the wet into the dry until thoroughly combined.
6. Pour the batter into the prepared pan.
7. Bake at 350°F for 40 minutes., until a toothpick comes out clean and the top springs back when touched. Cupcakes take about 30 minutes.
8. Cool in the pan for 15 minutes, and then remove to a cooling rack to finish cooling.
9. Frost with Chocolate Buttercream Frosting (below).

*Note: If not using Dutch processed cocoa powder, add ½ teaspoon baking soda.

continued on page 234

Chocolate Buttercream Frosting

4 ounces 100% dark chocolate
4 ounces (1 stick) butter
½ cup of your favorite syrup sweetener
1 teaspoon pure monk fruit or stevia
2 teaspoons vanilla extract
⅛ teaspoon almond extract (optional)
Pinch or two of sea salt

1. In a saucepan over low heat, heat the chocolate with the butter until melted together.
2. Remove from heat and stir in the rest of the ingredients.
3. Let rest on the counter until it cools to room temperature.
4. Use as is or whip until fluffy. Whipping it results in a lighter color frosting.

Note: Double this recipe for a four-layer cake.

Tip: For Milk Chocolate Frosting: Replace the butter with heavy cream or coconut cream, chill, and whip until light and fluffy.

German Chocolate Cake

. . . .

Years ago, when I first started baking grain/starch-free, I always used my food processor, nuts and shredded coconut, along with other whole foods. I still often prefer this method, but you may prefer to use the blender and flours instead of whole nuts. For this reason, I've converted most of my recipes to the blender for broader appeal. This one is no different as it can be made in the blender as well. Simply trade out the whole nuts for flour and stir it in last. Or, you can always use the tamper with the blender if you have a Vitamix. You won't taste the dates, but don't forget to make sure they're completely pitted before using. This cake is a very favorite of mine and for my own nostalgic reasons I always make it with my food processor.

Makes 2 (6-inch round) 1 (7-inch springform), 1 (8-inch round), or 12 cupcakes

Ingredients

1 rounded cup of your favorite nuts or 1¼ cups nut flour (about 4 ounces)
1 rounded cup shredded coconut (about 2½ ounces)
⅔ cup pitted dates (about 3 ounces)
2 cups chopped apple or zucchini, or a blend of both (about 10 ounces), no need to peel
4 large eggs
¼ cup cocoa powder
1 teaspoon pure monk fruit or stevia
1½ tablespoons vanilla extract or paste
1 teaspoon espresso powder or almond extract (optional)
½ teaspoon sea salt
1 rounded tablespoon coconut flour
2 teaspoons baking powder or 1 teaspoon baking soda

1. Position your oven rack to the middle portion of oven and preheat it to 350°F.
2. Spray a 7-inch round springform pan with cooking spray. Measure and cut a 7-inch round piece of parchment paper and fit it into the bottom of the pan.
3. In your food processor, fitted with the S blade, add the nuts and coconut and blend until very fine and pasty; stop and scrape as necessary
4. Add the dates and apples and syrup and blend a couple of minutes.
5. While blending, add the eggs, one at a time, and the rest of the ingredients while blending.
6. Pour the batter into the prepared pan.
7. Place on the middle oven rack and bake about 35 minutes, until a toothpick comes out clean and the top springs back when touched.
8. Cool in the pan for 15 minutes, and then remove to a cooling rack to finish cooling.

continued on page 237

Coconut Pecan Frosting

½ cup butter
½ cup water
1 cup soft dates (about 5 ounces)
½ cup of your favorite syrup sweetener
¼ teaspoon pure monk fruit or stevia, or to taste
Pinch of sea salt
1 cup shredded coconut
1 cup chopped pecans
1 teaspoon vanilla extract (optional)
¼ teaspoon almond extract (optional)

1. Melt the butter and the water together in a small pot.

2. Add the dates, syrup, stevia, and salt to your blender.

3. Once the butter is melted, pour over the contents of the blender and blend until smooth.

4. Return to the pot and simmer for 3 or 4 minutes, remove from heat and stir in the coconuts and pecans and extracts.

5. Taste for sweetness and adjust as needed.

To Frost: Spread the frosting on the tops of the cakes, layering them together.

Tip: Even if your dates are pitted, I recommend cutting them in half to make sure there are no fragments left behind before tossing them in your blender.

Carrot Cake Cupcakes

So, this looks like a lot of ingredients for the simple carrot cupcake. Okay, so it is a lot of ingredients, but it's so easy to toss them all in your food processor and whip up this bit of deliciousness. This cake is even wonderful made the day before. Just let it rest, covered, on your counter, and smother with frosting before serving.

Makes 12 cupcakes, or 1 (8-inch round) or 2 (6-inch round) cakes

Ingredients

1 cup roughly chopped carrots (about 5 ounces)
1 cup shredded coconut (about 3 ounces)
½ cup coconut flour
2 tablespoons egg white powder
⅔ teaspoon pure monk fruit or stevia
1½ tablespoons cinnamon
¼ teaspoon allspice
½ teaspoon sea salt
1 teaspoon baking soda
4 large eggs
1 cup full-fat coconut milk
1 tablespoon lemon juice
1 tablespoon vanilla extract

Stir-in Ingredients

½ cup drained, chopped pineapple, or 1 peeled, shredded apple
⅔ cup shredded carrots
½ cup raisins or currants
½ cup roughly chopped walnuts or pecans

Cream Cheese Frosting

½ cup very soft cream cheese
¼ cup very soft butter or palm shortening
2 tablespoons of your favorite syrup sweetener
½ teaspoon vanilla extract
¼ teaspoon almond extract
¼ teaspoon pure monk fruit or stevia

1. Position your oven rack to the middle portion of oven and preheat it to 350°F.
2. Line 12 muffin cups with cupcake liners, or coat your cake pan(s) with coconut oil and cut a piece of parchment paper to fit it into the bottom of the pan(s).
3. In your food processor, add the carrots and coconut and blend until very fine; stop and scrape as necessary.
4. Add the rest of the ingredients and blend until smooth, stopping to scrape as needed.
5. Remove the blade and add the stir-in ingredients, using a rubber spatula to combine well.
6. Scrape the batter into your prepared pans, or use a large ice cream scoop to fill each cupcake holder with about ⅓ cup of batter.
7. Bake until a toothpick comes out clean, about 45 minutes for the cakes, or 30 minutes for cupcakes.
8. Cool in the pan for 10 minutes, then remove to finish cooling on a cooling rack.

For the Frosting

1. In a small bowl use your handheld mixer to whip the cream cheese until smooth and free of lumps.
2. Blend in the butter, syrup, extracts, and monk fruit. Whip until fluffy, chilling if necessary.

Note: Double the frosting recipe if making a two-layer cake.

Chocolate Orange Walnut Torte

....

I so love walnuts. I so love chocolate. If I had to marry one, I don't know which I'd choose. I guess I really don't have to worry about that since I'm already married anyway. As I may have already mentioned, I can be somewhat immature at times. I think it just goes hand in hand with raising a husband and boys (c'mon, you know I'm teasin' guys!). This cake does bring out my more refined side, which is a good thing, on occasion.

Makes 1 (9-inch) torte or 12 mini tortes

Ingredients

1½ cups walnuts (about 5 ounces)
1 cup roughly chopped sweet potato or yam (about 5 ounces)
1½ cups chopped thin-skinned oranges, such as Valencia (about 7 ounces)
4 ounces 100% chocolate (such as Guittard)
1 teaspoon stevia or pure monk fruit
½ teaspoon baking soda
½ teaspoon sea salt
4 large eggs
½ cup of your favorite syrup sweetener

1. Preheat the oven to 350°F.
2. Liberally butter a tart pan or spray with coconut oil cooking spray.
3. In your food processor, fitted with the S blade, blend all of the ingredients except the eggs and syrup to a thick, semi-smooth paste.
4. Process and scrape sides as needed.
5. Add the syrup and eggs, one at a time, through the top of the processor as it is blending.
6. When all the eggs are blended in, remove the blade and spoon the batter into prepared pan(s).
7. Bake for about 35 minutes until the top puffs. Don't overbake.
8. Cool completely before removing from the pans.

Sweet Whipped Cream

1½ cups heavy whipping cream
Sweetener to taste
2 tablespoons Grand Marnier liquor (optional), or 1 teaspoon vanilla extract

1. Whip together all ingredients with your handheld mixer until fluffy.
2. Place a dollop of whipped cream on each cake and garnish simply with a walnut half or drizzle with chocolate sauce.

Note: If you don't have thin-skinned oranges, use their zest, then peel them and discard the peel.

Gingerbread Cake

....

This is a wonderfully spicy gingerbread that warms the cockles. Not my cockles, your cockles. I'm going to look up cockles now . . . Okay, I'm back, wow, I had no idea how many different origins the word cockles could have. First of all (I know you want to know this), a cockle is a type of shellfish/mollusk, kinda like a clam and its shell is sort of heart-shaped. So it could've originated from the Latin word "cordis," which means "heart," or the French word "couquille," which means "shell." Also, a kiln has a chamber referred to as a cockle, so it could mean the chamber of our heart is warmed as it is in a kiln. When something "warms the cockles of your heart," it refers to something good or wonderful that makes your heart beat fast and delights you. Like this cake at Christmas time, or anytime for that matter. Just shoot me an e-mail me if there's any other word I can clarify the meaning of for you.

Makes 1 (8 x 8-inch square) cake

Coconut oil or ghee for the pan

Dry Ingredients

1¼ cups almond flour
¹/₃ cup coconut flour
2 teaspoons baking powder
½ teaspoon sea salt
2 tablespoons ground ginger
¼ teaspoon cinnamon
⅛ teaspoon black pepper (optional)

Blender Ingredients

4 large eggs
1 medium-sized orange, with peel, deseeded
    and roughly chopped (about 1 cup)
1 chopped apple (about 1 cup)
1 (2-inch) piece of fresh ginger
½ cup molasses
1 teaspoon pure monk fruit or stevia
2 teaspoons vanilla extract

1. Preheat oven to 350°F and brush an 8 x 8-inch baking dish with coconut oil or ghee.
2. In a medium-sized bowl, whisk together the dry ingredients and set aside.
3. Blend the wet ingredients in your blender until smooth.
4. Whisk this mixture into the dry ingredients.
5. Pour the batter into the prepared pan and bake until the top is firm to the touch and a toothpick inserted in the center comes out clean, about 40 minutes.
6. Finally, you must serve this with sweet whipped cream.

Sweet Whipped Cream

1¹/₂ cups heavy whipping cream
¹/₄ teaspoon pure monk fruit or stevia
1 teaspoon vanilla extract

1. Whip the ingredients together with your handheld mixer until fluffy.
2. Place a dollop of whipped cream on each cake and garnish simply with a walnut half or drizzle with chocolate sauce.

Red Velvet Cake

. . . .

This is usually the all-time favorite cupcake I'm asked to make. The raw beet provides this beautiful color and the flavors are delicious. I prefer the bright color and sweet cherry flavor of these without cocoa powder, but if you prefer a more traditional look and taste, go ahead and add 2 tablespoons of cocoa with the dry ingredients. Make sure you peel, or, at least scrub the beet well before chopping, otherwise it may be a little "earthy" tasting, if you know what I mean. Also, be careful when chopping the beet—the color can stain. Lastly, don't substitute baking soda for the baking powder or the color will change.

Makes 12 cupcakes or 1 (8-inch round) cake or 1 (7-inch springform) or 2 (6-inch round) cakes

Dry Ingredients

1½ cups almond flour
¼ cup coconut flour
1 tablespoon egg white powder
2 teaspoons baking powder
½ teaspoon sea salt

Blender Ingredients

4 large eggs
¾ cup peeled and chopped sweet potato (about 4 ounces)
¾ cup peeled and rough chopped raw beet (about 1 medium)
1 cup pitted, previously frozen or fresh cherries (about 5 ounces)
1½ teaspoons stevia or pure monk fruit
1 tablespoon fresh lemon juice
2 tablespoons vanilla extract
1 teaspoon almond extract

1. Position your oven rack to the middle portion of oven and preheat it to 350°F.
2. Line your muffin pan with 12 cupcake liners and set aside.
3. In a medium bowl, whisk together the dry ingredients and set aside.
4. In your blender, blend together the wet ingredients until smooth.
5. Whisk the wet into the dry until thoroughly combined.
6. The batter should be the consistency of thick pancake batter. If it seems too thin, sift and whisk in another tablespoon of coconut flour.
7. Use an ice cream scoop to measure the batter into the muffin cups.
8. Bake cupcakes for about 30–33 minutes (40–42 minutes for a cake) or until a toothpick comes out clean and the top springs back when touched. Cover with parchment paper or aluminum foil if they begin to brown too much.
9. Cool in the pan for 10 minutes, and then remove to a cooling rack to finish cooling.
10. Top with Fluffy Cream Cheese Frosting (see the following recipe).

continued on page 245

Note: The type and age of your baking powder will affect the color of the baked cake. Use one that has cream of tartar as an ingredient and it will keep a nice pink hue. Or, add a $1/4$ teaspoon cream of tartar to the baking powder. I don't use food coloring in this recipe, but if you want a really bright pink color, and you don't have cream of tartar on hand, use a drop or two of non-toxic color. Definitely don't substitute for baking soda or it will turn greenish.

Fluffy Cream Cheese Frosting

$1/2$ cup very soft cream cheese
$1/4$ cup soft butter or melted palm shortening
2 tablespoons of your favorite syrup sweetener
$1/2$ teaspoon vanilla extract
$1/4$ teaspoon almond extract
$1/8$ teaspoon pure monk fruit or stevia

1. Use your handheld mixer to whip the cream cheese until smooth and free of any lumps.

2. Blend in the butter, syrup, extracts and monk fruit.

3. Whip until fluffy, chilling if necessary.

Note: Double the frosting recipe if making a two-layer cake.

Hummingbird Cake

We have a fountain that we built ourselves (except for the pretty center part that has a pineapple on top where the water squirts out—we bought that part because sculpting is not in our background). Humming-birds love to play and take baths in it. I wish I could say that I invented this cake while I watched the little hummingbirds play in my pineapple fountain, but we'd all know I was fibbing again, so I won't do that. I'm not sure where a hummingbird cake recipe first appeared. I think it was a homemaker magazine contest way back whenever. It's a bit revised here, of course, but I think this cake and frosting recipe is the real contest winner.

Makes 1 (8-inch round) cake or 1 (7-inch springform), or 2 (6-inch round) cakes, or 12 cupcakes

Dry Ingredients

⅔ cup almond, or other nut flour
⅔ cup coconut flour + more for dusting
2 teaspoons baking powder
½ teaspoon sea salt
1 teaspoon cinnamon

Blender Ingredients

3 large eggs
1 cup shredded coconut (about 3 ounces)
2 ripe bananas
2 teaspoons vanilla extract
½ teaspoon stevia or pure monk fruit
¼ cup pineapple juice
1 cup fresh, canned, or previously frozen crushed pineapple

1. Preheat the oven to 375°F and position your oven rack to the middle portion of oven.
2. Grease and dust your cake pans with coconut flour (or line a muffin pan with 12 cupcake liners).
3. In a large bowl, whisk together the dry ingredients, sifting the coconut flour and baking powder to remove any lumps.
4. In your blender, blend the eggs, shredded coconut, bananas, vanilla, sweetener, and pineapple juice until smooth. The coconut will not blend completely smooth.
5. Add the pineapple and blend or pulse to crush it into small pieces.
6. Pour the wet ingredients into the dry and combine well. Pour the batter into the prepared cake pans.
7. Bake until a toothpick inserted comes out clean, about an hour, or about 35 minutes for cupcakes.
8. Cover with aluminum foil to prevent over-browning the top.
9. Cool in pan for 30 minutes; remove to finish cooling on a rack to prevent sogginess.

Hummingbird Frosting

½ cup very soft cream cheese
½ cup soft butter
1 tablespoon pineapple juice
1 teaspoon almond extract
⅓ teaspoon pure monk fruit or stevia, or to taste
2 teaspoons sweet potato flour
½ cup crushed pineapple (strained)
½ cup chopped pecans, toasted

1. Use your handheld mixer to blend the cream cheese and butter together until smooth.
2. Add the pineapple juice, extract, sweetener, and sweet potato flour, and whip until combined.
3. Stir in the crushed pineapple. Frost the cooled cake, then top with the toasted, chopped pecans.

Lavender Honey Cake

. . . .

Using the different colors of sweet potatoes and vegetables is so much fun. This doesn't have an ounce of food coloring in it. I know they make non-toxic colors now, but who cares? While I enjoy juicing every day, sometimes I would rather just eat a piece of cake, especially when they're such a pretty color. I usually peel the sweet potato for a more delicate flavor, but don't bother peeling the apples.

Makes 1 (8-inch round) cake or 1 (7-inch springform) 2 (6-inch round), or 12 cupcakes

Dry Ingredients

¾ cup coconut flour
1 tablespoon finely minced lavender flowers
2 teaspoons baking powder
1 tablespoon egg white powder
½ teaspoon sea salt
¼ cup egg white powder

Blender Ingredients

4 large eggs
1 cup roughly chopped purple sweet potato
   (about 5 ounces)
2 chopped apples (about 12 ounces)
6 tablespoons melted butter
½ cup honey
1 tablespoon fresh lemon juice

1. Position your oven rack to the middle portion of oven and preheat it to 350°F.
2. Line your muffin pan with 12 cupcake liners and set aside.
3. In a medium bowl, whisk together the dry ingredients and set aside.
4. In your blender, blend together the wet ingredients until smooth.
5. Whisk the wet into the dry until thoroughly combined.
6. The batter should be the consistency of thick pancake batter. If it seems too thin, whisk in another tablespoon of coconut flour.
7. Bake for about 40 minutes, until a toothpick comes out clean and the tops spring back when touched. Cover with parchment paper or aluminum foil if it begins to brown too much.
8. Cool in the pan for 15 minutes, and then remove to a cooling rack to finish cooling.
9. Top with Honey Buttercream Frosting (see recipe below).

Note: The type and age of your baking powder will affect the color of the baked cake. Use one that has cream of tartar as an ingredient and it should keep a nice, bright hue. Or, add a ¼ teaspoon cream of tartar to the baking powder. Don't substitute for baking soda or it will not keep the nice color.

Honey Buttercream Frosting

½ cup soft palm shortening
½ cup soft butter
1 whole egg or ¼ cup egg white powder
   (optional)
1 rounded tablespoon sweet potato flour
4 tablespoons honey
½ teaspoon pure monk fruit or stevia, or to taste

1. Use your handheld mixer to whip the shortening until smooth and creamy.
2. Add the rest of the ingredients and whip until fluffy.

Note: If using egg white powder, you may need to whip longer for it to soften and dissolve.

MARSHMALLOW WHOOPIE PIES

. . . .

We all know that whoopies are not really pies at all. They're more a cross between a cake and a cookie, so why on earth are they called pies? And, for goodness sake, should they be in the cake, cookie, or pie section? Believe me, these are big mysteries in my brain. One thing I do know, however, is that somehow whoopie pies have the ability to bring everyone back to their childhood. Happy times, with memories of eating them or, maybe not-so-happy times when big brother smashed yours in your face. I'm not sure which memories you may have, but a good ol' whoopie pie will bring 'em back.

Makes about 8 whole whoopie pies

Dry Ingredients

¼ cup coconut flour
⅓ cup cocoa powder
1½ teaspoons psyllium husk powder
1 teaspoon baking soda
⅔ teaspoon sea salt

Blender Ingredients

4 large eggs
1 cup pumpkin puree
¼ cup water
1 teaspoon pure monk fruit or stevia
1 tablespoon vanilla extract
1 teaspoon almond extract

Filling Ingredients

1 cup water
2 teaspoons gelatin
½ cup egg white powder
2 teaspoons sweet potato flour
½ teaspoon pure monk fruit or stevia
½ cup of your favorite syrup sweetener
1 teaspoon vanilla extract
1 teaspoon almond extract
1 cup palm shortening

1. Position your oven rack to middle portion of oven and preheat it to 350°F.
2. Line a sheet pan with parchment paper or a baking liner and set aside.
3. In a small bowl, whisk together the dry ingredients, sifting as necessary to remove any lumps.
4. In a medium bowl, whisk together the wet ingredients. Sprinkle in the dry ingredients and whisk to combine.
5. Using an ice cream scoop, place dollops of batter on the cookie sheet. Bake for 15 minutes.
6. Cool on pan until firm enough to move to a cooling rack or paper towels.
7. Place filling on top of one "pie" and then cover with another.

For the Filling

1. Heat the water in a small pan until very hot to the touch.
2. Add the gelatin, egg white powder, and sweet potato flour to the bowl of your stand mixer.
3. Turn the mixer on low and add the hot water, mixing until the gelatin is melted.
4. Add syrup and extracts and blend until room temperature. Add shortening and whip until fluffy.

If it's a warm day, you may need to chill the mixture first and then whip until fluffy.

Tip: If you haven't yet purchased sweet potato flour, you can replace it with 3–4 tablespoons of cooked and mashed sweet potato (I usually keep already baked ones in my fridge for snacks). If you're out of pumpkin puree, replace it with 2 cups roughly chopped zucchini blended in your blender with the other wet ingredients and reduce water to 2 tablespoons.

Old-Fashioned Yellow Cake

. . . .

We often let guests rent our property for their "farm-style" or "country" wedding. Cakes decorated simply with fresh flowers, homemade pies, and of course cupcakes, are really popular choices for their dessert. We had to stop allowing a full bar at these events because some of those city folk would get feelin' a wee bit too relaxed and would do some weird things. I guess, for some reason, they seemed to think they're celebrating out in the "boonies" so's they can get all wild and crazy. Well, maybe they are out in the boonies, but even us "boonie" folks have limits. I think this is the only cake that I actually add a little fat in the form of butter to because I prefer to just use the whole foods and I don't like heating fat if I don't have to. Anyhow, I'm pretty sure you'll get wild and crazy about this cake, butter or not.

Makes 1 (8-inch round) cake, or 1 (7-inch springform), 2 (6-inch round), or 12 cupcakes

Dry Ingredients

1½ cups almond flour
¼ cup coconut flour
2 tablespoons egg white powder
1 teaspoon baking soda or 1 tablespoon baking powder
½ teaspoon sea salt

Blender Ingredients

4 large eggs
1 cup chopped yellow sweet potato (about 4 ounces)
2 cups chopped yellow summer squash or apple (about 9–10 ounces)
6 tablespoons melted butter
1½ tablespoons vanilla extract or paste
1 tablespoon fresh lemon juice
1⅓ teaspoons stevia or pure monk fruit

1. Position your oven rack to the middle portion of oven and preheat it to 350°F.
2. Spray an 8-inch round cake pan with cooking spray. Measure and cut an 8-inch round piece of parchment paper and fit it into the bottom of the pan.
3. In a medium bowl, whisk together the dry ingredients and set aside.
4. In your blender, blend together the wet ingredients until smooth.
5. Whisk the wet into the dry until thoroughly combined.
6. Pour the batter into the prepared pan.
7. Bake about 35 minutes, or until a toothpick comes out clean and the top springs back when touched. Cover with parchment paper or aluminum foil if it begins to brown too much.
8. Cool in the pan for 15 minutes, and then remove to a cooling rack to finish cooling.
9. Frost with Chocolate Buttercream Frosting on page 234, or the following Easy Vanilla Buttercream Frosting.

Tip: The yellow squash makes a beautiful yellow cake, but if you don't have squash on hand you can substitute them with apples and a few pinches of turmeric to do the trick, and without leaving a detectable flavor.

continued on page 254

Easy Vanilla Buttercream Frosting

½ cup room temperature heavy cream or full-fat coconut milk
½ cup cold butter or soft palm shortening
¼ cup of your favorite syrup sweetener
1 tablespoon vanilla paste or extract
½ teaspoon pure monk fruit or stevia, or to taste
1½ tablespoons sweet potato flour
¼ cup egg white powder (optional)

1. Add the cream, butter, syrup, vanilla, and sweetener to a tall, narrow bowl.
2. In a small bowl, stir together the sweet potato flour and egg white powder and sprinkle over the contents in the tall bowl.
3. Use your handheld mixer to whip until fluffy.

COOKIES & BROWNIES

I was once a cookieholic. There was even a time when I could put away half a pack of Oreos. Yes, I admit I had issues, but I have truly changed my ways. Now, thankfully, I can eat cookies to fill my heart's (and stomach's) desire and not hurt my body. I usually use my food processor to make my cookie doughs and brownie batters. The benefit to the food processor is that it makes these just one bowl clean-up, and who doesn't like that? However, if you prefer to use your blender instead, the egg, melted butter, and syrup in most of the recipes allow for easy blending also. I love using super nutritious dates in cookies for their sweetness and chew, and if you have date-haters in your household, just don't tell them they're eating dates, because they won't even taste them. If you buy the ones that have been pitted and already soft, there's no need to soften them in water first. I've found pit pieces on occasion, so it's best to cut them in half to make sure before tossing them in your blender. The syrup and added fat also helps get that spread and chew we all love. Almond flour makes great cookies but several recipes use coconut as well, and while we can buy plantain flour and sweet potato flour, I find it more cost effective and simple to just toss in the whole food instead.

BLONDIES

If you love macadamia nuts, use them here, but almond flour gives a more traditional taste. Either way, you'll love these chewy bars. I use psyllium here for a bit of a chew and to give a nice little "skin" to the top of the Blondies. It may puff a bit in the oven, but once removed from the heat, will settle down.

Makes 9–12 brownie squares

Dry Ingredients

1 cup macadamia nuts, or 1¼ cups almond
    flour*
2 tablespoons coconut flour
½ teaspoon baking soda
½ teaspoon sea salt
2 teaspoons psyllium husk powder

Optional Stir-in Ingredients

½ cup chopped macadamia nuts, white or
    chocolate chips, shredded coconut, dried
    cranberries or cherries

Blender Ingredients

3 large eggs
1 cup roughly chopped yellow sweet potato
    (about 5 ounces)
6 large dates (about 2 ounces)
¼ cup soft or melted coconut oil or butter
1 tablespoon vanilla extract
1 teaspoon stevia or pure monk fruit

1. Preheat your oven to 350°F and lightly brush an 8 x 8 x 2-inch pan with oil or butter.
2. Stir together the dry ingredients in a medium-sized bowl.
3. Add the blender ingredients to the blender and blend on high until smooth.
4. Pour the blender ingredients into the dry ingredients and stir well to combine.
5. Stir in any other stir-ins.
6. Spread the batter into the prepared pan.
7. Bake for about 25 minutes until golden and puffy.

*If using whole nuts, add them to the blender with the other blender ingredients.

Butter Pecan Cookies

. . . .

These cookies are delicate and buttery, like wedding cookies. Ice cream sandwich wedding cookies. I mentioned that we occasionally host weddings on our unique little piece of land in the southern California countryside. Our oldest son and his wife, Charity, were the first to exchange their vows under what we now have named the "kissing tree." There have been dozens since and it's always fun to see what décor the bridal party comes up with. It's very rustic, so mason jars and photos with the chickens, goats, and piggy are always popular. Although we once overheard a guest from Orange County complain that he'd been told to "park next to a pig," as he stepped out of his fancy car. Well, can you imagine? What nerve! That snob was lucky to be parked next to our Mr. Chuckles.

Makes about 12 cookies

Ingredients

1¼ cups pecans
¼ cup sweet potato flour, or coconut flour
½ teaspoon baking soda
5 tablespoons soft butter
¼ cup of your favorite syrup sweetener
1 teaspoon vanilla extract
¼ teaspoon pure monk fruit or stevia

1. Preheat the oven to 350°F and line a cookie sheet with parchment paper.
2. Process the pecans, flour, and baking soda in your food processor until mostly fine and powdery.
3. Add the rest of the ingredients and blend just until combined.
4. Chill the dough if necessary.
5. Scoop out about 2 tablespoons of dough and place on the cookie sheet.
6. Bake until edges start to brown, about 10–12 minutes.
7. Let the cookies cool completely on the cookie sheet before transferring to a plate.

Chewy Brownies, Nuts or Not!

Sometimes we need choices. And sometimes we just need a late-night chocolate fix. This may mean we'd rather not pull out the blender or food processor during the commercial break. Plus, it's just good to have choices, right? And, while this book is full of nuts, because I believe them to be awesome, I also know a few of you may have some unfortunates in your lives that cannot eat nuts. This is the perfect recipe for you to cheer up those poor souls. Hopefully, they're not allergic to coconut! I prefer to use Dutch processed cocoa for my brownies, for the deep color and smooth chocolate taste. Regular cocoa or 100% baking chocolate will do nicely in a pinch. Our dog, Blue, was never picky when it came to chocolate, so ever since the disappearing Christmas fudge incident, we had to make sure we always hid the brownies in the microwave. Yes, I own a microwave, but I only use it to melt butter or reheat a cold cup of coffee.

Makes 9–12 brownie squares

Oil or butter for pan

Dry Ingredients

½ cup cocoa powder, or 4 ounces 100% chocolate
2 tablespoons coconut flour, or ⅔ cup nuts, or ¾ cup nut flour
1 tablespoon psyllium husk powder
½ teaspoon baking soda
½ teaspoon sea salt

Blender Ingredients

½ cup pumpkin puree, or 1 cup roughly chopped yam, sweet potato, or zucchini (about 4–5 ounces)
½ cup of your favorite syrup sweetener
½ cup melted butter or coconut oil
3 large eggs
1 tablespoon vanilla extract
¾ teaspoon stevia or pure monk fruit

Stir-in Ingredients

½ cup chocolate chips
½ cup walnuts (optional)

1. Preheat your oven to 350°F and coat an 8 x 8 x 2-inch pan with oil or butter.
2. If using a fresh vegetable, whole nuts, and/or chocolate *rather* than cocoa and canned pumpkin, just toss everything into your food processor and blend until smooth, scraping as needed. Proceed with step #6. Otherwise:
3. Whisk together the dry ingredients in a small bowl.
4. Whisk together the wet ingredients in a medium sized bowl.
5. Whisk the dry ingredients into the wet ingredients until it's a smooth batter.
6. Use a rubber spatula to stir it for about 30 seconds.
7. Stir in the chocolate chips and walnuts, if using.
8. Spread the batter into the prepared pan.
9. Bake for 20–23 minutes; be careful not to over-bake.

Chocolate Rocky Road Cookies

. . . .

It can be a toss-up when it comes to a quick chocolate fix around here. Brownies or these cookies? I must say the gooey mini marshmallows kinda make me swoon, but healthy they're not. The store-bought ones are made with sugar and corn syrup, which I don't eat, so as much as I love them, I often leave them out and just enjoy the walnuts. I do have a recipe for healthy marshmallows, but they rarely last long enough to add to these cookies. Once in a while, a mini-marshmallow probably won't kill us. Dunking advice? Nut milks are great; my favorite is a coconut/almond blend or macadamia. I also like to pour about 2 tablespoons of heavy cream into a tall glass and top with ice cold water. Hey, don't knock it till you try it!

Makes about 18 cookies

Dry Ingredients

3 tablespoons coconut flour
½ cup cocoa powder
½ teaspoon sea salt
1 teaspoon baking soda
1 teaspoon instant espresso powder

Stir-in Ingredients

½ cup each walnuts, chocolate chips, and miniature marshmallows

Blender Ingredients

1 cup roughly chopped sweet potato or yam (any color, about 4–5 ounces)
½ cup soft, pitted dates (about 8 large or 2½ ounces)
1 large egg
½ cup melted butter
½ cup of your favorite syrup sweetener
⅔ teaspoon stevia or pure monk fruit
1 tablespoon vanilla extract
⅔ teaspoon almond extract

1. Preheat your oven to 350°F and line your cookie sheet with parchment paper.
2. In a medium-sized bowl, sift together the dry ingredients and set aside.
3. Add the wet ingredients to the blender and blend until smooth.
4. Pour the contents of the blender into the dry ingredients and stir well to combine.
5. Stir in the walnuts, chocolate chips, and marshmallows.
6. Use an ice cream scooper to drop onto the prepared cookie sheet.
7. Bake for about 12–14 minutes.
8. Cool before removing from the pan.

Tip: If you want to make these in the food processor, just blend the sweet potato and dates together for a minute first, then add the rest of the ingredients and blend until smooth, stopping to scrape as needed. No need to melt the butter either.

Coconut Snowball Cookies

....

The name makes you think you should only eat these during the holidays, but don't let it keep you from making these yummy morsels any time of the year. These are fun to make with kids because they like rolling the dough into balls. You can substitute the potato for another colored root veggie if you'd like to—I won't try to stop you. If you like coconut, you will love these cookies.

Makes about 15 cookies

Ingredients

1 cup shredded, unsweetened coconut
¾ cup chopped sweet potato, about 4 ounces
2 tablespoons coconut flour
⅓ cup cream cheese
2 tablespoons virgin coconut oil
1 tablespoon vanilla extract
1 teaspoon coconut extract
½ teaspoon almond extract (optional)
½ teaspoon pure monk fruit or stevia
½ rounded teaspoon sea salt
Shredded, sweetened, or unsweetened coconut for coating

1. Preheat your oven to 350°F and line a cookie sheet with parchment paper.
2. In your food processor, puree the coconut, sweet potato, and coconut flour until almost pasty.
3. Add the rest of the ingredients except the additional coconut for coating, and puree until creamy.
4. Chill, if necessary, then drop by rounded tablespoonfuls onto your cookie sheet.
5. Roll each into a ball and coat with the shredded coconut.
6. Bake for about 14 minutes, just as the coconut is beginning to toast.
7. Cool on pan before removing them to a rack or paper towel to finish cooling.

Jammies

....

These thumbprint cookies are a favorite around here. It's kinda difficult to imagine why jam nestled in a banana-cream cheese cookie wouldn't be everyone's favorite. If loving these cookies is wrong, I don't wanna be right.

Makes about 12 cookies

Ingredients

1 cup almond or other nut flour
2 tablespoons coconut flour
½ teaspoon sea salt
1 egg
1 small, barely ripe banana (about 3 ounces)
¼ cup cream cheese
1 tablespoon vanilla extract
1 teaspoon almond extract
½ teaspoon stevia or pure monk fruit
Approximately ⅓ cup jam (page 57)

1. Preheat your oven to 350°F and line a cookie sheet with parchment paper.
2. Toss everything (except jam) into your food processor and blend until smooth.
3. If necessary, chill until firm enough to handle.
4. For each cookie, drop about 1 tablespoon of dough onto the cookie sheet.
5. With slightly dampened hands, roll each dough into a ball.
6. Use a small measuring spoon or your finger to gently press into each dough ball to make a deep hole.
7. Fill each hole with your favorite jam (or bake first and fill with raw jam once cooled).
8. Bake for about 15 minutes, or just until the cookies are beginning to turn golden.
9. Cool on pan before removing them to a rack or paper towel to finish cooling.

Note: My favorite jams to fill these cookies with are apricot, berry, and lemon curd. I also like to sprinkle a little powdered erythritol over the tops.

No-Oatmeal Cookies

. . . .

Well, I still eat an occasional oat now and again, but with these cookies I don't miss the oats one bit. These taste and look like the real thing. You can always add a sprinkling of oats just for appearances if you sometimes live dangerously, like me. My husband loves these sandwiched with the filling for Whoopie Pies (page 258), like those bad ones he got in his lunchbox back in the day. These taste so much better and will definitely brighten any lunchbox, any day.

Makes about 12–16 cookies

Ingredients

1 cup roughly chopped peeled yellow sweet potato (about 5 ounces)
1 cup shredded coconut (about 2 ounces)
1 cup walnuts (about 3 ounces)
1 egg
½ cup softened coconut oil or palm shortening
½ cup of your favorite syrup sweetener
⅔ teaspoon stevia or pure monk fruit
2 teaspoons vanilla extract
1 teaspoon almond extract
2 tablespoons coconut flour
2 teaspoons cinnamon
½ teaspoon sea salt
1 teaspoon baking soda

Optional Stir-ins

½ cup raisins or dried cranberries
½ cup walnuts

1. Preheat the oven at 350°F and line a cookie sheet with parchment paper.
2. In your food processor, fitted with the S blade, blend sweet potato, coconut, and nuts until somewhat finely ground.
3. Add the egg, coconut oil, sweeteners, and extracts, and blend together well.
4. In a small bowl, stir together the rest of the ingredients and add to the food processor while blending.
5. Remove the S blade and stir in the raisins or cranberries and walnuts (if using).
6. Use an ice-cream scoop to drop batter onto the prepared cookie sheet; gently press down each mound with your damp palm, if desired.
7. Bake for about 16–18 minutes until turning golden brown.
8. Cool before serving, as these cookies are delicate when they're warm.

No-Sugar Cookies

. . . .

I happen to prefer big, soft, chewy sugar cookies, so call me lazy, but I don't often make roll-out cookies, because, well, I'm lazy. But if roll-out cookies are your thingy, just add a smidge more coconut flour, chill the dough, and roll away. I tend to like just doing drop cookies and getting on with the decorating part cuz (aside from eatin' 'em) that's the part the kids love. And unless you need to make blue cookies, you can leave the food coloring on the shelf when making these. Baby spinach, pink or yellow beets (red beets for Valentine's is my favorite), carrots, I've even used blueberries for the purple color . . . the sky's the limit.

Makes 18 cookies

Ingredients

1 cup roughly chopped root vegetable like sweet potato, beets, or carrots (about 5 ounces)
2¼ cups almond flour, divided
1 egg
⅓ cup soft butter or palm shortening
⅓ cup cream cheese
1 tablespoon vanilla extract
1 teaspoon almond extract
1½ teaspoons pure monk fruit or stevia
1–3 tablespoons coconut flour (depending on vegetable/fruit's moisture content)
1 teaspoon baking powder
½ teaspoon sea salt

1. Preheat your oven to 350°F. Add the vegetable to your food processor and process into small pieces, scraping the sides as needed.
2. Add half the almond flour, along with the egg, butter, and cream cheese, and process until smooth, stopping to scrape as needed. Blend in the rest of the almond flour, extracts, and sweetener.
3. Stir together the coconut flour, baking powder, and salt. Sprinkle in and blend until well incorporated. Chill the dough until it's firm enough to handle, if necessary.
4. Drop about 1–2 tablespoons of dough onto a parchment-lined cookie sheet, roll into balls, and gently flatten with the palm of your hand.
5. Bake for 10–12 minutes, depending upon the size and thickness of the cookie.

Notes and Tips:

1. The amount of coconut flour and sweetener may vary depending on the vegetable/fruit you choose. If the dough is moist and too sticky to handle, stir or knead in 1–2 tablespoons more coconut flour; chill or let rest long enough for the coconut flour to absorb moisture.
2. You may need to chill the dough in between rolling if you have warm hands or it's a warm day.
3. You can also roll the dough up in waxed paper and chill or freeze and cut into slices.
4. The cookie tops will "crackle" more if you brush them with egg before baking.
5. For green cookies, use ¾ cup roughly chopped white sweet potato and ¼ cup packed baby spinach.
6. Yes, you can use plantain instead of a root vegetable!

Chewy Nut Butter Cookies

. . . .

Sometimes I get a major craving for peanut butter cookies. I don't know what it is—I must be deficient in something that makes me crave them. Can a person be deficient in peanuts? I know I must be deficient in chocolate because I'm often craving that too. When these cravings hit at the same time, you know what that means: I have to add a few dark chocolate chunks to this dough before baking. I like sweet potato flour in these cookies, but if you haven't bought sweet potato flour yet, go ahead and use the coconut.

Makes about 16 cookies

Ingredients

⅔ cup soft butter or palm shortening
2 eggs
½ cup of your favorite syrup sweetener
2 teaspoons vanilla extract
1 teaspoon stevia or pure monk fruit
3 tablespoons coconut flour or sweet potato flour
1 teaspoon baking soda
½ teaspoon salt
1 rounded cup peanut butter (just peanuts!), or your favorite nut butter

1. Preheat your oven to 350°F and line a cookie sheet with parchment paper.
2. Use your handheld mixer or food processor and blend all of the ingredients except the peanut butter until smooth.
3. Add the peanut butter and blend until combined and batter becomes thick.
4. Chill until firm.
5. Use an ice cream scoop to drop balls onto a parchment-lined cookie sheet.
6. Roll them into smooth balls with your hands, and then use a damp fork, or dip it in a granulated sweetener to make a criss-cross pattern as you push down the dough ball.
7. Bake for about 16 minutes, or until just turning brown.

REAL Chocolate Chip Cookies

· ·

This is a cookie recipe that goes back to the early days of my grain-free baking. When this cookie received the approval sign from my youngest son, Christian, I knew I'd done it right. Christian has been a cookie monster (like his mom) since I can remember, so he can be one tough cookie critic. That's okay with me because who wants to eat a less than delectable chocolate chip cookie anyway? Aside from Christian, who is now 6'5", these cookies are also favored by a few "little people" around who refer to me as "Nonna." That's all I can say about that or you might start trying to figure out things about me that you don't really need to know. Anyway, a REAL Chocolate Chip Cookie that these little people could eat anytime was number one on my recipe list.

Makes about 20–24 cookies

Ingredients

⅔ cup roughly chopped sweet potato (about 3 ounces)
3 large, soft pitted dates
½ cup soft or melted palm shortening, butter, or ghee
2 cups almond flour
½ cup of your favorite syrup sweetener
1 egg
1 tablespoon vanilla extract
1 teaspoon baking soda
½–⅔ teaspoon stevia or pure monk fruit
½ teaspoon sea salt
½ cup chocolate chips (see Resources for preferred options, page 296)

> *Tip: Using palm shortening or ghee makes a chewier cookie than butter does. If you use ghee, you will taste it in the cookie so make sure you love ghee!*

1. Preheat your oven to 350°F and line a cookie sheet with parchment paper.
2. Add the sweet potato and dates to the bowl of your food processor and process until very small pieces.
3. Add the butter and continue processing until fairly smooth, stopping to scrape down sides as needed.
4. Add the almond flour and syrup and process for another minute.
5. Add the egg and the rest of the ingredients and process a few seconds until combined.
6. Stir or pulse in the chocolate chips.
7. Remove the blade and chill dough until firm enough to handle.
8. Use an ice cream scoop to place about 2 tablespoons of cookie dough for each cookie.
9. With damp hands, gently press on top of each cookie to flatten slightly.
10. Bake for about 13–15 minutes, until golden brown.

Note: Adjust the amount of stevia/monk fruit according to the sweetness of the syrup you use. The date caramel on page 100 is delicious as the "syrup" in this recipe. If you use it, omit the dates and reduce the vanilla to 1 teaspoon.

Tip: You can roll the cookie dough into a cylinder, cover with plastic wrap, refrigerate, slice, and bake.

PIES, PIES, PIES: Okay, so I have already told you that I rarely eat breakfast in the morning. But I must confess, if there happens to be a pie lying around, I will eat it with my morning coffee. This is because when it comes to me, pie and willpower, they just don't go together. I see a pie, and willpower is out the window. Now are you beginning to understand why I had to start cooking and baking this way? If I hadn't, I probably would be in the doctor's office so much I wouldn't have had time to bake anything and would've been forced to eat Twinkies. See what a horrible, vicious cycle can happen if you're not careful? We all love pie so let's eat "good-for-you" pies.

Chocolate Cream Pie

Banana Cream and Chocolate Cream are favorite pies of all four of my sons, but I had to narrow my pie recipe selection down, so Banana Cream took the hit.

Makes 1 (8–9-inch) pie

Ingredients

3 ounces unsweetened 100% chocolate
1¾ cups heavy cream or full-fat coconut/nut
   milk, divided
1 tablespoon gelatin
2 cups packed baby spinach
2 teaspoons pure monk fruit powder or stevia

2 teaspoons vanilla extract
½ teaspoon almond extract
¼ teaspoon sea salt
One pre-baked Could Be Graham Cracker Crust
   (page 290)

1. Break the chocolate into a few pieces and place in your blender.
2. Pour the cream into a small saucepan and sprinkle the gelatin on top. Let soften a minute, then warm and stir until the gelatin is melted.
3. Pour the hot cream mixture on top of the chocolate, let set a minute, then add the rest of the ingredients. Blend on high until smooth and thick, about a minute.
4. Pour into the pre-baked crust and chill until firm. Top with Sweet Whipped Cream (page 240).

Deep Dish Coconut Cream Pie

If you're one of the unfortunate souls, too young to even remember reruns of Gilligan's Island, then let me just be the one to tell you that you really missed out! You must Google this or turn on the Nickelodeon channel on your TV, so I can prove to you that being just a tad bit older has its rewards. Those of you who remember, tell me I wasn't the only one who was jealous of Ginger and Mary Ann when Gilligan swooned over their homemade coconut cream pies? Well, I know he'd be swoonin' over this pie if he got to taste it. This pie would even snag that slim, good looking, serious ol' Professor.

Important tip: make sure you taste the brand of coconut milk you choose, because some of them taste much better than others.

Makes 1 deep dish (9- inch) pie

Ingredients

1 can full-fat coconut milk
2 large eggs
1 rounded tablespoon gelatin
1 cup roughly chopped yellow summer squash or peeled zucchini (about 1 medium or 4 ounces)
½–⅔ teaspoon pure monk fruit or stevia
1 teaspoon vanilla extract
½ teaspoon coconut extract
¼ teaspoon almond extract (optional)
⅛ teaspoon sea salt
1 pre-baked Old-fashioned Pie Crust (page 293)
1½ cups unsweetened shredded coconut

Topping Ingredients

2 cups coconut cream or heavy cream, or a blend of both
½ teaspoon pure monk fruit or stevia
¼ cup virgin coconut oil, melted
1½ teaspoons sweet potato flour*
½ cup sweet coconut flakes

1. Add the coconut milk, eggs, and gelatin to the blender and blend until smooth.
2. Pour this mixture into a medium-sized saucepan and heat and stir until very warm to the touch and the gelatin has dissolved.
3. Pour this mixture back into the blender, add the rest of the ingredients, except the crust and shredded coconut, and blend again until smooth.
4. Add the coconut and pulse a few times.
5. Pour this mixture into your pre-baked pie crust and chill while you whip the topping.

For the Topping

1. In a tall medium-sized bowl, use your handheld mixer to blend the cream with the sweeteners.
2. While blending, slowly add the coconut oil and whip until stiff peaks form.
3. Top the pie with this whipped cream mixture and sweet coconut flakes, toasted, if desired.

*If you don't have sweet potato flour yet, chill the can of coconut cream and just use the thick cream, omitting the liquid from the bottom of the can.

Fruit Pie in the Raw

. . . .

This is a true summer treat, and strawberry and peach are two of my favorite pies to keep raw. If we can keep the squirrels from stealing every last peach from our tree, we may get a peach pie this year. Let me tell you, those squirrel families are huge. They're also tricky, hungry, and wily little critters. I use nuts so much, I'm not sure why we never planted any nut trees, but it's probably a good thing because the squirrels would've made off with those too. Use a color coordinated jam here, depending on the type of fruit/fruits you're putting in the pie—such as the apricot/peach jam on page 57 for a peach pie. I used the strawberry/cherry jam for the pie pictured here.

Makes 1 (8–9 inch) pie

Ingredients

One pre-baked pie crust of choice
About 4 cups fresh or previously frozen fruit
½ cup water
1 teaspoon gelatin or agar
½ cup fresh jam
1/3 cup of your favorite syrup sweetener
Zest and juice of ½ orange or lemon
1 teaspoon vanilla extract (optional)
Pure monk fruit or stevia, if desired
Dash of sea salt

1. Cut the fruit into the sized pieces you want in your pie and set aside.
2. Add the gelatin to the water in a small saucepan over low heat, whisk and stir until dissolved.
3. Turn off the heat and stir in the rest of the ingredients. Taste for sweetness and add sweetener according to the sweetness of your fruit and your taste.
4. Pour this mixture over the fruit and gently toss to coat.
5. Turn into a previously baked pie crust and chill until ready to serve.
6. Serve with whipped cream, or: slowly pour 1 cup heavy cream into 4 tablespoons very soft, whipped cream cheese and a 1/8 teaspoon stevia or monk fruit and pipe it around the edges of the pie.

LEMON CHIFFON PIE

. . . .

I am such a lucky gal that my property has not just one, but two lemon trees! I confess to favor the Meyer tree because of its sweet, juicy flesh and thin skin, which works perfectly for this pie. This pie is so refreshing and always says springtime to me, so it's often offered to the Easter Bunny when he stops off to bring his colored eggs. If you're too busy coloring eggs or painting your toenails and just don't want to deal with a food processor, this recipe will also work in the blender. Or, forget about both of those machines and simply juice and zest the lemons. With so many choices, what will you do?

Makes 1 (9-inch) pie

Ingredients

¼ hot cup water
2 teaspoons gelatin
Juice of 3 Meyer lemons + half of one peel
2 eggs, separated
¼ cup clear syrup, such as VitaFiber or honey
1–2 teaspoons pure monk fruit or stevia
1 teaspoon vanilla extract
⅛ teaspoon cream of tartar
⅔ cup heavy cream or coconut cream
1 pre-baked Shortbread Cookie Crust (page 292)
Fresh berries for topping

1. Stir the gelatin in the water until it's dissolved.
2. Add gelatin mixture, lemon juice, one half of a peel of one lemon, egg yolks (no whites!), monk fruit or stevia, and vanilla to your blender and blend until smooth.
3. Whip the egg whites and cream of tartar in a small bowl until semi-stiff peaks form, about 2 minutes.
4. Fold into the cooled lemon mixture.
5. Whip the cream in the empty egg white bowl and fold into the mixture.
6. Pour into the pie crust and refrigerate several hours until firm. Top with fresh berries.

Peanut Butter Banana Pie

. . . .

Wow. This pie knocked the socks and shoes right off me. I swear, one bite and I was barefoot! Okay, I'm just kidding, but it's true how yummy this pie is. If you prefer more peanut taste and less banana flavor, switch the blended banana for one plantain and omit the sliced banana altogether. That may work great for your household, but it wouldn't roll in mine, as I have too many banana lovers who would complain far too loudly. Feel free to mix and match crusts to suit your taste buds. Also, this pie is pictured with the Old-fashioned Pie Crust (page 293) because I doubled the recipe to make an outlandish deep-dish pie that we could devour after the picture was snapped, but it's also wonderful with the Shortbread Cookie Crust (page 292).

Makes 1 (9-inch) pie

Ingredients

1 pre-baked crust of choice
3 medium-large "just ripe" bananas
8 ounces cream cheese, softened
1 teaspoon stevia or pure monk fruit
1 teaspoon vanilla extract
1 cup heavy cream, whipped
1 cup chunky peanut butter
Honey roasted peanuts, for garnish

Chocolate Peanut Butter Ganache Ingredients

¼ cup of your favorite syrup sweetener
2 tablespoons smooth peanut butter
2 tablespoons cocoa powder
1 teaspoon vanilla extract
Stevia drops to taste

1. Process one banana, cream cheese, sweeteners, and vanilla in your food processor, fitted with the S blade, until smooth.
2. Add the whipped cream through the top while blending.
3. Add the peanut butter and pulse to blend in.
4. Remove the S blade and stir gently to finish combining all ingredients.
5. Slice the remaining 2 bananas into "coins" and layer them into the bottom of the pre-baked crust.
6. Pour the filling over the bananas and smooth the top.
7. Chill in the refrigerator while you make the Chocolate Peanut Butter Ganache (see recipe below).
8. Drizzle the ganache over the top of the chilled pie and garnish with honey roasted peanuts.

For the Ganache

1. Stir ingredients together in a small bowl until smooth; warm in the microwave a few seconds, if necessary.
2. Thin with a little water if needed.

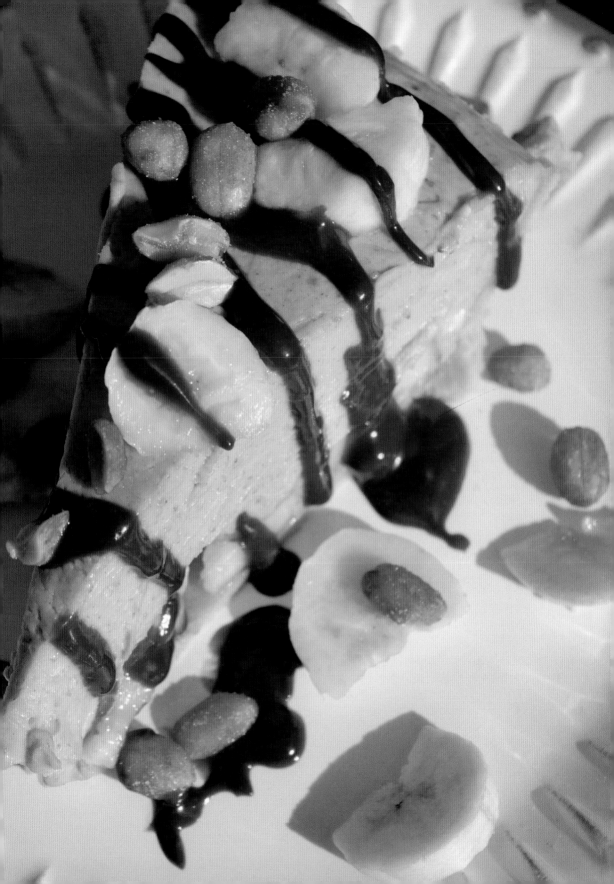

Sweet Cherry Pie

. . . .

My husband had a traumatic event happen over and over during his childhood. I think it's what made him so mean (you know I'm teasing again . . . right?). He claims that his mother (he had eleven siblings, by the way) had a mischievous sense of humor and would often ask after dinner, "Who's going to get the cherry pie on top of the refrigerator?" Then, all the kids would clamor to get there first—only to find the top of the refrigerator empty. Apparently, they fell for this little trick over and over. Obviously, she had a really poor sense of humor, but other than this, she was, by all accounts, a wonderful mother. I understand it's scarred him horribly, but his brothers and sisters all seem well-adjusted and normal, so maybe there's still hope for him. I'm not fond of pitting cherries, so I usually opt for the frozen ones because I've had to bake plenty of cherry pies over the years to make up for his childhood trauma.

Makes one (9-inch) pie

Ingredients

2 pounds pitted dark cherries, fresh or frozen
1½ tablespoons gelatin or agar
½ teaspoon cinnamon
Pinch of sea salt
1 tablespoon lemon juice
2 teaspoons vanilla extract
½ teaspoon almond extract
½ teaspoon stevia or pure monk fruit
1 pre-baked Old-Fashioned Pie Crust (page 293)
1 egg, for brushing

1. When you make one of the pie crusts, don't forget to brush the crust with the gelatin egg wash (see page 295).
2. Simmer the cherries with any juices in a covered saucepan for about 15 minutes.
3. Use a ladle to transfer about ½ cup of the juice from the pan to a small bowl.
4. In another small bowl, stir together the gelatin, cinnamon, and sea salt, sprinkle and whisk this mixture into the juice until dissolved, then stir back into the cherries.
5. Stir in the lemon juice, extracts, and sweetener.
6. Pour the filling into the prepared pie crust and top with the top crust. If the top crust is not already baked, brush both sides with more egg wash and cut a pattern of slits to allow steam to escape.
7. Bake at 350°F until the top crust is golden brown, about 20–25 minutes.

SWEET CRUSTS: The following pie crusts have all been made without grains or starches. And you thought your days of eating pie crust were over? These crusts are so delicious they'll remind you of those favorite pies you grew up eating.

TOP CRUST FOR A TWO-CRUST FRUIT PIE

I use the gelatin egg wash to protect my crust from the moisture of the filling. Fruit pies can be very wet, so sometimes (but not always) I'll cook and thicken the filling on the stove top first. Then, I'll fill the pre-baked pie shell and top with an unbaked top crust and bake until it's golden. Oddly, the bottom crust doesn't get over done, even if I don't pre-cook the fruit. Use one of these techniques for the best crispy results.

1st Method:

1. Roll out the second half of the dough to fit the top of your pie pan, 8–9 inches.
2. Brush with egg, then invert onto a cookie sheet that has been lined with a piece of liberally buttered parchment paper.
3. Use fork tines to decorate the edges and prick air holes in half a dozen places.
4. Brush the topside liberally with egg wash, sprinkle with granulated sweetener, if desired.
5. Bake this alongside your bottom pie crust until golden, about 25 minutes.
6. To assemble, simply place this on top of the pie once it's filled with your cooked filling.

2nd Method:

1. Fully pre-bake the bottom crust.
2. Move the oven rack to the highest position.
3. Between waxed paper sheets, roll out the top crust large enough to fit over the edges of the bottom crust.
4. Liberally brush both the top and bottom crusts with the gelatin/egg wash.
5. Fill the pie and invert the top crust, pressing it around the edges to adhere to the bottom crust.
6. Cut air holes, and brush the entire top crust with the egg wash
7. Sprinkle with sweetener, if desired, and bake on the top rack until golden, about 25 minutes, protecting the edges as needed.

Note: The second method does not produce quite as crisp a top crust.

COULD BE GRAHAM CRACKER CRUST

. . . .

Yes, nuts are a good option when you're fresh out of graham crackers. I love all types of nuts, but I think my favorite is the walnut. Well, pecans come pretty darn close. I don't use walnuts for this crust because they're a little soft, but any of these other three choices work great.

Makes one (9-inch) round crust

Ingredients

1½ cups pecan pieces, chopped Brazil nuts, or hazelnuts
3 tablespoons coconut flour
3 tablespoons sweet potato flour
¼ teaspoon sea salt
3 tablespoons cold butter, diced
2 tablespoons honey
⅛–¼ teaspoon pure monk fruit or stevia
1 teaspoon vanilla extract
1 teaspoon cinnamon (optional)

1. Preheat oven at 325°F. Butter an 8 or 9-inch round pie pan and set aside.
2. Process the nuts into a fine meal in your food processor.
3. Add the rest of the ingredients and pulse to combine.
4. Press mixture into the buttered pie pan.
5. Bake for 15–18 minutes.
6. To keep the crust from becoming soggy, once it's cooled, brush with a gelatin wash (page 295) before filling.

Note: You can substitute the monk fruit or stevia for ⅓ cup granulated sweetener and use all coconut flour if you haven't bought sweet potato flour yet.

> Tip: For a more "graham cracker" crust, add 1 teaspoon cinnamon.

Just-Like-Oreo-Cookie Crust

I cannot even begin thinking about Oreos again, so let's get right to the recipe and you can even leave your food processor in the cupboard.

Makes one (9-inch) round crust

Ingredients

1½ cups pecan meal or almond flour
⅓ cup Dutch processed cocoa powder
6 tablespoons coconut flour or sweet potato flour
¼ teaspoon sea salt
1 large egg white
6 tablespoons melted shortening
2 teaspoons pure monk fruit or stevia
1 teaspoon vanilla extract

1. Preheat oven at 325°F. Butter a 9-inch round pie pan and set aside.

2. In a medium-sized bowl, whisk together the dry ingredients.

3. In a separate bowl whisk together the wet ingredients.

4. Combine the wet and dry ingredients and press mixture into the buttered pie pan.

5. Bake for 15–18 minutes.

Shortbread Cookie Crust

Makes one (8–9-inch) round crust

Ingredients

1⅓ cups blanched almond flour
¼ cup sweet potato flour
¼ cup coconut flour
½ teaspoon sea salt
6 tablespoons butter
½ teaspoon pure monk fruit or stevia
1 teaspoon vanilla extract

1. Preheat oven at 325°F.

2. Butter a 9-inch round pie pan and set aside.

3. Combine all of the ingredients in a bowl. It will look like a crumble of pea-sized pieces.

4. Press mixture into the buttered pie pan.

5. Bake for 15–18 minutes. Cover loosely with aluminum foil or parchment paper halfway through baking

Tip: To keep the crust from becoming soggy, once it's cooled, brush with a gelatin wash (page 295) before filling.

Old-Fashioned Pie Crust & Pastry Dough

. . . .

Baking the top pie crust separately really gives you a nice crunchy top crust, but sometimes we just need that old-fashioned look, so, again, a gal (or guy) needs choices . . . and you can even change your mind, I'm not judging. You can use this traditional pie crust for any of your favorite pies. Starting the crust in a cold oven and baking it at a moderate temperature helps keep the crust from puffing up, and there's no need to poke it all over with a fork. Use a crust protector or aluminum foil if necessary. The saturated fat makes a tender, cookie-like crust. I like the flavor ghee gives this crust, but palm shortening or lard also work great; butter is fine, but it may not be quite as crispy. If you own a pizza stone, pop it in the oven to heat while you make your pie dough. Baking grain-free pie crusts on the stone helps crisp the bottom before the edges and top are too brown. Before I owned a pizza stone, I would place the crusts on the floor of my oven for the first half of the cooking time—that works too!

Makes 2 (8 or 9-inch) pie crusts, or 1 deep dish 9-inch crust

Ingredients

1½ cups roughly chopped white or yellow sweet potato, with or without skin (approximately 7 ounces)

1 teaspoon sea salt

4 tablespoons ghee, butter, palm shortening, or lard + extra for the pan

3 cups almond flour, divided

2 tablespoons coconut flour

For a sweet crust, add:

½–1 teaspoon stevia or pure monk fruit

2 teaspoons vanilla extract

1. Do not preheat the oven. Adjust the oven rack to the lowest position and set a pizza stone or cookie sheet in to heat.
2. Brush the insides of your pie pan with melted butter or ghee.
3. Add the sweet potato and salt to your food processor, fitted with the S blade, and process to very small pieces, stopping to scrape the sides down.
4. Add the fat of choice and 1 cup of the almond flour, and continue to process until smooth.
5. Add the rest of the almond flour and process until it comes together into a ball. Stop to scrape the sides if necessary. You should see very few, if any, small bits of the sweet potato in the dough.
6. Place half the dough (or all of it for a deep-dish pan) onto a sheet of waxed paper. Top with a second sheet of paper and roll the dough out to fit your pie pan. If it's a warm day, it may be best to chill the dough at this point to make it easier to handle.
7. Gently pull off the top piece of paper, replace it back onto the dough (this is to make peeling it off once it's in the pan easier), turn over, and pull off the other sheet.
8. Lightly place the pie pan upside down over the crust, slip your hand under the crust, and invert it onto the pie pan, or use the rolling pin method to place the crust into the pan. Gently peel off the second sheet of waxed paper (chill, if necessary).
9. Press it into the pan and crimp the edges of the crust, trimming as needed.
10. Heat the oven to 350°F. Bake until just golden, about 20–25 minutes.

continued on page 295

To keep the crust from becoming soggy, once it's cooled and before filling it, brush with the egg wash.

For the egg wash:

2 tablespoons water
1 teaspoon gelatin or agar powder
1 egg

1. Heat two tablespoons of water until very hot.
2. Whisk in gelatin until melted.
3. Whisk in egg, whisking until very well incorporated.
4. For a single crust pie, brush the crust with the egg wash five minutes before the end of baking and again as soon as it comes out of the oven.

Tip: Be patient and let the food processor do its job. Make sure you stop and scrape the sides as needed so it chops and blends evenly into a dough. You can usually tell the dough is ready by the change in the sound of the food processor and how it rolls to one side like a ball of dough.

Ingredient and Kitchen Resources

Apple Fiber & Pectin

Prescribedforlife.com
Amazon.com

Baking Goods (Silpats, etc.)

williams-sonoma.com
Amazon.com

Baking Powder and Baking Soda

Hainpurefoods.com
Bobsredmill.com

Blanched Almond Flour

Honeyville.com
Sunorganicfarm.com
Aldrinalmonds.com

Blenders

Cuisinart.com
Vitamix.com
Blendtec.com

Bread Loaf Pans

Fatdaddios (Amazon.com)
Magicline (Cheftools.com)

Broth

Bone: kettleandfire.com
No-bone Broth: chefv.com

Butter/Ghee

Purityfarms.com
Tinstarfoods.com
Kerrygoldusa.com
Greenpasture.org

Chocolate Products

Dagobachocolate.com
Enjoylife.com
Lilyssweets.com
Nativasnaturals.com

Coconut Products

Wildernessfamilynaturals.com
Tropicaltraditions.com
Nutiva.com
Nuts.com

Cultured and Fermented Products

Wildways.com
Bodyecology.com
Culturedfoodlife.com

Dairy Products

Organicpastures.com
Claravaledairy.com

Dairy-free Cheese

Kitehill.com

Date Products

Shieldsdategarden.com
Ilovedatelady.com
Therawfoodworld.com
Organicfruitsandnuts.com

Dried Egg Whites

Roseacresfarms.com
Jayrobb.com
Juilianbakery.com

Extracts

Flavorganics.com
Moutainroseherbs.com
Nielsenmassey.com

Flours

Plantain Flour: Barryfarms.com
Sweet Potato Flour: Northbaytrading.com

Food Processors

Cuisinart.com
Kitchenaid.com

Gelatin

Bernard Jensens (Amazon.com)
Greatlakesgelatin.com

Grass-Fed Meats

Eatwild.com
Applegatefarms.com
Grasslandbeef.com

Monk Fruit and Stevia Sweeteners

Lakanto Monk Fruit Liquid: Bodyecology.com
Pure Monk Powder: Julianbakery.com
Sweetleaf.com

Nuts

Nuts.com
Organicfruitsandnuts.com
Sunfood.com (Jungle peanut butter)
Traderjoes.com (Valencia peanut butter)

Organic Produce

Organicfruitsandnuts.com
Localharvest.org
Eatwellguide.org

Palm Shortening and Lard

Fatworks.com
Spectrumorganics.com
Nutiva.com

99% Purity Psyllium Husks

Indusorganics.com
Organicindia.com

Sea Salt and Seasonings

Mountainroseherbs.com
Livesuperfoods.com
Frontiercoop.com
Spicehunter.com

Syrups, Honey, and Fruit Spreads

Vitafiber.com (IMO syrup) Amazon.com
Maplesource.com
Waxorchards.com
Reallyrawhoney.com
Honeygardens.com
Madhavasweeteners.com

Sweeteners

Allulose: Bettertaste.com
Lakanto.com (Bodyecology.com)
Swervesweetener.com
Organiczero.com
Norbusweetener.com

Variety

Shoporganic.com
Amazon.com
Thrivemarket.com

Bibliography

Belay, Amha and Gershwin, M.E., *Spirulina in Human Nutrition and Health.* Boca Raton: CRC Press, 2008.

Bowden, Jonny PhD, CNS. *The 150 Healthiest Foods on Earth.* Beverly, MA: Fair Winds Press, 2007.

Bragg, Paul and Patricia ND, PhD. *The Miracle of Fasting.* Santa Barbara: Health Science, 1975.

Brand-Miller PhD, Wolever MD PhD, Colagiure MD, Foster-Powell MN. *The New Glucose Revolution.* New York: Marlowe and Company, 2002.

Campbell, T. Colin PhD, and Campbell, Thomas N. II. *The China Study.* Dallas: Benbella Books, 2006.

Campbell-McBride, Natasha MD. *Gut and Psychology Syndrome.* Cambridge: Medinform Publishing, 2004.

Chilton, Floyd H. PhD with Laura Tucker. *Win the War Within.* New York: Rodale, 2005.

Cousins, Gabriel. *Conscious Eating.* Berkley: North Atlantic Books, 2000.

Cousins, Gabriel. *Rainbow Green Live-Food Cuisine.* Berkley: North Atlantic Books, 2003.

D'Adamo, Peter MD. *Eat Right for Your Type.* New York: Penguin Group USA, 1996.

Davis, William MD. *Wheat Belly.* New York: Rodale, 2011.

Diamond, Harvey and Marilyn. *Fit For Life.* New York: Warner Books, 1985.

Ehret, Arnold. *Rational Fasting.* New York: Benedict Lust Publications, 1971.

Elias, Thomas. *The Berzynski Breakthrough: The Century's Most Promising Treatment . . . and The Government's Campaign to Squelch It.* Los Angeles: General Publishing Group, 1997.

Fallon, Sally. *Nourishing Traditions.* San Diego: Promotion Publishing, 1995.

Fitzgerald, Randall. *The Hundred Year Lie: How Food and Medicine Are Destroying Your Life.* New York: Penguin Group USA, 2006.

Furhman, Joel, MD. *Fasting and Eating for Health.* New York: St. Martin's Press, 1995.

Gates, Donna. *The Baby Boomer Diet.* Carlsbad: Hay House Inc., 2011.

Gates, Donna. *The Body Ecology Diet.* Atlanta: B.E.D. Publications, 1996.

Goldberg, Burton and Larry Trivieri, Jr. "Cronic Fatigue, Fibromyalgia, and Lyme Disease." alternativemedicine.com. New York: Celestial Arts, 2004.

Haggen, Bruce C.,PhD, *How to Live to Be 100 in Spite of Your Doctor.* Souix Falls: Haggen Publishing, 2006.

Howell, Edward, M.D. *Enzyme Nutrition: The Food Enzyme Concept.* Wayne, NJ: Avery Publishing Group, 1985.

Hyman, Mark Dr. *The Blood Sugar Solution.* New York: Little, Brown & Co, 2012.

Kaufman, Doug A. *The Fungus Link.* Rockwell, TX: Media Trition, 2000.

Lipski, Elizabeth MS, CCN. *Digestive Wellness.* New Canaan: Keats Publishing Inc, 1996

Mercola, Joe MD. "Killer Sugar: Suicide with a Spoon." Mercola.com 9 Jan 2000 http://articles.mercola.com/sites/articles/archive/2000/01/09/killer-sugar-suicide-with-a-spoon-sugar-dangers.aspx.

Null, Gary PhD. *Parasites: The Complete Encyclopedia of Natural Healing.* New York: Kensington Publishing, 2005.

Null, Gary PhD. *Power Aging.* Stamford, CT: New American Library, 2003.

Rubin, Jordan S. *The Maker's Diet.* New York: Berkley Publishing Group, 2004.

Saputo, Len MD and Nancy Faass MSW, MPH. *Boosting Immunity.* Novato: New World Library, 2002.

Somers, Suzanne. *Knockout: Interviews with Doctors Who Are Curing Cancer—And How to Prevent It in the First Place.* New York: Crown Publishing, 2009.

Thompson, Robert, and Kathleen Barnes: *The Calcium Lie: What Your Doctor Doesn't Know Could Kill You.* Brevard, NC: Take Charge Books, 2008.

Urschel, Harold C. III MD. *Healing the Addicted Brain.* Naperville: Sourcebooks Inc., 2009.

Wallach, Joel D., and Ma Lan. *Dead Doctors Don't Lie.* Franklin, TN: Legacy Communications, 1999.

Walsh, William J. PhD. *Nutrient Power: Heal Your Biochemistry and Heal Your Brain.* New York: Skyhorse Publishing, 2012.

Watson, Brenda ND, and Smith, Leonard MD. *Gut Solutions.* Clearwater, FL: Renew Your Life Press, 2003.

Williams, Louisa MS, DC, ND. *Curing CASPERS: Chronic Auto-Immune Stealth Pathogens Evolved from Resistant Bacteria Syndrome.* 2013. e-book.

Wright, Jonathan V., and Alan R. Gaby. *Natural Medicine Optimal Wellness.* South Salem, NY: Vital Health Publishing, 2006.

Acknowledgments

. . . .

First of all, I'd like to thank the Universe for giving me spirit, and Life for always kicking me in the butt! Thank you to Coleen O'Shea, my intrepid agent, for believing in me and the roller-coaster ride that became this book. Thank you to my very talented editor, Leah Zarra, and the team at Skyhorse Publishing for bringing this book to life, and to Lara Asher for your continued support.

A super special thank you, thank you, thank you to my dearest Tom, Thom, Thomas, Tommy, Thomasina, Animal, husband, business partner, and dearest friend. I'm sorry for any time I have ever called you something other than these names, I swear I didn't mean it. Thank you for your unwavering encouragement through the years, putting up with my crazy ideas, and your willingness to take on even crazier projects. Thank you for the early morning runs to the grocery store, for your top-notch editing skills, your opinionated photography remarks, for rubbing my feet and feeding the dogs more than me. Thank you for your love, patience, and understanding, and for being the man I can always count on to have my back. I love you, love you, love you!

Hugs, kisses, and thanks to all of our sons, Joshua, Jeremiah, Jacob, and Christian, for at least pretending to listen to me once in a while, for giving me incredible inspiration, for encouraging me and loving me and letting me just be Ma. And for all those years you made sure we rarely had a dull moment—I love you all dearly!

Thank you, dear Jake, for your patient photography skills and artistic eye—even though shooting food isn't your favorite subject, you managed to come through with honors. We both know I couldn't have done this without your help.

To Derek, for always being ready to lend a hand and for your great photography skills and attitude.

Thank you, Jahara, for your earnest desire to make all things better, encouraging words, stylistic eye, helping hands, and inner (and outer) beauty.

Much love and gratitude to my "daughter" Andrea and the "gals" in my sons' lives, for showing me in so many different ways, the strength, and belief it takes to heal.

Thank you to Dr. William Davis (author of *Wheat Belly*) for the timely 20-minute telephone conversation I will always appreciate, and Dr. Kellyann Petrucci (author of the *Bone Broth Diet*) for your earnest enjoyment of our baking mix products. And thank you to Greg and Risa for taking a leap of faith with us!

Thanks to my sister-in-law, who sparked this whole book idea when she told me she didn't like using her food processor! And to all of my extended family supporters and my wonderful taste testers (you know who you are!) and my beautiful friend, Cathy, for encouraging me with excitement and positivity.

And, finally, my heart will also forever hold a special place for some whose lives taught me so much about suffering, illness, pain, and dependence, as well as tenacity, dignity, strength, gratitude, and hope: to Roy and Rae Ellis, whose remarkable love story will someday be published; my dear friend Julie, for her encouragement; my friend, Tony; my sister, Leslie; my brother, Steve. And special thanks to my mother, Hope, for reminding me that "sometimes you have to toot your horn to be heard." Toot, Toot!

The END

About This California Country Gal

When Annabelle Lee discovered the starches in gluten-free recipes were giving her what she calls a "Starch Belly," she began a mission to recreate her family's favorite recipes using real, whole foods. Once she realized cutting grains from her diet also gave her relief from painful autoimmune symptoms, she knew she was on the path she would stay on forever.

As mom to a busy household of four hungry boys and wife to a husband she lovingly refers to as "Animal," Annabelle made a lot of sandwiches in the kitchen of their family farmhouse. To share her growing list of recipes, Annabelle began blogging as California Country Gal.

Today, the boys are grown and Annabelle's delicious and unique bread recipes have grown into a line of baked breads for the food service industry. Her Breads and Baking Mixes were recognized at the Natural Products Expo West trade show in 2015 as "next" trending items in the industry. You can purchase the mixes on the company website, Californiacountrygal.com, on Amazon, and at select retailers both online and in stores.

Visit her today at facebook.com/CalCountryGal, on Instagram @CaliforniaCountryGal, or contact her at info@californiacountrygal.com.

"Silly people . . . grains are for the birds!"

Conversion Charts

METRIC AND IMPERIAL CONVERSIONS
(These conversions are rounded for convenience)

Ingredient	Cups/Tablespoons/Teaspoons	Ounces	Grams/Milliliters
Butter	1 cup = 16 tablespoons = 2 sticks	8 ounces	230 grams
Cheese, shredded	1 cup	4 ounces	110 grams
Cream cheese	1 tablespoon	0.5 ounce	14.5 grams
Cornstarch	1 tablespoon	0.3 ounce	8 grams
Flour, all-purpose	1 cup/1 tablespoon	4.5 ounces/0.3 ounce	125 grams/8 grams
Flour, whole wheat	1 cup	4 ounces	120 grams
Fruit, dried	1 cup	4 ounces	120 grams
Fruits or veggies, chopped	1 cup	5 to 7 ounces	145 to 200 grams
Fruits or veggies, pureed	1 cup	8.5 ounces	245 grams
Honey, maple syrup, or corn syrup	1 tablespoon	0.75 ounce	20 grams
Liquids: cream, milk, water, or juice	1 cup	8 fluid ounces	240 milliliters
Oats	1 cup	5.5 ounces	150 grams
Salt	1 teaspoon	0.2 ounce	6 grams
Spices: cinnamon, cloves, ginger, or nutmeg (ground)	1 teaspoon	0.2 ounce	5 milliliters
Sugar, brown, firmly packed	1 cup	7 ounces	200 grams
Sugar, white	1 cup/1 tablespoon	7 ounces/0.5 ounce	200 grams/12.5 grams
Vanilla extract	1 teaspoon	0.2 ounce	4 grams

OVEN TEMPERATURES

Fahrenheit	Celsius	Gas Mark
225°	110°	¼
250°	120°	½
275°	140°	1
300°	150°	2
325°	160°	3
350°	180°	4
375°	190°	5
400°	200°	6
425°	220°	7
450°	230°	8

INDEX